The Text Is Myself

Wisconsin Studies in Autobiography

William L. Andrews
General Editor

The Text Is Myself

Women's Life Writing
and Catastrophe

MIRIAM FUCHS

THE UNIVERSITY OF WISCONSIN PRESS

The University of Wisconsin Press
1930 Monroe Street
Madison, Wisconsin 53711

www.wisc.edu/wisconsinpress/

3 Henrietta Street
London WC2E 8LU, England

1   3   5   4   2

Printed in the United States of America

Library of Congress Cataloging-in-Publication Data

Fuchs, Miriam.
The text is myself: women's life writing and catastrophe / Miriam Fuchs.
p. cm.—(Wisconsin studies in autobiography)
Includes bibliographical references and index.
ISBN 0-299-19060-9 (cloth: alk. paper)—
ISBN 0-299-19064-1 (pbk.: alk.paper)
1. Autobiographical fiction—Women authors—History and criticism.
2. Autobiography—Women authors. I. Title. II. Series.
PN3448.A8 F83 2003
809′.93592072—dc21
2003005656

To the women paddlers

Lanikai

Kumulau

Bora Bora

What was the organization of illusion, of memory? Who knew even his own divided heart? Who knew all hearts as his own? Among beings strange to each other, those divided by the long roarings of time, of space, those who have never met or, when they meet, have not recognized as their own the other heart and that heart's weaknesses, have turned stonily away, would there not be, in the vision of some omniscient eye, a web of spidery logic establishing the most secret relationships, deep calling to deep, illuminations of the eternal darkness, recognitions in the night world of voyager dreams, all barriers dissolving, all souls as one and united? Every heart is the other heart. Every soul is the other soul. Every face is the other face.

Marguerite Young
Miss MacIntosh, My Darling

Contents

Illustrations and Figures

Acknowledgments

This book has evolved over a long period of time. It has taken slightly different directions as other studies in the field have been published and in response to the suggestions of colleagues who have read selected chapters. My greatest debt is to Joan Douglas Peters, who listened to all of my initial ideas, translating them back to me in much more lucid form. In addition to keeping me intellectually on track, her standards served as inspiration for what was possible and gave me unwavering encouragement and challenge. Our friendship has taught me much about responsibility, courage, and survival, in ways that go far beyond what can be said in a paragraph of public acknowledgment. And I should add that while she helped in all ways with this manuscript, its faults remain entirely my own.

An enormous debt is to Ellen G. Friedman. Our friendship, dating back to graduate school, grew over many years while our jobs changed and our paths geographically diverged. But nothing stopped us from working collaboratively in the 1980s or from keeping our friendship intact—not even recent obstacles stronger than either one of us could have predicted. She will understand why I acknowledge her for her loyalty and strength and thank her and her husband Max Friedman for their visits over the past year.

Many people in Hawai'i and colleagues at the University of Hawai'i have given intellectual and personal support. Very special thanks go to friends Pat and Robert McHenry for coming to my aid in ways that enabled me to finish this book on schedule; no request was ever too mundane or too lavish—as well as for enjoyable times in numerous obscure locations. I am grateful to Charlene Avallone and Chip Hughes for their persistence and their willingness to answer my calls for neighborly and personal favors. The Department of English and the College of Languages, Linguistics, and Literature granted a number of research reductions and travel grants pertinent to this study. My sincere thanks go to Dean Joseph O'Mealy for his professional encouragement and his personal friendship over the years; to Cristina Bacchilega for her steadfast support; Valerie Wayne and Susan Schultz for staying in touch in various ways; Kathy Phillips for offering counsel during the writing process; Reinhard Friederich for helping with German translations; and Peter Nicholson for his visits. Director of the University of Hawai'i Study Abroad Program Sarita Rai is to be thanked for her support, her energy, and for insisting upon our weekly breakfasts.

Though I only list their names, each of the following persons came forward to offer assistance or support in a meaningful way: Steve Canham, Suzanne Kosanke, Cynthia Franklin, Laura Lyons, Ann Rayson, Margaret and Glenn Mann, Mark Heberle, and Mark Wilson. In addition, Craig Howes, director of the Center for Biographical Research and editor of *Biography*, made valuable comments on selected early chapters and has been a wonderful colleague. Stan Schab, managing editor of *Biography*, was enormously helpful in assisting with the final stages of this project and has become a good new friend.

I wish to thank William L. Andrews, executive editor of the Wisconsin Studies in Autobiography series, and Raphael Kadushin at the University of Wisconsin Press for their early interest in the project; Sheila Moermond for managing an efficient review process; Erin Holman for her editorial help; and the two readers for their comments and reviews.

Many friends provided encouragement as well as time away from the demands of scholarship. Suzi Mechler helped in crucial ways with humor and affection. I am very glad to acknowledge Mary and Dave Lerps for being such gracious and dependable friends; Mollie and Phil Foti for making participation in the 2002 World Sprints possible; Mauli Aspelund Olds for friendship and for sharing her knowledge of Hawaiian culture. Pauline MacNeil, Alexandra Avery, and Lani Twomey should all be mentioned for their help and camaraderie. And, of course, loving appreciation goes to my friend Suzanne Gilbert for her thoughtfulness and her generous, loyal spirit.

There is no satisfactory way to thank Michael E. Carney; I can do no more than express profound gratitude for his patience, his compassion, and his formidable skills. And many thanks to Suzanne Ditter for her competence and ability to make others feel comfortable in difficult times.

Finally, I cite my brother, Sy Fuchs, for insisting on a strong bond throughout our adult years and for making our closeness a significant, enduring element in both of our lives.

The past two decades are inconceivable without the presence of Alan Holzman. I want to thank him for being an unexpected and loving companion, who worked miraculously to weave together our dissimilar paths into the rich fabric of our long partnership. Without him, there would be no book. Nor would there ever have been a multitude of discovered museums, Kaua'i hikes and waterfalls, New Zealand treks, lessons in fine wine, adventures from Rangirora to Kithnos, or an extended family of siblings, children, and grandchildren. While the future is unknown, our shared past is certain, and my gratitude and love are immeasurable.

An abbreviated version of the third chapter was published as "Mapping Catastrophe: Topography, Tropology, and Testimony in H.D.'s *The Gift*," in F. Regard, ed., *Mapping the Self: Space, Identity, Discourse in British Auto/Biography* (Saint-Etienne, France: PUSE, 2003).

Sections of the chapter on Grete Weil's *The Bride Prince* initially appeared in "Recalling the Past and Rescuing the Self," in *Shofar* 17.2 (Winter 1999): 73–83.

This project was supported by a grant from the Hawai'i Council for the Humanities, an affiliate of the National Endowment for the Humanities.

The Text Is Myself

Introduction

The idea for this study had a specific starting point. It was H.D.'s memoir of childhood, *The Gift*. Reading it quickly while working on a project in the late 1980s, I did not stop to analyze its disturbing images of fire, shooting stars, and death that appeared intermittently and sometimes without discernible cause. Nor did I scrutinize its shifts in time and style—that is, until the book's final chapter. However, in the seconds needed to read the first two paragraphs of that chapter, every preceding episode was torn from the context of the distant past. Whatever conflicts H.D. had recorded from childhood, her last few pages revealed that the drama in her life *while* she was writing—bombs falling overhead in London—was powering the style and substance of all of her reminiscences.[1] Caught in the midst of the German-British air war, H.D. found her immediate experience of World War II bearing down on her memoir of life at the turn of the century in Pennsylvania. For a reader, the memoir itself seems to detonate in the space between a question that H.D. asks as a child and the answer she listens for but does not hear. The child does not hear it because the author neglects to write it. The noise around her is deafening, concentration impossible. She hears, rather than a dialogue from memory, a building close to her Chelsea flat getting hit by a bomb and come crashing to the ground. Catapulted from childhood, H.D. suddenly locates her adult self. It is January 17, 1943, and her autobiographical voice has been working mnemonically all along to help her withstand the terrors of a possible direct attack.[2] Recalling her grandmother's enigmatic recounting of ceremonies of exchange between Native Americans and Moravians,

H.D., in a sense, has been searching for models where contending sides move toward mutual tolerance and peace.

In the chapters that follow I argue that like H.D., all the writers I examine in various geopolitical sites and cultures, more than presenting just their own life stories, are seeking safe ground and ultimately survival. Consequently they pursue narrative scripts that offer glimpses of reconciliation as well as a means of resistance or protest. Under this pressure, the autobiographical impulse develops according to necessity. The impulse may manifest itself as biography, fiction, or biographical fiction; these may recede into autobiography; and autobiography may be a pretext for trying to reconstruct what the catastrophe has damaged. The case studies I have selected show ways that creative women have responded to larger struggles that affected them profoundly but precluded their direct participation and could readily have consigned them to utterly passive roles. I further argue it is catastrophe that causes their gender, race, location, and political and personal histories to intersect in imagined, imaginative, or patently strategic life stories.

My plan for highlighting catastrophe and thereby showing the notable differences between catastrophe and crisis is to focus on texts written by women. All of these texts are sensitive to ways in which women are vulnerable to violence—bodily, materially, genetically, by cultural prescription or enforcement. All of the texts reveal a dynamic correspondence between catastrophe's onset and ways that women reconceptualize exposure to violence through gender-specific displacements. Gender is invariably reflected back through visions of order that construct feminist configurations of power and prerogative. In making a decision to emphasize women's lives and texts, I do not mean to say that this category of writing is linked irrevocably to gender or that it will ultimately be defined by women's practices. I *do* wish to demonstrate that such writing is especially compelling to persons who are, or believe themselves to be, susceptible to events beyond their own determining. This condition certainly crosses the gender divide to incorporate ethnic, religious, political, indigenous, and racial groups, and all of these warrant study relative to catastrophe narratives. But it is no secret that when women are victims, elements concerning gender are present *along* with other elements; and this is my own particular interest and commitment. Moreover, as Americans become increasingly aware of catastrophe as a global phenomenon to which no one is immune, there is less justification for examining only one national literature. With attention focused on women, it is possible to look at catastrophe from the Pacific to the Americas to Europe throughout the twentieth century within this single volume. The five selected women all suffered limited political, diplomatic, religious, social, or medical authority and present a wide range of catastrophes and creative responses. By looking at them separately and then relative to one another, we see how their texts commingle ideas on disaster with stories that each disaster unleashes. The recollected narratives acknowledge and, indeed, celebrate and pay tribute to other women who faced comparable challenges and in whom the authors come to recognize themselves. In limiting my study to catastrophe life writing by women, I thus offer one way of introducing and thinking about the implications of this category of life writing.

I began with my own experience of reading *The Gift* as a way of illustrating the drama in these life writing works, for my purpose is to trace representational activities and to examine instances in which the writer's immediate material circumstances are a primary element of the work. By looking closely at the critical moments of writing as they are revealed in the text along with the developing story, I hope to demonstrate the paradoxical relationship between life writing intentions and the available genres for carrying them out. As an external factor that triggers the project, the circumstance determines the parameters of these projects in overt and sometimes puzzling ways. The nature of the circumstance can make the correspondence between intentionality and genre extremely hard to discern. Indeed, the resulting images may be so far removed from the woman that we do not realize her autobiographic relationship to them. I therefore argue that the distance between the subject and the images that represent the writer foregrounds the role that substitutive, distantiating discourses come to play.

For these reasons, I examine women who were galvanized to work creatively because they were exposed to intense political conflict, war, or personal upheaval reflecting a panorama of global disasters for which the twentieth century is certain to be remembered: expansionism, racial and religious persecution, dictatorship, world wars, exile, political incarceration, and incurable illnesses and epidemics despite scientific and technological advances. Regardless of their cultural or economic situations, these women were embroiled in or else deeply affected by events beyond their ability to readily cope. Each had reached a life juncture at which self-representation became imperative. Ranging from just before the twentieth to a few years before the twenty-first century and from areas as distant as London to Honolulu, the works I examine begin with *Hawaii's Story by*

Hawaii's Queen (1898), an autobiography by Lili'uokalani, who was the last Hawaiian *ali'i* to govern before American annexation.[3] They follow with the autobiographical memoir *The Gift*, written between 1940 and 1944 by the American expatriate H.D. in London; the biographical fiction *Artemisia*, written mainly during World War II by the Italian writer Anna Banti; the more recent novel *The Bride Price* by the German writer Grete Weil; and the autobiographical memoir *Paula* by Isabel Allende, exiled from Chile and now living in the United States.[4] H.D. and Allende are best known for their work in genres other than life writing, H.D. in poetry and Allende in fiction. Lili'uokalani, who many readers will be unfamiliar with, is a central figure in the history of Hawai'i. Her life and work exemplify ways that gender, class, and race intersected with Western institutional powers in the battle over annexation and had implications for other once-independent islands in the Pacific. Weil and Banti, though notable in their own countries, are less known in the United States despite accessible translations of their writings. Addressing Philippe Lejeune's declaration that "in spite of the fact that autobiography is impossible, this in no way prevents it from existing," *The Text Is Myself* looks at this exemplary and diverse group of women for whom the recording of their lives or a particular period of their lives would seem an unlikely, if not impossible, accomplishment.[5]

I use the words "unlikely" and "impossible" because these women found themselves in what Sander L. Gilman and Steven T. Katz might describe as periods of "disequilibrium."[6] In the introduction to their essay collection, these editors survey historical, cultural, and national situations of collective "stress" and "crisis" as they are linked to virulent periods of anti-Semitism, hence their title, *Anti-Semitism in Times of Crisis*. Like Gilman and Katz, I rely on the words "stress," "crisis," and occasionally "disequilibrium" but not, as they do, to signify how communities historically have used "categories of difference" in order to sanction persecution. As should become clear, I am especially concerned with differentiating "crisis," as a decidedly broad term, from specific situations of catastrophic dimensions. I use the term "catastrophe" for situations that occur rapidly, with immediate and shocking effects and, additionally, that bar direct intervention. The conditions confronting these five women were extreme and certainly come under the category of "catastrophe." This term resonates more profoundly, I think, with the proximity of disaster, while at the same time it often points toward explicit world events. "Catastrophe" also differentiates my focus and choice of subjects from other full-length studies of crisis and life writing.

As I do here, Suzette Henke in *Shattered Subjects: Trauma and Testimony in Women's Life-Writing* limits her discussion to women and looks across national borders.[7] But Henke concentrates on how the conflicts portrayed in the texts evince particular kinds of psychological traumas. She is especially interested in traumas that occurred during childhood, and she uses them as a basis for studying Colette, H.D., Anaïs Nin, Janet Frame, Audre Lorde, and Sylvia Fraser. Henke's perspective highlights their feminist life narratives for how they exhibit post-traumatic stress disorders as clues to the ways in which their lives unfolded. Viewing the writing as a method of healing and as a therapeutic activity, Henke discusses her primary texts to illustrate forms of "scriptotherapy." I do not follow a psychoanalytical approach or attempt to draw a series of psychobiographical portraits. Rather, I examine the literary projects as purposeful and *performative* responses to debacles that affected individuals in the midst of composing and that also extended nationally or internationally in some way. This means that, for the most part, my case studies do not come under the rubric of representations of individual post-traumatic stress disorders. The work of Cathy Caruth on trauma, temporal delay, and dreams and recurrence is therefore beyond the boundaries of this study.[8] So, too, is Leigh Gilmore's examination of "limit-cases," focusing on fictional and metaphoric representations that enable an engagement with past traumas. Whereas Gilmore discusses life writing that returns to past traumas "to represent a self who can differ from the identity trauma imposes," the texts I offer here are much closer in time to the affective events, and their metaphoric modes have a different relationship to them.[9] My analytical lens stays fixed on the correspondence between the writing environment and the text these authors produced because of it. As a picture of this correspondence comes into focus, I regard in each instance how life writing dimensions expand to fit the histories, protagonists, and scripts that these women devised and strategized in order to confront catastrophic events.

Susanna Egan's use of "crisis" in *Mirror Talk: Genres of Crisis in Contemporary Autobiography* comes nearer to my own use of "catastrophe" than Henke's psychoanalytically weighted "trauma" does. But there are important distinctions that "catastrophe" generates and maintains.[10] Setting the groundwork for the way she looks at crisis, Egan summarizes points made by Jean Starobinski and Anthony Paul Kerby. Crisis, for Starobinksi, refers to a radical change that took place in the author's life and warrants retelling, while Kerby distinguishes crisis as the basic conflict or tension that drives the narration.[11] Egan adds to their past-tense locus to explain that the crises motivating the texts she examines extend forward from the past into the present where they linger and stay unresolved. Crisis "is an unstable condition seeking change," a condition that is "current and continuing." To define the word in these terms opens up discussion to a wide survey of literature, because it is the persistent condition that leads to such life writing, characterized by instability, the textual presence of the body, generic experimentation, and dialogism whereby "one person is formed in relation to another."[12]

My own approach works somewhat in reverse in order to demonstrate the existence and importance of catastrophe narratives. The selections that I examine belong to a circumscribed category, and I hold to a restrictive definition, emphasizing the activity of writing as eruptive, not cumulative. Rather than look for past conflicts lingering on into the present, I concentrate on life writing characterized by a volatile occurrence *in* the present time of the writing or close enough to be a significant element in the mnemonic, creative process. This means that the occurrence is unanticipated or at the very least unpredictable in timing, destructiveness, and long-term results. Significantly, because catastrophes represent a breakdown of logic, they are far from being inevitable. Indeed, as the twenty-first century has already shown, catastrophes often introduce threats extreme enough to be incomprehensible, and the "disequilibrium," to return to Gilman and Katz's term, has extraordinary potency. Because the subject matter in catastrophe narratives is contingent on dire events that have just occurred, are occurring, or threaten to take place imminently, the prose may be uneven in style or tone or disjointed in organization. Catastrophe narratives are therefore highly responsive texts. Responsiveness involves confronting horrific circumstances, and confrontation generally involves submerging or displacing those circumstances into other narratives and personae.

The Holocaust was a crisis of unimaginable magnitude, and its horrors extend so far beyond conceivable bounds of human cruelty that it is important to see how survivors and their families live in a condition that is also catastrophic. Lyotard does this by situating survivors' past on "this side of the forgotten, much closer to the present moment than any past." Lawrence L. Langer uses the term "duration" to stress similarly that the Holocaust remains perpetually immediate, "not to be dredged from memory because it is always, has always been there."[13] These views contradict Starobinski's position that a radical change, followed by a series of experiences, leads to a new understanding or stage of life; cause-and-effect does not operate here because past and present converge. I use Grete Weil's work to illustrate this phenomenon from the perspective of someone who successfully fled the Nazis but whose husband was caught and put to death. Her work is a particularly vexing example of how survival itself can be experienced as a form of catastrophe when the terrible contradictions of identity from half a century earlier remain inexorable, unresolved, and disruptive. Writing as an old woman, Weil attempts to transform her memories and losses into a "new understanding." But because the Holocaust remains too close and will always be too close, the contradictions continue to erupt rather than ever be resolved. The author finds herself rejecting, then acknowledging her Jewish identity, gesturing toward contemporary Israel, then distancing herself from it. *The Bride Price* is a belated attempt to push out of "duration" and generate a developmental script for oneself—as a developing character. Weil rewrites a chapter of Jewish biblical history in order to open it up so that she, as a feminist and a Jew who declares her loyalty to Germany, can somehow fit into a Jewish context.

This study also examines ways in which life writing about terminal illness—whether written by the dying person or collaboratively—can also be a form of catastrophe narration. When death is not the consequence of a long illness but rather an anomalous event of horrendous proportions, it has dimensions of catastrophe that inevitably affect the writing of the narrative. To illustrate the powerful role that catastrophe may play in certain illness narratives, I take up the case of Isabel Allende's *Paula*. Part catastrophe, part crisis narrative, *Paula* records how Allende's daughter has an attack of porphyria, a metabolic and enzyme-related disorder, which is eventually fatal. Going into convulsions, Paula loses consciousness and goes into a coma. Rendered incapable of cognition or communication, she can neither tell her own story nor collaborate in her mother's account. Conventional dialogue is impossible, and there is no way to grasp Paula's suffering from Paula's perspective; in any event, that perspective would depend upon the patient's being aware of herself. From the perspective of the life writing work, the attack of porphyia that felled Paula *was* the crisis and is already in the past when Allende begins to write; the situation contains no constructive or reconstructive narrative possibilities. Instead, the catastrophe is what occurs, or more regrettably does *not* occur, *now* in Allende's present, which adheres to Langer's sense of duration. So the questions that I raise address ideas of absence within presence and autobiography as failed biography as well as a form of catastrophe narration.

Lili'uokalani, H.D., Banti, Weil, and Allende were all involved in heavily contextualized life writing activity, one that connects all of them despite the different catastrophes they experienced and the different cultures in which they lived and their relative position within them. These are, respectively, the loss of a country and delegitimation of its indigenous culture due to American expansion; the air battles of World War II; Allied and Axis fighting in northern Italy; the loss of a husband by genocide and a late-life stroke and coma; and a daughter's terminal illness linked emotionally to political violence and exile. These situations caused the authors to locate themselves, and something of their histories, in projects reflective of their oppressive conditions. The projects afford us insights into their lives not necessarily because they contain a plethora of autobiographical data—a number of them are only minimally autobiographical—but because we witness how their books answer to appalling news or events and then serve as mechanisms of negotiation. Some of these books are more successful than others in strengthening the women's resolve, endurance, or spiritual faith, but all refer in some fashion—explicitly or obliquely—to the heightened tensions the writers suffered while composing in the midst of catastrophe. Moreover, we discover details other than what continuous, less anxiety-ridden retrospective works would expose, for we experience the women in the interludes, during which they are making progress while they also call attention to what they are doing. Representations take place through a particular genre but are ultimately more expansive and far reaching. I thus refer to them in a more encompassing sense as an activity, a form of social behavior set off by material conditions and meant as a rebuttal and protest to the actuating conditions. I align myself with Barbara Harlow's view of autobiographical work that derives from social struggle as "constitut[ing] a new social history as well as a new literary corpus."[14] Like Michael M. J. Fischer, I approach life histories and representations as *inhabiting* diverse formats rather than simply *being* them.[15] The sum of these life histories or representations is greater than the whole, for by utilizing the genre (or genre combinations), each of these women acts socially, resistantly, and, by her own criteria, ethically.

Since their goals extended beyond traditional autobiographical expression, these women were not preoccupied with leaving behind completed, polished records of themselves. Committed to their projects as a way of resisting calamity, they had little reason to follow Western male traditions of autobiographical and biographical writing, which stress that the complete (or nearly completed) life be worthy of reproduction and then of admiration by contemporary and future generations. Liliʻuokalani initially may seem the most intent of the five women to adhere to Western formulas for self-representation. But despite emphasizing public achievements, *Hawaii's Story by Hawaii's Queen* is a shrewd example of writing back to catastrophe by exploiting prescriptive autobiographical modes. Liliʻuokalani depicts herself as a singular personage in ways that her own people would immediately recognize as counter to Polynesian traditions and values that put the community before the individual. She places herself and her life in the center of her story but, purposefully, in order to accomplish something different from traditional self-presentation. She was attempting a remarkable goal: to gain legitimacy from her readers on the American continent and then influence Americans' political sentiment and both houses of the American Congress. Nothing was further from her goal, and from the goals of any of these women, than merely recording a life well lived.[16] The traditional criterion that one's (male) life be a model for readers to emulate is out of the realm in which these women functioned. The life details that they provide served purposes more pressing than rounding out the richness of their experiences or showing that their lives deserve to be praised.

We know, moreover, that many women, because they lived private and socially marginalized lives, wrote autobiographical works that, in contrast to Western paradigms, tell partial stories—of their childhood, their position in the family, their role in the community with which they identified themselves. As many critics have observed, women's stories often stress collective, communal, and female consciousness.[17] In their works, Liliʻuokalani, H.D., Banti, Weil, and Allende also avoid privileging individualism over all other attributes and seek interdependent or plural relationships. They do this, however, not because they led insular lives but quite the opposite. They were accustomed to functioning politically, publicly, artistically, or professionally, and, to a large extent, their activity made them vulnerable to the disastrous occurrences that, in turn, triggered their projects. Whether they portray their lives relative to one other person or embedded in the life of a community, the isolation they experienced because of the catastrophes they faced is tempered by their looking outward. Most importantly, these women wrote partial life stories rather than teleological unities, illustrating ways that women have produced narratives that address conditions over which they lose control or never had control. Their protagonists do the unexpected, shifting themselves onto other narrative scripts or focusing on themselves idiosyncratically in order to carry out their real intentions. The works I examine illustrate this type of identic expansiveness through a reliance on displacement and plurality. Banti, Weil, H.D., and Allende clearly invoke a shared or interdependent subjectivity, since female characters other than the authors are present and the reciprocal correspondences are fairly evident. Lili'uokalani assumes a plural subjectivity though it is more abstract and dispersed, since as queen she embodies the spirit and the history of all her people. The characteristics of the "I" for all these women are part of a process that incorporates diverse permutations and juxtapositionings of selves and forms. The process shows them moving off from unguarded, vulnerable positions toward strongly voiced, larger, albeit segmented, constructions. The texts are often marked by breaks or narrative imbrications, suggesting the urgencies of catastrophe and the invocations of a plural, expansive, and gendered referentiality borne of catastrophe.

If catastrophe operates as a factor to trigger the work, the ongoing nature of the event can affect the genre-producing activity once the initial stages are under way. Looking at direct references to material conditions, I trace how external events are not only linked to the project as a whole but how they come to operate internally as part of the rhetoric and structure. Sometimes an external event will interrupt the writing process and lead these women, when they resume, to move across their own time and spatial borders and draw into their chapters pieces of history, fiction, documents, biblical renarratization, biographical fiction, and biography. The various displacements resuscitate characters from pages already destroyed (Banti rewriting a lost manuscript) and exhibit the writer replacing one body with her own (Allende narratively substituting herself for her daughter) or one catastrophe with another (Weil troping her medical condition into a version of Nazi persecution). These changes range from being calculated for political effect (Lili'uokalani depicting herself to meet Americans' expectations) to being the result of fear and defiance (H.D. writing to endure air raids and bomb attacks). They may also seem digressive, but only if viewed from either an excessively strict autobiographical perspective or from the perspective of any single one of the deployed genres. The changes are quite consistent as a pattern of partial or dispersed stories interacting with, and intercepted by, their social contexts. In effect, because the framework for each project is materially present, it is doubly situated outside and inside of the work; the larger problem, not one of psychic collapse, concerns representation and narrative choices.

Whatever the differences, the movements among genres, discourse levels, or modes of seeing and reading evince each book's extratextual emotional beginnings and reveal a correspondence between the whole life and partial views and between the unitary "I" and other subjectivities. The catastrophe creates a need for substitution, while substitution leads to metaphoric and tropological representations, which then pluralize and relativize the "I."

As readers we know, of course, that referentiality is never exact. There must always be distance and narrative transference between the life as it was led (or is being led) and its signifying language or signs.[18] Kristeva's analysis of metaphorical objects is useful in this regard because it characterizes metaphor as dynamic and in flux, a "movement towards the discernible, a journey towards the visible."[19] Writing in "Freud and Love: Treatment and Its Discontents," Kristeva describes how a sense of self develops through metaphoric and metonymic identification. As she explains, the introduction of a "metaphorical object" presents numerous possibilities of identification, direct and indirect. The object may itself serve as a model or contain within it a relevant pattern. "Incorporation" of the object, meaning assimilation, can also occur, in which case identification is deep enough for Kristeva to call it "fusion."[20] Although the discussion is more psychoanalytical than my own critical analyses, Kristeva's observations that the positioning of other persons and parts of things and phenomena contribute to one's subjectivity are relevant here. The "I" envisioned by each of these women avoids locating itself singularly or wholly. It emerges through an interplay with substitutive tropes, images, or extensions that are reflective and sometimes deflective but always necessary objects of identification.[21] After the external occurrence releases the project, so to speak, it becomes a subject of representation and therefore a literary or visual trope. For this reason, I illustrate throughout this study how events once drawn into the composing process provoke a simultaneity of the metaphoric and the literal, proximity and distance, self and others, autobiography and biography, life writing and fiction. I also discuss the bodies of these women as both a thing and a trope, from which other tropes and substitutions derive. Because it is the body that has been divested of authority or subjected to literal pursuit and attack, the mind that experiences the body under siege and works to textualize or visualize this is perhaps the most dynamic and paradoxical representation of all.

The text I initially examine is Liliʻuokalani's *Hawaii's Story by Hawaii's Queen*. Liliʻuokalani took over the monarchy in 1891 after her brother, Kalākaua, elected in 1874 by Hawaiʻi's legislature to be king, died while abroad. She was, in addition, a gifted composer and musician who, by her own count, wrote hundreds of songs for her people.[22] But over a hundred years of Anglo-European influence came to a head during her reign. She was forced to abdicate in 1893 and lost a series of political struggles that made it possible for her adversaries to end the Native monarchy. American or non-Polynesian inhabitants declared Hawaiʻi a provisional government in 1893 and in 1895 a republic. The U.S. Congress was voting on annexation in the summer of 1898. Liliʻuokalani understood all too well that her country, on the brink of extinction, was in a catastrophic period; if a political demise was imminent, a cultural demise would follow. A catastrophe of this magnitude actually taking place had been unimaginable in earlier decades. Since 1893, however, she had been forced to abdicate, put on trial, convicted of misprision, and incarcerated in one form or another for nearly two years. Liliʻuokalani wrote most of *Hawaii's Story by Hawaii's Queen* in a narrow interval—between late 1896, when her house arrest ended, and 1897—in time to be reviewed in U.S. newspapers and read by congressional delegates. Her efforts did not prevent annexation, of course, and Hawaiʻi became a U.S. territory. A century later the debates on Native sovereignty are everywhere.[23] They are certain to continue, gaining energy with the Apology Bill of 1993 and a U.S. Supreme Court Decision in 2000 concerning race and voting eligibility in the state's Office of Hawaiian Affairs.[24] It would be hard to predict how and when Native Hawaiians will determine their political status, but this much is certain: almost all Hawaiians were against annexation, and Liliʻuokalani wrote *Hawaii's Story by Hawaii's Queen* while she was under enormous pressure to make this message unambiguous to American readers.[25] The range of discourses and emotional intensities derive from the conditions that fueled the writing. Every page of this remarkable book and every one of its addresses to "you" assume the reader has no knowledge of the author's political and spiritual role and knows nothing of the Hawaiians' opinions on annexation. Liliʻuokalani's work is an eloquent political argument presented in the guise of autobiography. To use Fischer's word, the genre "inhabits" the project but is not the sum of its parts.

   H D. wrote *The Gift* as a strategy to withstand the destruction around her caused by a war four decades after Liliʻuokalani's political battles and eight thousand miles away. In contrast to Liliʻuokalani, whose text was a unique response to catastrophe (she never wrote anything similar to it), H.D. had been writing autobiographically for many years before she began *The Gift*. By the 1940s she had long since abandoned the crystalline poetry that once made her Ezra Pound's exemplary Imagist in favor of longer poetical works and autobiographically figured fiction. *Palimpsest* was published in 1926, *Hedylus* in 1928, and *Nights* in 1935. She had also written the autobiographical fictions *Paint It Today* and *Asphodel* in the 1920s, though neither was published until after she died.[26] Theoretically, she might well have begun her memoir of this period of early childhood at another time and in another place. But if H.D. had written *The Gift* in calmer years, either long before or long after the Luftwaffe attacks of the early 1940s, it would scarcely resemble the text we have today. *The Gift* draws disconnected episodes from childhood into the narrative, moving not from the past forward but rather from the present backward. It is the presence *in the present* of possible death that launches H.D. to uncover what she had forgotten for decades and then overlay it with references evocative of modern warfare.

Artemisia, too, was the result of its author's exposure to military attacks in World War II. Anna Banti was the pen name of Lucia Longhi Lopresti, a prominent art and literary critic in Italy who wrote fiction and short stories from the late 1930s until shortly before her death in 1985. *Artemisia*, the work for which she is best known, is most often acknowledged as a biographical fiction of one of the few women painters of the Renaissance, Artemisia Gentileschi. (Americans unfamiliar with Banti's treatment of Gentileschi may recall the film *Artemisia*, written and directed by Agnes Merlet, which came to the United States in 1998.) But *Artemisia* is also autobiographical. Indeed, Banti's story is a skeletal frame for Artemisia's historically based fiction. Banti lived in Florence when the Allies and the Germans were fighting in northern Italy in 1944. She wrote, or more accurately rewrote, parts of the manuscript in the aftermath of the bombardments that destroyed her house and the original pages of *Artemisia*. She worked on the second manuscript from 1944 to 1947 and refers often to the differences between the two versions. With Florence in disarray and herself in need of shelter and food, Banti had a second life story to refer to, and this was of her own devastating losses. She combines what she remembers from her first *Artemisia* manuscript with references to her own and others' suffering because of the immediate wartime catastrophe. The newly introduced autobiographical passages are both interruptive and productive in relation to the Renaissance story. They establish a dialogue between the two women, between their artistic ambitions and losses, and between the genres that present this information.

Like Banti, Weil wrote of her experience of World War II, but from the perspective of someone who fled her country to escape victimization. From the 1940s to her death in 1999, she published five novels and a number of short story collections under the long shadow of the Holocaust, including the translated *My Sister, My Antigone, The Bride Price,* and, in 1997, *Last Trolley from Beethovenstraat.*[27] *The Bride Price: A Novel* (1991) devotes many pages to a fictional recounting of the life of King David based on pertinent sections of the Old Testament. As successful as this biblical and feminist renarratization may be, Weil's purpose is not primarily novelistic. There is too much other material that readers must account for and too many intercalated autobiographical chapters. These personal sections recount parts of Weil's twentieth-century life story and reflect provocatively upon the renarratized biblical discourse. Weil explains in the eight chapters that are about herself—which are interspersed between thirteen long novelistic chapters—that as a child and as a young woman raised in Germany by German parents, she did not practice Judaism or ever consider herself Jewish despite having Jewish grandparents. She and her husband nonetheless fled to Holland—where they lived together until 1941, when he was taken to Mauthausen and killed there. Weil makes it clear that she has suffered each day of the second half of the century with a sense of disbelief that has never diminished, bringing to mind Langer's description of duration. Although she feels driven to record her wartime experience, the intensity prevents her from developing it into a completed teleological narrative. Most especially, it is the personal medical catastrophe she suffers while writing and visualizes as a collective wartime torture that impedes her progress in one direction and creates a position and self-image contradicting the earlier ones. *The Bride Price* is two stories: one autobiographical and the other a recasting of some of the most patriarchal and militaristic chapters of the Old Testament, the biographical story of David. Each story expands within the folds of the other so that Weil's recurrent attempts to write about her life move across one narrative implicitly into the other. Her autobiographical chapters and her Old Testament revision bifurcate each other as Weil seeks possibilities for female rebelliousness and protest and, in the process, reflects upon contradictions of prewar and postwar identity, diaspora, and homeland and what constitutes being and believing oneself to be Jewish.

In her books before *Paula*, Allende was able to transmute the events of her life and the politics of her birth country, Chile, into fictional narratives. After fleeing the regime of Pinochet and going into exile in Venezuela, Allende used military rule as a backdrop for her first novel, *The House of the Spirits* (1982), which she describes as "triggered ... by the desire to recover the world that I had lost after I had to leave my country and live in exile." Allende explains that her second novel, *Of Love and Shadows* (1984), also "was triggered by anger, anger and sadness, at the abuses of the dictatorship."[28] *Paula*, however, breaks this pattern of containment, because Allende in no way uses her daughter as a subject for sustained creative fiction. In the months she watches over her, Allende writes for the first time autobiographically and, to a lesser extent, biographically, telling herself that she is composing a journal to Paula that will necessitate a response, hoping against overwhelming odds that dialogue will one day be possible. Despite Allende's hope that one small improvement will lead to another until Paula breaks out of the porphyria-induced coma, the relationship of life writing, catastrophe, and the stasis of duration is consistent throughout. In fact, *Paula* is two discrete parts (and an epilogue). One part is written while the author perceives her daughter as poised to break out of a neurological catastrophe, the other major part when she recognizes that Paula has crossed a threshold into a perpetual crisis condition. In the former there are possibilities of sudden reversal and renewal, but in the latter hope is nearly gone. To write and publish this book was surely a painful accomplishment, because it was wholly dependent upon Paula's debilitation. Nearly all Allende's drafting took place in the duration of the coma, with Paula a living presence both within and outside of the specific project. Allende is forced to regard her daughter as a contested body or territory invaded by an invisible adversary she is not equipped to fight and which is argued over by innumerable physicians. Only in the epilogue does Allende finally accept the transformation from catastrophe into unchanging crisis when she recounts the details of Paula's death from a retrospective site, making it possible to narrate the agony (and beauty) of her daughter's last moments.

CATASTROPHE, SELF-REPRESENTATION, AND TROPES

Self-representation that occurs in response to immediate and alarming conditions is distinguished by its "troubles."[29] Because the "troubles" are powerful enough to destroy everything that is materially and spiritually familiar, women facing this threat look past their own time and place and represent themselves by moving broadly into tropological and metaphorical forms.[30] However, whatever the new representations may be—other women, sites, or genres—these never actually replace, never completely stand in for the subject or representation that preceded them because these women mean to address, not flee, their material surroundings. Earlier, unfinished stories come back, and present time can infiltrate the interior or embedded narrative as these women call attention to the activity of troping and substitution. Experiencing conflict and often conflicted themselves, they create through partial and multiple substitutions, which, given their conditions, seem more suitable than a leisurely developed, uninterrupted, unitary representation. This also means that Kristeva's idea of resolution and "fusion" coming out of metaphoric identification is too extreme to take place. But de Man's view of autobiography as a series of tropological substitutions (which therefore incorporate fiction) helps to explain the relationship of tropes to self-representation. De Man sees the troping movement away from the person behind the signature as centrifugal, capable of "infinite acceleration" and, presumably, of infinite distance.[31] Rather than expect fusion to take place, the reader or viewer must finally decide if, and when, the tropological progression pushes the work beyond any discernible kind of self-representation and draws it entirely into the realm of fiction or the scope of another subject. This implies that certain techniques, even those that are novelistic and distantiating, if autobiographically motivated, may be deployed for self-representational purposes. Women, writes Sidonie Smith, "secure themselves, dislodge themselves, or refashion themselves" by using "various technologies of subjectivity." The "technologies" and modalities vary, but the process of securing, dislodging, and refashioning indicates the importance of tropological extensions for life writing in catastrophes.[32] They help women with limited control over sudden and overpowering circumstances to establish a working distance from them. The number and types of narrative tropes and surrogates may therefore be in proportion to each woman's commitment to tell her story under pressure in whatever way becomes feasible. The writers I examine do not try to conceal the tropological elements of their work. Using tropes, they rely on framebreaking devices, story segments, and intertextuality to invoke a shifting, composite, collective, or palimpsestic subjectivity that counteracts the constraints and unique pressures they otherwise face.

THE BODY AND THE BODY'S TROPES

Of all the tropological substitutions that serve as additional "sites" for the autobiographical persona, the body is the most important and complex. It operates as a trope but is more than a trope, because the bodies of most of these women are bodies actually under siege—physically removed from office, imprisoned, under attack, hunted down, debilitated, exiled, or powerless while watching another body terminate. Experiences within history and the textual discourses about them therefore converge or almost converge in very conspicuous ways. Along these lines, Leslie Adelson proposes that the body is the primary site of history and historical discourse and asks in *Making Bodies, Making History:* "What is history if not the accounts of human bodies in and over time? History without bodies is unimaginable."[33] Once the body is foregrounded in historical or rhetorical discourse, the differences between subject and object—or thing and trope—are severely problematized, for "the body is so many things all at the same time. Sometimes the victim of history, it is always the object of historical construction, the site of historical experience, the arbiter of all cognition, and the material ground of freedom. It is a thing and a sign, an inside and an outside, a boundary constantly crossing itself."[34] The women who are my case studies similarly experience themselves as "a thing and a sign," as one thing to themselves and another thing to those responsible for the catastrophe. We therefore witness an important autobiographical event as it is taking place in the writing process—self-positioning and self-insistence in a variety of forms and sites while events threaten to diminish the women further or in some cases lead to their death.

Women in oppressive and sudden circumstances recognize these contradictory dimensions of themselves. Sometimes the sites on which they extend themselves are separate and discrete; other times they are a battleground of "multiple, conflicting subjectivities within the same body."[35] Lili'uokalani, for example, writes herself as a single autobiographical character and starts with the details of birth. Her unitary body, however, functions primarily as a referential or cultural code because she knows the kind of self-imagery American readers will expect of a Polynesian ruler, especially of one who is a woman. Initially she embodies and confines her identic complexities into "stereotypic bodies of knowledge" in order "to activate models of what is *vraisemblable*"—lifelike and in line with expectations of a Caucasian readership.[36] But being "so many things," among them politically motivated, tactical, and adept at turning the signs of exotic interpellation to her own purposes, Liliʻuokalani writes herself through a series of additional discourses. Her body changes as each textual site—from diplomatic letters, political documents, international treaties, to genealogies—produces different historical constructions that insist upon her racial body, her royal body, her political body (and body politic), and her spiritual presence. These plural bodies within Liliʻuokalani's autobiographically presented body emerge gradually and are perhaps more formidable because of the time they require to develop as simultaneously and plurally constituting Liliʻuokalani. They are powerful images that allow Liliʻuokalani and the culture and history she embodies to prevail, at least rhetorically, over the illegality and immorality of annexation. In particular, they allow her to address catastrophe as it occurs while the manuscript is under way and to alter her rhetorical strategies in response.

With H.D.'s body in immediate danger, or else threatened with danger for much of the writing time, the sense of the represented body throughout *The Gift* is both literal and figurative. The textual troping of the imperiled body moves in two directions. The first is toward damaged or deceased bodies of female victims. It develops mostly in the author's maternal and paternal genealogies of infants, children, and aunts who died young and often without explanations; yet the most affecting image is the unnamed little girl who burns to death when her dress is ignited during a school Christmas celebration. Underlying a second direction is H.D.'s active desire to construct defensive body images to counteract those occurring in the first direction. The most important images of female bodies are those that ordinarily would be most vulnerable to external violence, the very old and the very young. In important sections, the interacting grandmother and child protagonist are linked together as survivors and privileged as body transmitters of historical lessons that counter the catastrophe of the intermittent, unpredictable risk of death by bombs.

Artemisia shifts its bodies and texts around so that they compete as well as support each other. Banti arranges the sections of this biographical fiction so that they absorb elements of her life experience. She then uses her own body to *embody* the voice and life of her historically based character Artemisia Gentileschi. The tropological sequences become involuted as the autobiographical body moves across three centuries into different bodies and voices. In fact, the concluding chapters sweep up the ambiguities of visual and literary representation, referentiality, and the body by narratively performing Artemisia's famous self-portrait. Throughout this book the "I" is aligned to various female bodies, not just to Banti's or to the protagonist's in the biographical fiction that gradually unfolds. Another body who insists upon recognition belongs to yet another "Artemisia," one who was destroyed during the fighting in Florence. Readers learn quickly that Banti's initial manuscript was in her home when it was destroyed in the summer of 1944. The text that exists today capitulates that first story (to the extent it can be recalled) and expands upon its protagonist, drawing into its biographical and fictional boundaries Banti's immediate war experiences. This means that *Artemisia* is strewn with female bodies whose sites are "real" and contemporary, autobiographical, historical and biographical, and intertextual. Artemisia's intertextual body actually voices instructions to the "I" that signifies Banti concerning how she wants to be re-represented in this new text. Banti the author is already in the process of recreating the "other" Artemisia, the one who was the Renaissance portraitist and self-portraitist, who precedes the Artemisia of the lost manuscript and is not identical to her.

Like Banti who moves beyond her twentieth-century body into the past, Weil establishes in *The Bride Price* a tension between her own contemporary body and one that she finds in the Bible and fictionalizes for her own purposes. Writing in her very old age, Weil is distressed at her body's mortal signs. A stroke has affected her memory. Her age has affected her concentration. Her contrary feelings about her life center on her body, as one lone material thing that managed to elude the Nazis. Numerous factors, including resentment and guilt, cause Weil to have difficulty finishing her book. By shifting over to a surrogate story, in which another old woman reflects back on *her* long and conflicted life, Weil is able to progress. She makes an inventive and dazzling choice: Michal, King Saul's daughter and King David's first wife, given by her father to David as a reward for vanquishing the body of Goliath.[37] Weil seems fortified by using Michal and grafting this sister image and trope—including Michal's aging body— onto the manuscript to express what Weil, in her own body and voice, does not or cannot. Thus, *The Bride Price* begins with Weil as a child living in Germany, but by the second chapter there are two stories moving on divergent but mutually supportive tracks. The result is a dialectical performance of the embodied voices of the fictional/biblical Michal and the writerly/autobiographical Grete. Both struggle against the infirmities of their deteriorating bodies to generate text and occupy textual space, which are tropological figures of their histories and lives. Moreover, each woman articulates what Smith calls "unofficial knowledges" of the respective political cataclysms of the eras they survived. Both scathingly comment on the bodies killed in the name of nation building, Michal on King David's wars to transform Judah into a nation-state of Israel and Weil on Hitler's racial, religious, and social cleansing.[38] The boundaries between the author's voice, her narrational voice, and "her" subject's voice are not identical, but all of them are indeed autobiographical, autobiographically inflected and autobiographically informed. With the body "so many things at the same time ... a thing and a sign, an inside and an outside," the significance between ontological and material bodies has minimal import.

Allende also foregrounds women's actual bodies as she focuses on her own healthy body as well as her daughter's comatose, deteriorating body. But her immediate body, as Allende textually incorporates it in *Paula*, is also a trope, an imagined substitution for Paula's body because it is able both to enact and to recollect physical, intellectual, and sexual activities.[39] The literal and tropological positioning of the mother who represents herself because the "Other" is inaccessible nearly breaks down. This is because Allende wants to pass beyond the trope and give her body over to Paula, doing away with herself so that her daughter may revive and so that both crisis and catastrophe can be experientially erased. This relationality is particularly troubling, however. The mother veers away from the daughter for many pages at a time and traces the body of her own life history— her marriages, children, her midlife writing career, and political exile from Chile to Venezuela in the years of Pinochet's repression and violence. Indeed, the richness and length of Allende's autobiographical sections, corresponding inversely to the daughter's comatose body, become a kind of crisis for the reader. But this is in large part because Allende imposes punishing restrictions on herself. Her dilemma is how to make her text center on Paula without actually telling Paula's story, for to do so would be to appropriate what is not hers. Allende wants to keep Paula physically, at least, in proximity and addresses each day's writing to her (except for the epilogue). But because she will not take anything more from her daughter than has already been taken, Allende turns to her own life narrative as a way to mark time until, she tells herself, Paula regains consciousness. Her writing thus "inhabits" the framework of autobiography, but her purpose goes beyond it toward a maternal ethical activity (as contradictory as the ethics may seem) that responds to Paula's disastrous medical condition and, because of it, a crisis in biography. Because Allende's greatest hope is to put an end to her writing when Paula returns to conscious life, the more pages she generates and the more she develops autobiographically, the less probable her daughter's recovery becomes. In terms of referentiality and tropological substitutions involving bodies and textuality, Allende's completion of *Paula* corresponds, ironically and tragically, to Paula's dying.

The complex changes that Lili'uokalani, H.D., Banti, Weil, and Allende enact suggest women regaining authority, finding voice, and restoring emotional equilibrium. Their range of life writing modalities and their ways of altering fixed subject positions illustrate what Sarah Cornell explains in another context about the variability of the authorial "I."[40] The ability, Cornell writes, "to 'slide unceasingly' from one position to another offers the writer maximal narrative mobility [and] guarantees continuity even when the narrating 'I' is passionately carried away to the point of disappearance." Certainly, this practice of sliding from body to body and voice to voice offers Banti and the other women I examine a way to struggle against their own possible disappearances and, in Allende's case, to struggle against the disappearance—into a coma—of her daughter's sentient subjectivity. These ambiguous body positions operate strategically or at least defensively. They simultaneously enable "a metamorphic connecting flow between the moments of disappearance and reappearance" and identic self positioning relative to the sources of power that influence or threaten them.[41]

Women who envision the female body, their own in particular, as both a material "thing and a sign" may do so in different ways, but they all present their corporeal bodies as capable of extension and multiplication. When this takes place, they "secure" themselves through a double motion that "dislodges" or generalizes them away (returning to Smith's terminology) from their immediate and emotionally distraught conditions. The sites on which they subsequently redistribute or displace themselves include the bodies of other women from history, from their ancestors, and from previous texts of their own. Finally, because the most important autobiographical fact to be communicated concerns survival, it bears repetition and insistence and explains why the body in these works appears in so many permutations. This leads to a paradox, however. To position one's body *in* the representational medium is to acknowledge its material facticity and existence, to insist upon a corporeal grounding in considerations of gendered identity.[42] Still, the body-in-the-text is not the same as the living body.[43] As close as it may seem, the textual body is a tropological configuration that performs its function and creates the illusion of the thing itself through figuration and metaphors of embodiment. Throughout this study, I investigate two interrelated, though differently inflected ideas. Representation that closely adheres to its subject and visualizes it without intervening screens or without shifting into other discourses does not necessarily produce exacting, dependable images. Conversely, representation that opens up to wider angles of knowledge from intertexts, palimpsests, historical and political documents, secondary discourses, and "neighboring or even incompatible genres" does not lead away from life writing purposes.[44]

POSITIONS

The highly responsive nature of the works I examine underscores the impact of different historical moments upon women's self-representational activities. The elements of a catastrophe will differ according to an array of influences—politics, culture, geography, history, genealogy, race, ethnicity, sexuality, religion, and nationality. But despite these differences and along with them, catastrophe is a leveling experience, one that clarifies, as much as or perhaps more than anything else, a discrepancy in power relations. Catastrophe also causes those in its path to regard themselves in exaggeratedly self-conscious ways, precisely because catastrophe exposes the limits of what they can constructively achieve. And catastrophe brings to the foreground literal and figurative bodies as women are threatened and as they have experienced a history of being threatened. Finally, catastrophe can be either an overt or subtle organizing principle of self-representational productions. This is because the conventional cause-and-effect formula of autobiography that operates from the past to the present reverses itself. It operates from the present back to the past or disperses expansively and tropologically in ways that are unpredictable.

In the chapters that follow, I argue that the characteristics of catastrophe lead to self-representational forms markedly different from others that are produced in less pressured, less threatening contexts. My goal here is to maintain a focus on gender and certain types of catastrophe, while bringing together life writing selections from disparate catastrophes over the course of a century. In doing so, I try to foreground cultural specifics while keeping in mind Lionnet's opening statements in *Autobiographical Voices: Race, Gender, Self-Portraiture*: "We women are so diverse and live in such varied cultural, racial, and economic circumstances that we cannot possibly pretend to speak in a single voice. It is by listening to a plurality of voices from various corners of the planet and across centuries that we will strengthen our ability to resist demeaning power structures."[45] To be sure, women may feel themselves especially vulnerable in catastrophic times, and historically this has tended to be the case. Under the domestic, social, and legal jurisdiction of males (although jurisdictional practices vary from one culture and historical period to another), women have had ineffective mechanisms for defending themselves and for taking active and resistant measures. All of the women covered in this study, albeit in different ways, suffered the loss of traditional or customary sources of protection or defense, regardless of their class, race, or national affiliation.[46]

The writings of many critics have helped to clarify my ideas during this project. No one can participate in the field of women's life writing without acknowledging the groundbreaking studies by Sidonie Smith and Julia Watson. In addition, Caren Kaplan's work on feminist, transnational autobiographies; Leslie Adelson's study of gender and bodies in history; and Smith's book on women's bodies and autobiographical practice were instrumental in my own thinking about genre border crossing and ways that the body serves in catastrophe as an autobiographical configuration.[47] Lionnet's work in finding space for "intersubjectivity and reciprocity" in postcolonial inquiry through a *métissage* of indigenous and Western cultural forms was pertinent while I was drafting chapter 1.[48] G. Thomas Couser's *Recovering Bodies: Illness, Disability, and Life Writing* offered a broad context of illness narratives—covering breast cancer, HIV/AIDS, physical disability, and deafness—for my focused examination of Allende's writing about porphyria. Although Barbara Harlow concentrates in *Resistance Literature* on the Middle East, Latin America, and Africa, the section on women, liberation, and autobiography was very useful while I was conceptualizing this study and especially as I embarked on the chapter on *Hawaii's Story by Hawaii's Queen*.[49]

The work of these and many other critics indicates how far we have come in seeing beyond our own national and ethnic borders. This applies especially to those of us who live in communities different from those in which we were raised. Like my colleagues at the University of Hawai'i, I try to engage in ongoing debates relevant to the location where we teach and to encourage students to do the same. In Hawai'i this means engaging ideas of nationalism, colonialism, and interethnic relationships that may not occur elsewhere in the United States, at least not in identical ways. These ideas derive from a history of incursive forces coming between the Hawaiians and their spiritual and traditional connections to the land:

European voyaging expeditions, competing colonialisms, a plantation economy, Western concepts of ownership, World War II, and, most recently,
American statehood. As someone whose mother lived in Russia while the
Czar was alive and whose paternal family perished in World War II, I
learned to view location as a site of potential danger, and genealogy as
a category of knowledge better left unknown. To be sure, I understood
that catastrophe and upheaval could happen at any time, but until then
one location was as good—or as dangerous—as another. With almost
two decades of living in a Pacific Island culture, I am constantly learning
new lessons in contrasting values, particularly regarding relationships to
the land, generational continuity, and ethnic-cultural communities. Attentive to events where I live and looking for related historical and cultural
circumstances, I certainly recognize that my work is tentative, subject
to discussion and revision. I hope that my errors eventually will be less
important than the conversations intended to help make certain issues
public and politically viable. I also hope that the women I study will find
a wider audience in the life writing community of scholars and readers.

　　All of these factors suggest that while my presentation is chronological, it is not meant to be developmental. The historical specificity of one
situation does not lead to that of the next, and I avoid positing a master
narrative of autobiographical works composed under the pressures of
catastrophe. Instead, by examining a cluster of works in which women
respond to material conditions by adapting and modulating rhetorical
forms, I demonstrate a variety of ways that sudden disaster problematizes
the link between autobiographical intentions and autobiographical genres.
I also emphasize the importance for life writing theory of differentiating
responses to protracted crises from responses to immediate, proximate,
and overwhelming catastrophe. To this end, although my chapters examine five diverse examples, each chapter pays close attention to changes
in the texts as the authors map their movements from catastrophe into
crisis or crisis into catastrophe.

　　I conclude by returning to the comment by Lejeune cited earlier in this
introduction: "In spite of the fact that autobiography is impossible, this
in no way prevents it from existing." Lejeune was not referring to the difficulties of life writing relative to catastrophe but to human nature as
equally hopeful and skeptical, believing and disbelieving. "Telling the
truth about the self, constituting the self as complete subject—it is a fantasy." But, he adds, "We *indeed know* all this; we are not so dumb, but once
this precaution has been taken, we go on as if we did not know it."[50] The

desire to believe and the desire to create so that others will believe encircle the necessary illusions of referentiality that are produced by life writing tropes. The women studied in these pages, who were pressured by circumstances and exigencies beyond their control, did not "go on as if [they] did not know it." They "went on" because they *did* "know it," and this freed them to envision self-representation, to return to H.D., as "things under things, as well as things inside things."[51] They "went on," using life writing genres in order to move beyond genres toward action, protest, and survival.

Queen Liliʻuokalani in the early 1890s. *Hawaiʻi State Archives*

CHAPTER ONE

Autobiography as Political Discourse

Liliʻuokalani's *Hawaii's Story by Hawaii's Queen*

T HERE IS A ROYAL PALACE in the United States, and it stands in the middle of downtown Honolulu. Known as ʻIolani Palace, it was the seat of government of Liliʻuokalani, who ruled from 1891 until her monarchy was overthrown in 1893. After she was tried in 1895 by a military tribunal, ʻIolani Palace served as her prison for eight months. And on August 12, 1898, it was here where the American flag was raised and the Hawaiian flag was lowered to signify the annexation of Hawaiʻi to the United States. A resistance movement had been operative at least since midcentury, and thousands of Hawaiians, including the ex-queen, continued to protest by boycotting the annexation ceremony. Six months earlier, though, Liliʻuokalani had shown her resistance in a very different way. Prompted by political events in the United States that had drastic implications for the Hawaiian population, she had written and quickly published *Hawaii's Story by Hawaii's Queen*.[1] The text of this autobiography begins in 1838, the year that Liliʻuokalani was born, and it ends in 1897, when she was nearly sixty years old and recently freed from months of house arrest that followed her palace incarceration. Her book received attention in the United States, and reviewers were impressed with what they took to be the former queen's sincerity. They also cited Liliʻuokalani for her "discretion" and "self-control," with one reviewer remarking that her manner and style proved that "the work of American missionaries . . . was not in vain."[2]

Although the author must have seemed very appealing to American readers, Liliʻuokalani's autobiographical protagonist is clearly the result of a well-planned, political performance strategy. She relied on autobiography to create sufficient space for her to discredit the political parties that overthrew her government and ultimately to stop annexation from ever taking place. In other words, Lili'uokalani composed her life story during a time of crisis and intended it as a response to that crisis. Like the life writings connected to crisis that Susanna Egan discusses in *Mirror Talk,* the driving force behind *Hawaii's Story by Hawaii's Queen* was instability. Conflict, which is integral to a climate of instability, may lead to immediate and long-range disturbances, but the basic instability endures and profoundly influences the way that people subjected to it must live and the way that many of them write. As Egan emphasizes, autobiographical representation in a context of crisis derives from a "current and continuing" situation. People respond to "the pressure of their lived experience" and their need for resolution, and thus their personal narratives are also crisis narratives reflecting the social and political pressures that operate on them.[3] Lili'uokalani responded to the pressures of her "lived experience." Arrested in January 1895 for treason, she was put on trial and declared guilty of misprision of treason. She not only served eight months in prison in 'Iolani Palace, but she spent an additional five months under house arrest in her private home, Washington Place, and then eight more months confined to the island of O'ahu. In late 1896, almost two years after her arrest, when she was finally allowed to leave Hawai'i, she traveled to Washington, D.C., for what she described as exile in a foreign land (94, 110). The trip was a cautionary move made once William McKinley, widely thought to favor annexation, had won the U.S. presidential election. Locked out of official politics but wanting the American public to understand her point of view, Lili'uokalani proceeded to work on a manuscript she had initially entitled "Recollections." She describes her early experiences by using conventions of the literary paradigm suitable for a woman writing autobiographically in the late nineteenth century—in other words, the conventions used by male writers. However, she does so as a subversive course of action. She portrays herself in ways that are familiar enough to convince Americans that she shares many of their social, religious, and cultural values, but she carefully reveals herself to be culturally different enough in order to convince them that Hawai'i should remain separate from their own country. By progressing *through* a paradigmatic script, Lili'uokalani develops herself as a woman with the trappings of late Victorian conventions, and then gradually as a woman who is defiantly *in*dependent of convention and critical of the forces that would colonize her and all Hawaiians.

But *Hawaii's Story by Hawaii's Queen* is more than an autobiography written in response to an ongoing crisis. In the later chapters the author makes a strategic, rhetorical shift and produces what I define as a "catastrophe" narrative. Unlike crisis, which may increase in intensity as time goes by because smaller conflicts and the continuing presence or buildup of tensions fuel it, catastrophe gains power from sudden impact and thus demands an immediate reaction. When catastrophe strikes, it produces a sharp break in ongoing, established patterns of conflict often because those who experience the break did not recognize that catastrophe was imminent. Hawaiians knew that the oligarchy of businessmen running their country was striving for annexation, and most Hawaiians also recognized that the new American president, William McKinley, favored it. But McKinley's decision to send an actual treaty to the U.S. Senate by June 1897, just a few months after his inauguration, was calamitous. It changed the terms of the long-standing political crisis for Hawai'i, and it triggered an unprecedented catastrophe as perhaps no other single event since the arrival of Captain James Cook in the late eighteenth century and the start of Western contact. McKinley's decision also meant that the future of Hawai'i would be determined by elected officials in the U.S. Congress, who knew little about Polynesian culture other than what they read in American newspapers and editorials, which was often inaccurate. In response to this sudden emergency development, Lili'uokalani altered her own course of action. She reacted aggressively and quickly by sending a formal protest to the U.S. State Department, without knowing who, if anyone, would read the document or what would subsequently become of it. Without official diplomatic status, she was only a private visitor temporarily living in exile in Washington, D.C. She was also an anomaly: a Polynesian woman of color from a group of small islands in the middle of the Pacific Ocean who was determined to influence the highest strata of American politicians and diplomats. While in Washington, she continued writing the autobiography that she had started before June 1897, in the period when annexation was still a long-standing possibility but not an imminent political fact. The manuscript was a place where she could respond at length to the one catastrophe that would push Hawai'i as she knew it into extinction, as soon as both houses of Congress agreed to vote on the issue.[4] After June 1897, when the annexation bill was made official and being widely discussed, Lili'uokalani worked on the last sections of her book, completing them by September 1897 while the outcome of the catastrophe was still uncertain. *Hawaii's Story by Hawaii's Queen* was available in January 1898 and ready to be a part of the debate.

This chapter argues that the author modified her autobiographical strategies when the political stakes were at their highest and the opportunities to influence the debates at their lowest. It examines the reciprocal relationship between intentionality and methodology by showing that Lili'uokalani, already using autobiography as a crisis narrative, steps up the writing process and changes her techniques when President McKinley's action poses the ultimate threat. The reader thus witnesses the evolution of the narrative from crisis to catastrophe through a textual transformation. In the latter part of the narrative, *Hawaii's Story by Hawaii's Queen* generically shifts away from a single-voiced autobiography subversively using a female bildungsroman and becomes a work of political heteroglossia, what Bakhtin explains as multiple voices articulating multiple ideologies in various levels of language.[5] This is achieved in the autobiography primarily through the introduction of diverse documents, which contain different and interrelating voices and points of view, and the embedding of political and cultural discourses directly into its text. A formidable strategy, it allowed Lili'uokalani to participate in the deliberations over Hawai'i's future while she was barred from doing so in her own body and public life. She argues intensely in the later chapters of the book, using documentary texts in place of characters, presenting languages, styles, and points of view so they clash and counter one other. At the same time, she is able to control the debate over annexation and colonialism in ways that she could no longer do in person. Shifting to a catastrophe mode finally gives the "I" the evidentiary weight for Lili'uokalani, in her closing discourse, to perform convincingly in her own voice, rather than as an autobiographical protagonist, and to appear to speak out directly and intimately to her readers in the United States.[6]

THE CRISIS NARRATIVE

Critics no longer argue whether autobiographical traditions were historically oppressive to women or whether race, nationality, and class exacerbate the problems when women must adapt their lives to a paradigm ill suited to their gendered experiences.[7] They concentrate instead on ways in which these factors pressure the old paradigm, and they generally assume that the more marginalized the woman, the more oppressive the paradigm and the more imperative the need for alternative genres. Addressing the issue of alternative genres, Caren Kaplan looks at "counterlaw or *out-law*" writing, which breaks the "most obvious rules of genre" and recasts itself to better serve the geopolitical cause of the writer.[8] Among the most politicized recastings of autobiography she studies are women's *testimonios* and prison memoirs. Without disagreeing over the importance of texts that overtly break generic prescriptions, I think that an autobiographical work that does not exhibit itself as "outlaw" can nonetheless accomplish outlaw goals, especially if one exhibiting itself as outlaw would fail. This is particularly true when the crisis needs coalition building more than it needs controversy because negotiations are occurring at the highest levels of politics that by nature tend to be conservative. *Hawaii's Story by Hawaii's Queen* is a case in point. Published and distributed in the United States for American readers, it was intended to create an understanding of the Hawaiians' point of view. By necessity then, it had to appear to be generically and politically conservative even though it is extremely bold on both these counts.[9] If considered "outlaw," *Hawaii's Story by Hawaii's Queen* could have been seen at the onset as highly critical of the United States and failed to gain the audience for which it was intended.

In the early chapters the crisis narrative interjects criticism within the parameters of the bildungsroman, effectively and subtly using this convention for subversive purposes. The bildungsroman was not an oppressive format, but a liberating one, because its very conventionality offered a framework for political activism once Lili'uokalani had met the terms of house arrest and was allowed to emerge from isolation. Adhering to genre prescriptions was an excellent strategy to compete for allies in the United States, just as her adversaries, whom she calls "foreign residents of American birth or sympathies," were doing by petitioning and sending their own emissaries to Washington (23). Some women in dire circumstances negotiate disaster by creating autobiographical substitutions so extreme that their original self-representational purpose is hard to discern; autobiographical intentions may lead into fiction, and biographical intentions are worked through *auto*biographical forms. In contrast, Lili'uokalani—from an extreme point of marginalization—does not immediately veer away from her storyline. She adopts autobiography not in spite of its traditional associations but *because* of the potential they offer in gaining broad exposure for the Hawaiian point of view expressed by a Hawaiian. Her "direct" story is consequently a tropological device, serving as a necessary substitute for participatory action. Whereas the life writing texts by women marginalized by fewer obstacles more obviously use tropes to impose distance between the crisis and the author, the early discourse in *Hawaii's Story by Hawaii's Queen* is subtly tropological. This is attributable to the fact that giving the impression of authenticity and accuracy is imperative. But the degree to which fusion, to use Kristeva's term, or even near-fusion occurs between Lili'uokalani as character and Lili'uokalani as ex-queen is less relevant than the fact that the character creates legitimacy for the person and thus for the political stance. There is no question that Lili'uokalani recognized the purposes that literary work could pragmatically serve. During her reign, for example, with political tensions mounting in 1892, she wrote to her niece and heir apparent: "You are studying literature. It will also be of *great advantage* to you. To be able to write a history, to compose a poem, to write anything which will prove a fertile & cultivated mind is an accomplishment which one in your station ought to be master of."[10] This warning to her niece Ka'iulani, that a creative offensive approach may be necessary for the next monarch uncannily foreshadows her own autobiographical project five years later. She may, in fact, already have been thinking about it.

The preliminary function of the early chapters is to create legitimacy for an author who will gradually move the discourse into undisguised criticism. It does this repeatedly because every other function of the text depends upon there being no serious doubts over Lili'uokalani's credibility. However, the narrating voice cannot establish itself as trustworthy by mere assertion, because the woman it represents has no standing in the international community. Her public reputation comes from the American press that "has seemed to favor the extinction of Hawaiian sovereignty" and, she adds, personally "treated me with coarse allusions and flippancy, and almost uniformly has commented upon me adversely, or has declined to publish letters from myself and friends conveying correct information upon matters which other correspondents had, either willfully, or through being deceived, misrepresented" (371). Gender, race, and her tenacity against the men who forced changes in Hawai'i's constitutions detrimental to the Native people, had made Lili'uokalani a subject of criticism and mockery. Misogynist and racist descriptions were common in the press and journalistic accounts, declaring her anything from a "baleful, degrading influence" to "a black pagan queen."[11] To draw a different picture, the narrator selects references and bits of history that build a rapport between her autobiographical character and readers and gradually create a sympathetic rapport between them and the author.

Even more urgent than establishing her intelligence is the need to alleviate suspicions that Lili'uokalani cannot be trusted, and religion becomes a vehicle for this purpose.[12] A spiritual and religious woman, Lili'uokalani uses religion tactically to bridge a cultural divide and counter the stereotyped and vitriolic representations of her in the media and by the pro-annexationists.[13] Treating religion rhetorically, she dramatizes and implies analogously through myth that her own religious beliefs have been entirely Christianized. On the first page the narrating voice, in line with the bildungsroman form, reviews her ancestral heritage. Giving little space to her parents and great-grandfather (all of chiefly lineage), she pays attention to a great-grandaunt instead. Also of chiefly lineage, "the celebrated Queen Kapiolani" was known for her devotion to Christianity, and thus she provides an extremely important link between Lili'uokalani and readers. The narrator tells the story of how this female ancestor vanquished the goddess of the volcano. Like a Crusader of the European Middle Ages, Kapiolani fearlessly entered pagan territory and descended into its boiling lava. She survived, and her action "broke forever the power of Pele, the fire-goddess, over the hearts of her people" and brought Christianity to her people. This story is necessary only in the context of its intended readers for whom the declaration of Christianity is important. Lili'uokalani had a deep knowledge of Polynesian history and storytelling, and her own attitude toward religion was encompassing and complex. She wrote an English translation of the *Kumulipo*, the Polynesian account of the Creation, while she was imprisoned and published it just before her autobiography; this edition is still used today.[14] By opening the autobiography with a Christianized myth that was scarcely older than Lili'-uokalani, the "I" establishes genealogical and gendered connections to a woman she expressly designates as "one of the first converts to Christianity." Noticeably absent from this account, however, is any personal statement to confirm that the writer unambiguously endorses its didactic lesson. The omission further suggests that the victory the text performs is only the most obvious of meanings. There is a subtext for those few readers who seek it. This is a personal narrative of a single Hawaiian woman, Lili'uokalani, who, against all apparent odds, rebels when necessary and takes an aggressive approach in order to act on her deepest beliefs. In other words, the values performed by the autobiographical script are not synonymous with those implicit in the subtext.

Adhering to the customary format, the autobiography also includes the story of the protagonist's birth and childhood, but, like many other parts of this narrative script, the segment is primarily a vehicle to corroborate the requisite character trait of sincerity. Focusing less on the actual birth than on events just afterward, the narrator takes a more daring tack than in the Pele account. Instead of camouflaging and merely alluding to differences of culture, the text goes in the opposite direction and draws attention to them. Then it skillfully manages that information so that it, too, can serve the performing script. The narrating voice introduces the Hawaiian *hanai* tradition of sharing children. It describes how the protagonist, just after birth, was taken from her parents' home and given to another *ali'i*, or chiefly family.

> But I was destined to grow up away from the house of my parents. Immediately after my birth I was wrapped in the finest soft tapa cloth, and taken to the house of another chief, by whom I was adopted. Konia, my foster-mother, was a granddaughter of Kamehameha I., and was married to Paki, also a high chief; their only daughter, Bernice Pauahi, afterwards Mrs. Charles R. Bishop, was therefore my foster-sister. In speaking of our relationship, I have adopted the term customarily used in the English language, but there was no such modification recognized in my native land. I knew no other father or mother than my foster-parents, no other sister than Bernice. I used to climb up on the knees of Paki, put my arms around his neck, kiss him, and he caressed me as a father would his child; while on the contrary, when I met my own parents, it was with perhaps more of interest, yet always with the demeanor I would have shown to any strangers who noticed me.... This was, and indeed is, in accordance with Hawaiian customs. (4)

As a highly calculated inclusion, this passage gives sanction to Polynesian traditions simply by acknowledging that the hanai practice exists. Why claim this history of the body when Lili'uokalani knows that readers in America will harshly judge it? The answer is that the information displays a narrator, and thus an author, who is quite willing to carry out the autobiographical obligations of frankness and sincerity, even at the risk of disapproval. As long as the "I" can show that she recognizes how problematic the sharing of children will be for readers who know little about Hawai'i, she can use the passage advantageously. On the one hand she says candidly that most of her siblings were adopted into the families of other chiefs. She seems to cast about for an "intelligible" rationale and finds that it is "not easy to explain its [the hanai custom] origin to those alien to our national life" (4). On the other hand, with a slight shift in perspective, she establishes the practice as a very positive phenomenon, one that contrasts with the dissension and rivalries brought about since her non-Hawaiian adversaries have fought for power to the point of obliterating such Native customs. It is, indeed, this hanai family system, which "cemented the ties of friendship between the chiefs" and "spread to the common people," that "has doubtless fostered a community of interest and harmony" within the Hawaiian population (4). Most shrewdly, by including this nonparadigmatic element within the sequence of her origins and birth, the "I" claims even broader authority than before to be restored to her role as queen. She displays chiefly lineage from four parents and establishes her position through four genealogical lines rather than just two. The slight gesturing toward an apologetic stance is clearly a narrational pose, and it solidifies her persona and makes her enunciating voice more persuasive.

Establishing authority for the narrating "I" makes it possible for the early chapters to undermine at intervals the values they otherwise seem to confirm. The most frequent device for accomplishing this is to turn the more intimate material outward by depersonalizing it and then using it for political commentary. The narration, which picks up details from a remembered incident, re-forms them into critical barbs and changes the tone of voice to match. Even though the interjections do not hamper the larger scheme that works to naturalize the protagonist, they do have a destabilizing effect. This can be seen, for example, in the passages where the narrator describes her education. A script of the maturing young protagonist should include passages on her education, and this one initially seems no different. The missionary-run boarding school that Lili'uokalani attends is geared to prepare the royal children to be future monarchs, and they learn subjects such as language and religious practice.[15] Quickly, though, the narrating voice becomes strained, and rather than continue to review her schooling, the "I" settles into a single memory and chooses her words very carefully. The teachers, she writes, were "especially particular to teach us the proper use of the English language; but when I recall the instances in which we were sent hungry to bed, it seems to me that they failed to remember that we were growing children" (5). The nascent sarcasm is one element of a paragraph that seems to promise an overview of the education but offers close to nothing. That is to say, the passage shifts into an account of the teachers in order to become a picture of their hypocrisy. At first the memory is secondary to the developing story, but then it enables the narrator to have her say without actually having to say it.

At the exclusion of other possible school scenes, the memory serves as a trope, one that foreshadows the way the narrative will soon analyze the native/foreigner dynamic. It establishes that dynamic in binary terms, which

stress the differences and keep the lines of the conflict easy to understand
and less complex than they actually were. In this instance the teachers
who neglect caring for the royal children ("including three future kings
and one queen") are a character trope for all the visitors who arrived in
Hawai'i on the pretext of improving conditions of the population. To
work the trope, the narrator makes her next memory very specific, that of
frequently being hungry while attending the Royal School:

> A thick slice of bread covered with molasses was usually the sole article
> of our supper, and we were sometimes ingenious, if not over honest, in our
> search for food: if we could beg something of the cook it was the easier way;
> but if not, anything eatable left within our reach was surely confiscated.
> As a last resort, we were not above searching the gardens for any esculent
> root or leaf, which (having inherited the art of igniting a fire from the fric-
> tion of sticks), we could cook and consume without the knowledge of our
> preceptors. (5)

The degree to which the story is accurate in every one of its details is not
the central point. What matters is that the teachers' neglect relegates the
students of chiefly rank to a state of powerlessness and that the narration
makes two acerbic points before it returns to the more benign memories
that dominate this part of the autobiography. One, the missionary couple, the Castles, closed their school and became very wealthy, breaking
ties with their mission and becoming entrepreneurs with another missionary family, the Cookes.[16] Two, the Castles' sons were active in the oligarchy that overthrew Lili'uokalani's government.[17] The experience of
education thus converges into a single trope that reflects all foreign visitors, who, purporting to have superior knowledge, are corrupt intruders
siphoning off the resources of Pacific lands.

Once the protagonist is shown to be credible in a series of domestic
and local contexts, the narrator places her into more consequential scenes,
and the individual life story is succeeded by a more overtly political
design. In it the adult Lili'uokalani is shown as the subject of respect on
a scale that far surpasses the expectations of her intended readers. The
narration, rather than focusing on cultural ties to other Pacific islands,
shrewdly emphasizes Hawai'i's place within the global community. It works
hard, for instance, to show ways in which the ali'i have been welcomed
enthusiastically into the European community of rulers. This point is
made in an early chapter where Prince Alfred, Duke of Edinburgh, visits

Honolulu in 1869, long before Liliʻuokalani becomes queen, and initiates a personal bond through their common interest in music. By her own count Liliʻuokalani wrote hundreds of songs, including "Aloha ʻOe," which was used in her lifetime as a national anthem (32) and remains today one of the best known of all Hawaiian songs. She informs readers that she can "scarcely remember the days when it would not have been possible for me to write either the words or the music for any occasion on which poetry or song was needed." Stressing that her ability was an inherited gift rather than a talent nurtured by missionary teachers, she adds: "To compose was as natural to me as to breathe; and this gift of nature, never having been suffered to fall into disuse, remains a source of the greatest consolation to this day" (30–31). In fact, historians now credit her for being the most prolific Hawaiian composer of the century.[18] More intent on using music to link these two individuals than on detailing her talent, the passage uses the figure of British royalty as a troping device to contest the popular image of Liliʻuokalani as uncultivated. Upon leaving, the Duke of Edinburgh privately shared with Liliʻuokalani two of his own musical compositions, a gesture that signifies his appreciation of her musical abilities and, even more importantly, exhibits a commonality between a royal male from the center of the colonial empire and royal female from the margins.

As a strategy this emphasis on the queen's social position and privileges serves pragmatic and performative functions. The book had to make a strong, positive impression to enable the narrator, in later chapters, to take issue with U.S. representatives and senators and to be taken seriously when discussing the policies of three U.S. presidents—Benjamin Harrison, Grover Cleveland, and William McKinley. To succeed at this the narration places the autobiographical subject in increasingly politicized scenes. This bolsters her credibility as an experienced and astute player in volatile diplomatic situations. Specifically, it moves her into European and American locales not because these make for an interesting story but because they are the contexts in which Hawaiʻi's future has to be discussed.

"Outlaw" autobiographies, as Kaplan notes, "are tied to a struggle for cultural survival rather than purely aesthetic experimentation or individual expression."[19] This means that each text adopts strategies that are workable at a particular site and that find a balance between form and function. *Hawaii's Story by Hawaii's Queen* is certainly an aggressive effort even if its autobiographical emplotment seems superficially to affirm Western practice and values. A case in point is the long stretch of discourse that follows a Hawaiian delegation to London in 1887 for Queen Victoria's Jubilee. Ten chapters lavish attention on the journey and its participants, among them King Kalākaua's wife, Kapiʻolani; Liliʻuokalani and her husband, John Dominis; and various attendants.[20] It contains anecdotes that readers would find appealing, and, more to the point, it situates the

Liliʻuokalani as princess. *Hawaiʻi State Archives*

indigenous monarchy prominently and globally. The magnanimous treatment the Hawaiian royal figures receive in Great Britain as well as America is contrasted to the contemptuous treatment they receive at home from persons who themselves have Anglo-American ancestry but no hope of ever achieving comparable status or respect. For emphasis, the narration describes the ceremonial events at great length, including the stopover in Washington, D.C. Not only do numerous senators and the secretary of state accompany the visitors while touring the area, but President Cleveland, known to disapprove of annexation, and his wife host them at the White House. Socializing with the president is merely a prelude to meeting with Queen Victoria, who privately receives the female visitors from Polynesia—Kapi'olani, the current queen, and Lili'uokalani, the sister of the king—as soon as they arrive in London.[21] All that is needed is a short scene in which a royal alliance, and a feminine one, is established, and this takes place as the royal bodies of the women signal a common identity. In a gesture of open affection and female bonding, the woman who rules the British Empire greets "*her sister sovereign*, Kapiolani" and kisses her on both cheeks (144; emphasis added). The gesture of female affiliation extends to Lili'uokalani, who receives a kiss on the forehead. This meeting is thus presented as something other than an official appearance, rather as an occasion for the three women to converse in private. Lili'uokalani recalls that the end of the meeting was as affectionate as the beginning, and more intimate: "The two queens exchanged kisses as before, and the Queen of England again kissed me on the forehead; then she took my hand . . . and said, 'I want to introduce to you to my children'; and one by one they came forward and were introduced" (145). Numerous other passages accomplish the same purpose, which is to establish the special treatment accorded the visitors from the Pacific and to demonstrate the respect they received from monarchs from around the globe.

The text's movement away from the autobiographical bildungsroman begins in the midst of this ultimate of legitimating contexts. Located in two juxtaposed passages, the shift is a sign that neither the structural principles nor the emphasis on the author's individuation will be needed, at least on a consistent basis. Thus, the real focus and purpose of *Hawaii's Story by Hawaii's Queen* come through just as Lili'uokalani's self-portrait is most distinguished. From this point on—until the unexpected catastrophe of McKinley's annexation bill affects the text dramatically—the "I" more overtly uses the text to serve as a crisis narrative. Its foremost function is to present the critical events that have coerced changes to the monarchy and its constitutions, with devastating results for the Hawaiian people. To embark on this *other* history, in which the female protagonist is given a smaller and smaller role, Liliʻuokalani fashions a different script. Its first scene places side-by-side the terrible events in Hawaiʻi that were occurring at the very same time as the public celebrations in Great Britain:

> This was to be our final interview [with Queen Victoria], and the afternoon with its pleasures soon passed away; we bade adieu to our royal hostess, wishing her with all our hearts many, many more years of prosperity as a sovereign, and content[ment] and peace as the woman whose name is respected and loved wherever the sun shines throughout the wide, wide world.
>
> Returning to our hotel, we received news which changed at once the current of our thoughts. This was of the revolutionary movement, inaugurated by those of foreign blood, or American birth, in the Hawaiian Islands during our absence. It was indeed a case of marked ingratitude; for this rebellion against constituted authority had been brought about by the very persons for whose prosperity His Majesty King Kalakaua had made such exertions, and by those to whom he had shown the greatest favors. On receipt of the intelligence, we decided that, instead of continuing our proposed tour, and visiting the continent of Europe, we would return at once to Honolulu. (173)

The juxtaposed passages contrast harmony abroad with disorder at home, associating harmony with monarchal tradition and the latter with revolution against it. The passages also shut down the continuous narration that thus far has been personal and autobiographical. Chapters entitled "A Sketch of My Childhood," "Some Incidents of My Youth," and "My Married Life" are now followed by chapters with titles indicating larger historical and political interests: "Invited to Conspire Against the King," "Hawaiians Plead for a New Constitution," and "Overthrow of the Monarchy." The chapter titles that continue to refer to the individual autobiographical subject make the obvious point of locating her in volatile and highly politicized scenes. These include "I Am Placed Under Arrest," "Imprisonment—Forced Abdication," "Brought to Trial," "Sentenced—My Prison Life," and "Released on Parole."

Critics are inclined to say that autobiographers in extremely trying circumstances or crises find new forms of expression because conventional ones fail to incorporate their lived experience. As the order these writers once depended on breaks down, elements such as chronology and character development lose relevance and applicability: "Failed narrative or disrupted processes of narrative," writes Egan, "posit the impossibility of traditional story."[22] In Liliʻuokalani's autobiography the disrupted narrative is quite different because it represents a willed decision, not a symptom of the impossibility of traditional narrative. The storyline breaks open for a more discursive approach when it seems acceptable and realistic to make the transition. The discourse thus becomes historical and historiographic, recounting history from the suppressed Hawaiian viewpoint and also commenting on the "official" versions of events widely available to the American public. The crises receiving this kind of historical treatment in *Hawaii's Story by Hawaii's Queen* are the rebellion that seriously impaired the indigenous monarchy when Kalākaua was king; the overthrow of the monarchy when Liliʻuokalani succeeded Kalākaua; the queen's trial; the forces that led to a Provisional Government before Liliʻuokalani formally abdicated; and the establishment of a Republic after she officially stepped down.

Because the "I" has created a solid base of credibility in the bildungsroman section, the narration makes little attempt to camouflage the stylistic changes and ideological emphases as it shifts into discourses that are primarily disputatious. Functioning as channels of historical information, these discourses give readers enough data to understand the indigenous points of view on all the major crises that Hawaiʻi suffered in the previous two decades. The narration introduces the shift simply by bringing the homecoming scene from Great Britain up short and suspending it in narrational time while inserting a second narration, with its own time and movement, in the space. The transformation takes place as follows: Liliʻuokalani, in the chapter "Ill News from Hawaii—Our Return," describes arriving home in July 1887 after weeks on steamships and after cutting short the royal visit to Queen Victoria's Jubilee celebration. She is greeted at the harbor by members of a new cabinet, whom she ominously notes as "all men of foreign birth," whereas in "the ministry directly preceding, three members had been native Hawaiians." The Hawaiians who also come to greet her exhibit "crushing sorrow" in their expressions, for "they knew, and we knew, although no word was spoken, the changes which had taken place while we had been away, and which had been forced upon the king" (175). Liliʻuokalani relates going immediately to see her brother at ʻIolani Palace. The drama is high, and they come face to face: "He appeared bright, and glad to welcome us back; yet we could see on his countenance traces of the terrible strain through which he had passed, and evidences of the anxiety over the perilous position, although this was only the commencement of the troubles preparing for our family and nation" (175–76).

Although the meeting above designates a climax in the storyline, the chapter is immediately aborted and replaced with another chapter, one that announces itself as an entirely different discourse. Opening with the statement, "It is necessary now to briefly review the events which had taken place in our absence of about three months abroad" (177), this new chapter is historical, informational, and argumentative rather than personal. Entitled "The Bayonet Constitution," it focuses on the oppressions of the Hawaiians throughout the century before it analyzes the crisis of spring 1887 when Kalākaua's monarchy was being pulled apart at the same time that its representatives were being enthusiastically welcomed in London. The chronological sequence of events is succinctly presented as just enough to clarify that King Kalākaua acquiesced to changes in the constitution *only* under threat of revolution and the end of his reign: "A conspiracy against the peace of the Hawaiian Kingdom had been taking shape since early spring. By the 15 of June, prior to our return, it had assumed a no less definite shape than the overthrow of the monarchy. . . . Although settled among us, and drawing their wealth from our resources, they [the participants] were alien to us in their customs and ideas respecting government, and desired above all things the extension of their power, and to carry out their own special plans of advancement, and to secure their own personal benefit" (177–78). As she tells it, the conspirators "rose one day *en masse,* called a public meeting, and forced the king, without any appeal to the suffrages of the people, to sign a constitution of their own preparation, a constitution which deprived the sovereign of all power, made him a mere tool in their hands, and practically took away the franchise from the Hawaiian race." As this passage does, the whole chapter makes it very clear that the new constitution was never desired or ratified by the Hawaiian population and that violence was required to coerce the king into signing it (180–81). Constitutions had long been at the center of the struggles for power. Proposed changes reflected tensions between the Caucasian oligarchy and the indigenous population, and underlying those tensions were the large numbers of people coming from countries other than the United States, including Japan and China. Whoever controlled the constitution determined voting suffrage, land ownership, and the economics of the islands. The constitution was what Liliʻuokalani turned her attention to as soon as she became queen. The events comprising this crisis are recalled in "Hawaiians Plead for a New Constitution," which is another chapter whose title also announces the autobiography's increasingly important communal and politicized frames of reference.

Once "The Bayonet Constitution" outlines the political tensions during Kalākaua's reign, it works rhetorically to construct its line of reasoning and, in the process, to set the pattern of subsequent chapters. "The Bayonet Constitution" uses a series of debate techniques that push scenic elements into the background and bring discursive ones forward—still keeping the face-to-face meeting between the king and his sister in the previous chapter suspended and unfinished. The enunciating voice, assuming that readers will need background information to respond to this new method of confronting the various crises, recounts all the significant events. The voice demonstrates that the government had always welcomed the advice and participation of "American residents who had cast in their lot with our people"—that is, until the "missionary party" took control over cabinet appointments and forced its own goals on those who disagreed with them (177). Now in a debate modality, the narrator makes theoretical concessions to the opposing point of view ("It may be true that they really believed us unfit to be trusted to administer the growing wealth of the Islands in a safe and proper way") only to turn the concession around to further her own thesis. If Hawaiians had a serious failing, it was not "incompetency" but rather their misplaced trust and shortsightedness "in not foreseeing that *they* [the Americans] would be bound by no obligations, by honor, or by oath of allegiance, should an opportunity arise for seizing our country, and bringing it under the authority of the United States" (178). Lili'uokalani drives home the immediate and long-term effects of the forced constitutional changes, which left the monarchy disabled and the Hawaiian population without adequate representation (180).

As though her adversaries are now on trial, the narrator offers evidence to prove their guilt. The tactic foreshadows subsequent chapters that do the same for other events and periods, including Lili'uokalani's reign after Kalākaua's death in 1891, the queen's attempts to address the imbalances of political power, her trial and guilty verdict, and her enforced abdication. The document in "The Bayonet Constitution," which the narrator places on formal exhibit, also introduces the masterful use that *Hawaii's Story by Hawaii's Queen* makes of appendixes. Referred to in the same chapter that executes the change away from personal narrative, "Appendix A" is the first

of numerous references in this part of the book calling upon discrete, supporting materials. These materials are organized in no fewer than seven
appendixes, most of which contain their own interrelating sections and
intertextual relationships. Brought in to the text at intervals, they repeat
and reconstruct events according to their own form and context and, while
adding information from new perspectives, always support the indigenous
arguments that are driving the narration. Therefore, to strengthen the case
against the Americans in Hawai'i, the "I" guides readers to the first appendix, which turns out to be a passage on the Bayonet Constitution and
resulting political turmoil, which was printed in an American newspaper. Calling the new government a "régime" that censored the press with
"military thoroughness" and implying that it falsified reports of public
court proceedings, this editorial from the *San Francisco Chronicle* makes
Lili'uokalani's partisan viewpoint look moderate while effectively rein-
forcing her criticism.[23] A final tactic for Lili'uokalani is to put on public
display new information that she has kept to herself. Rather than cite the
details, she creates a stronger impact by offering them rhetorically in a
question-and-answer format: "Why did the king give them [his adver-
saries] his signature?" The answer is that the king signed the constitution
because a clandestine group privately threatened to assassinate him if
he refused. All of these details and the persuasive techniques in which
they are presented put together a compelling case against further loss of
Hawaiian rights and reveal a strong, continuing Native resistance to all
efforts to join the country to the United States. The argument builds in
momentum as different discourses and rhetorical devices come into play
and fortify each other through cross-references and connecting links. The
pattern recurs in other chapters as well, but it is especially dramatic here
where it is first introduced. This is because two new discourses are put
into place in the midst of an especially emotional passage in the personal
narration. The exchange between the royal brother and sister, who are just
about to greet each other, is suspended for the duration of the introduced
discourse, which is itself interrupted when it refers to material in the
appendix.

   The appendixes are doubly important as a way to publicize information about Hawai'i's crises that people outside the highest levels of diplomacy did not know and thus to rehistoricize them. The documents and
letters contained in the appendixes shed light on the constitutional crisis
that Lili'uokalani's brother experienced and on the queen's later attempts
to change that constitution that she inherited. In turn, the materials

review the crisis that Liliʻuokalani triggered once she was queen and that led to her overthrow and trial as well as reproduce relevant documents. These include letters by the queen to two presidents (Benjamin Harrison, who submitted an annexation treaty to Congress, and Grover Cleveland, who rescinded it) and a plethora of information that bolsters the explicit arguments in the central part of the book and the implicit arguments in the first part. The supplementary sections achieve all this without cramming the central text with detail, and thus the book remains highly readable for the broad spectrum of readers it was intended. With texts as diverse as the annexation treaty sent to Congress in 1897, while Liliʻuokalani was writing, to detailed genealogies of Hawaiʻi's royal families, the appendixes function historiographically. They broaden the picture of nineteenth-century Hawaiʻi at the same time that they deepen it, and together these approaches clarify the effects of U.S. expansionism in the Pacific.[24] Finally, the appendixed materials comment on, and enable the narrating voice to comment directly on, previous and more widely known versions of the calamitous events that were directly and indirectly sanctioned by America. By the time Liliʻuokalani returns to the partially described dramatic moment that triggered this extensive debate, the personal details concerning her and her brother have lost much of their relevance. With her personal story no longer the major pretext of the book, she brings back the abandoned moment only as a platform for starting the next chapter, "Invited to Conspire Against the King," and for examining critical events that took place soon after her return from Great Britain.

The efforts devoted in this part of the autobiography to gathering evidence and refuting the allegations and rationales of the annexationists do not, however, completely erase the autobiographical story. Vestiges of the bildungsroman that occur in the historicized arguments may seem casual or superficial, but they are usually suggestive commentaries or illustrations of the argument being made. For example, the information that Liliʻuokalani's young niece left Hawaiʻi for Europe in 1889 seems irrelevant in a chapter that focuses on the king's political troubles. Her departure, though, validates Liliʻuokalani's assessment of the gravity of the crisis, and the fact that the niece is still living abroad confirms that the dangers have intensified since then. A later chapter that recounts Liliʻuokalani's social activities of an 1896 visit with the Boston cousins of her husband is much less casual than it appears. These are the people who edited and published *Hawaii's Story by Hawaii's Queen,* and the narration makes it clear that they admired Liliʻuokalani and worked assiduously to put her case before the American public. Even the death of Lili'uokalani's husband in 1891 is adroitly situated to confirm the larger argument that is unfolding. Inserted between two chapters, both of which recall the queen's difficulties with members of her cabinet, these pages on John Dominis implicitly contrast his kinship with the Native population to the cabinet members' hostility to the same group. The narration suggests—through the figure of the mourned husband—that trust and comradeship are still possible in a bicultural or multicultural Hawai'i. In fact, it establishes a close link between Lili'uokalani's brother and her Italian-American husband, who dies seven months after Kalākaua. The narrator makes a point of saying that her husband was buried with the ceremonies reserved for deceased sovereigns and, further, that he was honored with the same funeral ceremonies as the king himself. National and racial differences are symbolically erased as the chapter asserts that Dominis, the prince consort, "was borne, with all the honors accorded to *his brother* the king, to his final resting place, followed by many sincere mourners" (225; emphasis added), and it implies that brotherhood among races is a desired goal despite the unconscionable treatment of the indigenous community.[25]

Throughout the autobiography the husband is used exclusively for iconographic and symbolic functions and is never given an individualized presence. He is a vehicle for grounding the literary persona of Lili'uokalani in ways that readers could understood—as a respectful wife and loyal caretaker whose opinions likewise could be understood and considered reliable. In contrast to what the autobiography describes, Lili'uokalani's surviving diaries and private letters point to a very difficult marriage, a disapproving mother-in-law, and a husband who was often distant to his wife.[26] The inconsistency is not unusual in the writings of women who lead public lives, with their autobiographies often giving accounts of events and emotions different from those in their private correspondence.[27] This is particularly true for women before the twentieth century, who were acutely aware of the expectations of the public, and even more so for a woman in Lili'uokalani's marginalized position. What de Man calls the "policing power" of readers, which is the tendency to judge whether the "author *of* the text" is consistent with the "author *in* the text," is a crucial factor in a book such as *Hawaii's Story by Hawaii's Queen* that aims to make an impact on history—and very quickly.[28]

With this goal always in view, the book exhibits very careful treatment of the husband and shares no intimate details of the marriage, not even in the chapter entitled "My Married Life." Dominis is less a flesh-and-blood character than a device for Westernizing the protagonist and keeping the "I" (both *in* and *of* the text) on familiar ground. Without even mentioning the racial differences of husband and wife, the text makes the point at the start of the book. Formal portraits are placed just after the title page, and these show a Europeanized and elaborately dressed queen and prince consort, both with a magisterial presence. The effect is striking, and it must have seemed inconceivable to readers that this was the same woman the press often condemned as a relic of barbarism.[29] Race, through the image of the husband, operates visually as a metaphor of Lili'uokalani's conventional domestic life. Married to a man whom any of her female readers in America would find suitable, if not desirable, as a husband, the author constructs one more piece of the bridge that, for her immediate purposes, links Polynesian and Anglo-European contexts.[30] The details of her life story are frequently used in this manner to further the text's symbolic and illustrative purposes. Autobiographical references are configured so that they function as transitional material, which comes between the more complex pages that review the constitutional and governing crises. Thus the individual life becomes mainly a mechanism for personalizing the historical arguments and making it easy for casual readers to progress through them.

Given the momentum toward politicizing all aspects of the text, the remaining autobiographical details, even those pertaining to the queen's body, have argumentative purposes. "Brought to Trial" is probably the most important chapter describing the queen's downfall. With the initial charge of treason changed to "misprision of treason," she was accused of knowing that "my people were conspiring to re-establish the constitutional government, to throw off the yoke of the stranger and oppressor; and I had not conveyed this knowledge to the persons I had never recognized except as unlawful usurpers of authority, and had not informed against my own nation and against their friends who were also my long-time friends" (278–79). At first the chapter seems to promise a detailed and very personal account of Lili'uokalani's trial. It quickly presents, for instance, the room where the trial was held and goes so far as to give the time, date, and names of many of the spectators and judges, including the first witness for the prosecution. But it also refers to the subject's body as a trope for the treatment her country suffered. Nowhere else in the autobiography is there such a direct correlation between gender and

subjugation. Only in the charged courtroom of men versus one Polynesian woman is the protagonist so completely objectified, humiliated, and
"othered," as she is publicly marked by the judges:

> The only charge against me really was that of being a queen; and my case
> was judged by these, my adversaries, before I came into court. I remember
> with clearness, however, the attack upon me by the Judge Advocate, the
> words that issued from his mouth about "the prisoner," "that woman," etc.,
> uttered with such affectation of contempt and disgust. The object of it was
> evidently to humiliate me, to make me break down in the presence of the
> staring crowd. But in this they were disappointed. My equanimity was never
> disturbed; and their own report relates that I throughout preserved "that
> haughty carriage" which marked me as an "unusual woman." (280)

Establishing her body as a site of political resistance, the narrator shows
that her country's dignity is represented by and concentrated in her own
body. She remains composed throughout the proceedings, saying nothing
to "their taunts and innuendoes" and waiting until the strategic moment
to address the court with shrewdness and eloquence. In fact, she writes
that her refusal to break under pressure infuriates her male judges and
causes them further to derogate her person. Smith, in *Subjectivity, Identity, and the Body*, describes how masculine privilege, when attempting to
make a single female body "abject," is also attacking the body of the community she represents. Lili'uokalani's material body, as a legitimating
symbol of her community, threatens "to contaminate the body politic"
that her adversaries are establishing.[31] Her body is a desired commodity;
whoever controls it ultimately controls the future. Lili'uokalani is found
guilty, and her body is further violated, officially sentenced to five years of
hard labor.[32]

The details that let the world know of this vivid instance of the queen's
humiliation ultimately serve another purpose; they enable the author to
do nothing less than rewrite history and restore portions of the public
record that had been suppressed.[33] Toward this formidable goal, the personal details that introduce the queen's trial are not sustained once the
trial's description gets under way. They are primarily meant to create a
sense of outrage so that readers will stay with the text as it undergoes a
massive change of discourse. As in other parts of the book that also function as crisis narrative, the story is aborted at a riveting passage and a documentary discourse is inserted. The shift is as dramatic as it is significant.

At the height of autobiographical intensity, the narration moves into historical text; thus, when the personal story seems most heavily invested, the "I" narrates herself out of the chapter. The rationale here is obvious. The maneuver transforms the text into what the author ultimately intends her book to be—a repository of little known and censored information pertinent to Hawai'i's sovereignty. The crisis narrative may read like autobiography first, for long stretches and then intermittently, but it is meant to be, and is always in the process of becoming, a material archive. It brings official documents and letters out from the reaches of the mid-Pacific and draws them to the geographical centers of international diplomacy and expansionism and places them directly in front of critics, supporters, historians, and the American public.

The inserted discourses, like those that occupy most of "Brought to Trial," carry even more force than the appendixes and are consequently the most pivotal materials in developing the argument of the book.[34] This is because the appendixes break the central narration in a less intrusive way. Footnotes inform readers which appendix they should examine, and readers may or may not choose to interrupt their progress through the chapter. But the material nested right in the chapter *must* be read. The chapter's early content is abandoned, and if readers turn away they learn virtually nothing about the most horrific of Hawai'i's crises, its female sovereign tried in 1895 by a military court under martial law.[35] With only a few paragraphs taking up the personal thread at the end, Lili'uokalani's formal statement to her judges becomes the primary text of "Brought to Trial." Embedding her defense and giving it a central position is an astute countermove, for it enables the statement to stand on its own with devastating results for her adversaries. It proceeds through one crisis to another, through her constitutional crisis in 1893 to her yielding the throne in 1895, through her submitting the case to the U.S. government for arbitration. Blistering in condemning her condemners, Lili'uokalani's statement manages to be eloquent in its rationales and forgiving of those who truly think they are fulfilling their public duty.

> As you deal with them [others also on trial for treason], so I pray that the Almighty God may deal with you in your hours of trial....
>
> I must deny your right to try me in the manner and by the court which you have called together for this purpose. In your actions you violate your own constitution and laws, which are now the constitution and laws of the land....

> I would ask you to consider that your government is on trial before the
> whole civilized world, and that in accordance with your actions and deci-
> sions will you yourselves be judged. The happiness and prosperity of Hawaii
> are henceforth in your hands as its rulers. You are commencing a new era
> in its history. May the divine Providence grant you the wisdom to lead the
> nation into the paths of forbearance, forgiveness, and peace, and to create
> and consolidate a united people ever anxious to advance in the way of civ-
> ilization outlined by the American fathers of liberty and religion. (285)

Most important for its impact in arguing for sovereignty even more than
the queen's innocence is the way that this rhetoric drives the statement
beyond the courtroom. For the most part the "I" has confined itself to
describing and defending Lili'uokalani's actions. But here, at the end of
the queen's formal document, and at its most dramatic section, the "I"
draws into its purview the accusers facing her at the trial *and* each reader.
Using repeatedly the second-person address, the "I" concludes brilliantly,
implicating all American readers as well as the audience in the courtroom
from years earlier.[36]

As powerful as the quoted statement may be, including it is only half
of the strategy. By using another document, namely the court's response
to the queen's statement, the chapter delegitimizes the whole trial, the
judges, their motives and procedures. This is because "Brought to Trial"
reprints the court's formal response to the queen's statement, specifically
the court's demand that her statement be amended to "withdraw" certain
information from the record. The objectionable details include the queen's
refusal to accept a government that ignores the will of the people, her
insistence that the electoral process was illegal, and her accusation that
those now in power flouted the laws of their own country, the United
States. Merely by quoting those passages that the court demands she expunge from the record, the author exposes its blatant practice of censorship and bogus system of justice. This further means that the embedded
discourse presents Lili'uokalani's charismatic defense not just once but
twice for emphasis, because it repeats the very points that the court most
desired to erase from official records: the queen's most powerful opinions
are presented first in the text of her own statement and again in the quotations of the court's response. The chapter thus embarrassingly exposes
the opposition and teaches a lesson in the politicized transmission of
Pacific history. It also evinces the author's overall archival purpose as she
recounts the drama of her trial. Working hard to counter the censoring

of events, Lili'uokalani makes additional information available to readers and preserves documents for future generations by shelving them, so to speak, in her work and public archive.

The controversial information provided here and elsewhere in the book leads the author to try other ways to maintain a favorable self-image and a positive connection with readers. As the "I" shifts into assertive and opinionated positions, she needs to prolong a delicate balance between the way she imputes blame on some of her readers and the way she asks for assistance from others. She succeeds in this by separating into two distinct groups the people who would read *Hawaii's Story*. She makes readers on the U.S. mainland the addressees of the text and places them apart from the action that is unfolding inside of the narrative. To this end phrases such as "the reader can judge," "I leave it to the reader to say," and "I trust those who read these pages" separate the mainland Americans she is trying to educate from the Americans and descendents of Americans in Hawai'i whom she is holding directly responsible. The enunciating voice is sensitive to the needs of this first group of readers, the mainland Americans; it explains practices that may seem odd and serves patiently as a guide. The choice of the third-person when referring to these readers helps the narrator assume their continuous presence in a gracious, formal way. Because these readers are kept at the periphery of the narrative, they are unlikely to feel threatened and more likely to allow the "I," at the right time, to challenge them into action to lobby their representatives in Congress.

In contrast, the second group of readers is portrayed as deeply involved in the story and complicit in the events that led to Lili'uokalani's downfall. This group is the American population in Hawai'i, and its most powerful members are fashioned into literary characters. Lili'uokalani is unconcerned with their responses to her book, since the battle lines are entrenched and the autobiography is unlikely to do anything but exacerbate their anger at her skilled mode of resistance, which they could never have anticipated. The goal is always to discredit this second group and gain the support of the first. She thus distinguishes between "Americans" and people whom she calls "Pseudo-Hawaiians," by which she means the Americans who settled in Hawai'i and sought power only for themselves. This division frees the "I" to use as much detail as necessary to expose the oligarchy and its supporters, and this is precisely what happens. She uses them as literary antagonists in the plot and sets the chronology and commentary in motion. By turning her adversaries into characters, the narrator can bury them deep inside the narrative and control them. She can depict them subtly, which she does with her first missionary-teachers, or cast them as villains, which she does with the men she believes to be responsible for the crises that have made her autobiography such a necessary project. With this group inside the storyline and the other group outside, the space between them widens. The narrator works at the gap, describing exactly what certain individuals have done to deceive Americans on the mainland. In Hawai'i these individuals "retained their American birthright" and "designated themselves as Americans"; but in Washington, where they are lobbying politicians, "they represent themselves as Hawaiians" (325). Mainland readers are in a position to criticize their own countrymen because statements such as these divide national identity into geographical factors instead.

CRISIS INTO CATASTROPHE

A single action can transform a crisis narrative into a catastrophe narrative. With the effects more extreme than those of a crisis situation, a catastrophe requires immediate attention and thus shifts the narrative attention from the past onto present time. The catastrophe in this case took place on June 16, 1897, when President McKinley submitted to Congress a treaty of annexation and set into motion both the annexationists and Native resistance organizations.[37] McKinley's action was not completely unforeseen, of course, but few people had accurate knowledge concerning what specific steps he would take concerning the situation in Hawai'i and at what point in his term of office something definitive might take place. Lili'uokalani's protests to his action take center stage in the space still available to her, namely her manuscript-in-progress. It is the responsibility of confronting the emergency head-on that ushers in a more literal, straightforward treatment of present-time events.

Documents especially take on a crucial role, and they create an intense dialogic interplay and heteroglossia in the book's closing chapters; some of these documents are placed right in the text while others continue to go into the appendixes. In numerous chapters of the catastrophe narration, the author sheds her autobiographical camouflage since the pressure is now greater and the time frame for writing is closing in on her. She takes liberties with her female persona, projecting feminine traits when they are strategically effective and other times keeping the contentious enunciating "I" disputing the assumptions and goals of the proposed annexation treaty. Catastrophe changes everything and leaves an imprint everywhere. It changes the tactics and much of the content of the writing that follows the catastrophe, and, importantly, it recasts the material in the crisis narrative as well. The earlier chapters look different, more like causal elements leading up to McKinley's action than simply as remembered conflicts over constitutions and monarchal prerogatives. Through this new context of catastrophe readers can see events such as the queen's forced abdication and trial as a prelude to the catastrophe, with nearly all of the episodes converging toward a single event: the treaty of annexation. The catastrophe not only forces additional interpretations onto the crisis narrative while it re-forms the remaining narrative but also brings to the fore the issue of collaboration. Subversive writing by persons not in power makes its way to publication through levels of editors and mediators. It is therefore logical to suppose that Lili'uokalani, facing the daunting task of responding in kind to a formal treaty, made strategic use of the aides with whom she surrounded herself; and unpublished correspondence points to persons close to Lili'uokalani, who, carefully consulting with her, effected editorial changes. Finally, in recasting crisis, catastrophe suggests that however long a crisis has been in place, it is by nature precarious and likely to explode at any time.

The changes the text undergoes show the impact of a highly charged, materialist context on the life writing enterprise. The changes also clarify the way that external events do not remain external but may be drawn into the project that is responding to catastrophe. As the final chapters reflect Lili'uokalani's counteraction to the American president, much of its material presents and literalizes the calamitous development simply by inserting the pertinent documents into the text. From this point on, the "I" methodically debates the provisions of the existing, proposed treaty and expresses to Americans the unfathomability of annexation from a Hawaiian point of view. Foregrounding this technique is the chapter appropriately entitled "My Official Protest to the Treaty." Relatively short, it is almost nothing *but* the protest, dated June 17, 1897, that Lili'uokalani sent to the U.S. secretary of state (she had two of her aides personally deliver it). The "I" in this discourse methodically objects, one-by-one, to the terms of the treaty, exposing the fallacies and inaccuracies of each of them. The protest document is also double-voiced insofar as it reflects two aspects of the author and the major conflicts of her life. It speaks through the "I" of an ali'i whose position relative to her people can never be altered by abdication or military tribunals. She is "I, LILIUOKALANI of Hawaii, by the will of God named heir apparent on the tenth day of April, A.D. 1877,

and by the grace of God Queen of the Hawaiian Islands on the seven-
teenth day of January, A.D. 1893" (354). The second voice reflects the "out-
law" queen who quietly left the island when her parole was over by
convincing the president of the Republic that she wished only to visit
relatives of her husband in Boston. The document embedded in the document that is *Hawaii's Story* serves two "speakers"—the woman who
refuses a life sentence of isolation and fights on Western terms and the
one who spiritually embodies her people and knows this connection can
never be severed. The internal dialogism in the enunciating "I" allows each
of these voices to enrich the other.

Lili'uokalani's protest, which is situated centrally in the text, does more
than make way for a cross-examination of the assumptions behind the
treaty. It also creates a rhetorical mode of address that allows the "I" to
speak out directly to her readers and thus reduce the distance between
them. This connection that the "I" nurtures—of sympathy, tolerance, and
respect—is essential because it carries out the function that the more
compliant autobiographical protagonist served in the earlier sections. The
"I" picks up the task and then goes beyond it to instill additionally a sense
of ethical and spiritual responsibility in the book's readers. Delivering a
formal address, it requests the president of the United States to withdraw
his treaty entirely from additional consideration. The "I" reaches out to
other people who, in contrast to McKinley, have not made up their minds
whether to colonize Hawai'i and are more inclined to consider each of the
assertions. The "I" urges these readers to take the matter into their own
hands:

> Therefore, I, Liliuokalani of Hawaii, do hereby call upon the President of
> that nation, to whom alone I yielded my property and my authority, to with-
> draw said treaty (ceding said Islands) from further consideration. I ask the
> honorable Senate of the United States to decline to ratify said treaty, and I
> implore the people of this great and good nation, from whom my ancestors
> learned the Christian religion, to sustain their representatives in such acts
> of justice and equity as may be in accord with the principles of their fathers,
> and to the Almighty Ruler of the universe, to him who judgeth righteously,
> I commit my cause. (356)

By invoking religion as a bridge between two different cultures, which she
also does earlier, the enunciating voice makes its appeal on the loftiest of
grounds. This is crucial since Lili'uokalani's written protest was likely to

anger readers by insisting that their democracy has acted unlawfully. It insists that the diplomatic and naval forces of the United States overwhelmed Hawai'i and that forty thousand people who do not want annexation have been silenced by a minority oligarchy. It avers that crown lands cannot be ceded to any other country and that the United States would be taking land that the current oligarchy in Hawai'i has no constitutional right to hand over. Each paragraph of her protest attacks at the nationalist core of its readers. The appeal afterward on the grounds of common religion is simply a shrewd, conciliatory gesture, one of the few means still available for maintaining a rapport in the wake of such volatile statements.

The last few chapters of the autobiography, all in response to President McKinley's June 1897 action and all part of the catastrophe narration, establish a dialogical opposition between the proposed treaty and the narrational discourses that critique it. These chapters are quite different from those of the crisis narration, for they exhibit a much tighter configuration of dialogical and documentary discourses. Ironically, though, the proposed treaty is as physically absent as its implications are forcibly present. Significantly and structurally the treaty is barred from a highly visible place in the primary discourse of *Hawaii's Story by Hawaii's Queen.* It is not presented as a chapter onto itself as the queen's protest to it is in "My Official Protest to the Treaty." Nor is the treaty embedded in a larger chapter as the queen's legal defense in "Brought to Trial" is. How, then, is the body of the catastrophic document made known? The narrator relegates it to the supplementary section of the book, where it is given the unceremonious and generic title of "Appendix D." Moreover, the only reference even to this location appears as little more than an afterthought, in the terse and final sentence of "My Official Protest to the Treaty" (357). This strategy has the effect of textually submerging the treaty and symbolically overwhelming it with oppositional dialogue. In effect, the very element responsible for this form of argument and struggle leaves only traces of itself, and these traces lack the power the document would have if it were made into a discrete chapter and given equal space. In that case there would be much more than the lone sentence between "My Official Protest to the Treaty" and "The Treaty Analyzed" directing readers to the back of the book; the entire treaty would be situated between the two chapters that are generated as detailed arguments against it.

Excluding the document from which all the elements of catastrophe unfold enables the narrative to respond without being textually contaminated by the treaty, if only in a symbolic way. The pertinent chapters effectively work off its absence to counterargue the premises of the treaty and delegitimate each of its seven articles. Becoming almost as dialogically compact as "My Official Protest to the Treaty," the subsequent chapter, "The Treaty Analyzed," embeds supporting documents into its own analytical sequence in order to corroborate and illustrate its thesis that any form of political union is unlawful. Thus, "The Treaty Analyzed," which is itself a dialogical response, contains additional forms of discourse, among them definitional, historical, and legal. Despite the chapter's opening rhetorical disclaimer that "anything like an extended criticism of the proposed treaty will not be attempted here," the discourses are amalgamated into just that—an extended criticism of the proposed treaty. The chapter evolves into a heteroglossia of conflicting voices and styles, all the while keeping the voice of "extended criticism" in control. For example, the narrating voice defines the term "crown lands" to clarify that land being "ceded" cannot legally be ceded. To confirm this definitional point, the narrator gives a historical summary of land ownership and use, referring to the cataclysmic change of policy fifty years earlier largely initiated by the missionaries, who now own large tracts of property.[38] An allegation concerning traditional land policies is then quoted from a well-known annexationist and is used to establish a platform for a much longer reply.[39] The replying speaker is not the narrating "I," but a more legalistic speaker whose commentary, now quoted, corrects the annexationist's point. The reply ends with a hypothesis to show that U.S. investment in Hawai'i would be extremely problematic. Once the chapter returns to the queen's enunciating voice, it picks up the legalistic tone and style from the embedded material. This "I" attacks specific parts of the treaty and uses various rhetorical modes, including quotation, rhetorical question, italicized phrases, and hyperbole, footnotes, and statistics in order to do so. These techniques, in conjunction with the different language styles and introduced content and history, result in a charged and articulate analysis, which is, of course, highly critical of the catastrophic document.

The narrator returns to autobiographical figuration and, hence, to readers' expectations as a way to counter any excess of invective or anger that comes through in the increasingly literal treatment of the hated treaty. Since one textual misstep could ruin the effect of her book, she makes a gendered appeal to readers in America, presumably anticipating their own positions and inspiring them to come to her defense. Rhetorically, the strategy re-grounds her in a very traditional way and serves as a double measure for securing readers' good will. The "I" reminds readers that she has been subjected to "vile and baseless slanders" (370) and "animosity, openly and secretly expressed, toward me, not only as a queen, but as a woman" (334). She describes being humiliated by the men of American birth or ancestry who put her on trial, publicly calling her "that lady." She even recalls being forced to sign the formal abdication document as "Mrs. Dominis," an appellation she never used and one that nullifies her ancestry by reducing her to wife and widow status: "All my official acts, as well as my private letters, were issued over the signature of Liliuokalani. But when my jailers required me to sign 'Liliuokalani Dominis,' I did as they commanded. Their motive in this as in other actions was plainly to humiliate me before my people and before the world.... There is not, and never was, within the range of my knowledge, any such a person as Liliuokalani Dominis" (275–76).[40] Writing her autobiography in Washington, a center of international power, she continues to identify herself by stressing her feminine vulnerability. She is but "one woman, without legal adviser, without a dollar to spend in subsidies, supported and encouraged in her mission only by three faithful adherents, and such friends as from time to time expressed to her their sympathy" (331). These self-characterizations, which come in the midst of the catastrophe narrative, illustrate perfectly Sidonie Smith's observation that women autobiographers tend to project on their own representation readers' cultural expectations concerning gender. "Particularly in the dramatic passages of her text," which are precisely where these self-references to feminine vulnerability are located, the narrator "reveals the degree of her self-consciousness about her position as a woman." Smith emphasizes that the self-consciousness comes from participating in an androcentric genre.[41] In this case self-consciousness starts with genre and gender and goes beyond them because the woman in question is attempting to influence the course of history. The strategies Lili'uokalani adopts here and elsewhere in the catastrophe section of the narrative are intended to foreground the role of gender at junctures where doing so will serve the most constructive purposes.

With momentum building as multiple voices and discourses interrelate and heighten one another's impact, the chapter entitled "The Treaty Analyzed" shifts over into autobiography only as a final maneuver for sustaining a positive self-presentation. The enunciating voice prefers to call what it offers just "one more bit of political history," but tactically the chapter's closing paragraphs use self-references as a way to return to the queen's own voice. Rather than her legalistic or debating voice, she brings out her distinctly feminine voice, with which readers probably feel most comfortable. She returns to a more intimate dialogue and additionally shows that the former queen and the American president remain on respectful terms. Reiterating this fact, at least from her own perspective, is necessary, for the author must remain at all times convincing or appealing enough for her viewpoints to carry persuasive weight. Toward this end the narrator describes meeting socially with President McKinley just one month after he sent the treaty to Congress and just after her aides brought documents from the Native resistance organizations in Hawai'i to the White House. She stresses his congeniality in her effort to set the record straight, because "upon no subject has the desire been more frequently shown to prejudice me and my cause in the eyes of the American people" than the relationship with the White House (365).[42] The details of the meeting aside, the author is attempting to equalize her own position as a (former) head of state despite differences of gender, race, nationality, and political beliefs.

When life writing becomes a discourse of catastrophe, its attention may turn to present time. The past does not disappear, of course, but exigencies that threaten survival militate against the rich detailing of the past that occurs in the crisis narration, especially in its beginning chapters. A turn to current time is precisely what happens in the catastrophe section of the book in both subtle and obvious ways. The discourses that center on June 1897 in order to critique the treaty are the obvious examples of a sustained focus on the present. More subtle is the extensive treatment that 1897 receives and that yields two notable consequences. The first consequence is to spread a narrow duration of time (primarily winter through summer) so that it occupies a disproportionately large part of the text. By focusing on these months, the narrator stretches them out across the six chapters that precede the discussion of the treaty. This keeps 1897 in the immediate foreground, by both following its course very slowly and then stopping time altogether in order to concentrate on McKinley's document. A whole chapter, "A New England Winter," is devoted to covering January 1897 when the author is in Boston. Another chapter describes early February, when she is back in Washington, and so forth until "My Literary Occupation" ends as it reaches the landmark date of June 16, 1897, when President McKinley sent the annexation treaty to Congress. At that point time stands still, and the chapter concludes by announcing that the next chapter will simply *be* the document of her protest. The second consequence is to work the text so that it performs the author's refusal to see this single year, 1897, as anything but anomalous. The year becomes a continuous presence and burden in this part of *Hawaii's Story by Hawaii's Queen*, if not eclipsing, then certainly lessening, the impact of the earlier narration of childhood, youth, and early adulthood and recasting it in a new light. The extended treatment of these few months also draws readers' attention to the enormous gap between the two cultures, regardless of Lili'uokalani's ability to live in both Hawai'i and America and perhaps even *because* of that ability. The more the "I" describes her travels in New England, receptions everywhere, sightseeing excursions, and daily encounters, the more a judicious reader wonders about the observations that she chooses not to give and all the customs she must leave behind in order to succeed as triumphantly as the text demonstrates.

The differences between the crisis and catastrophe narratives, caused by the task of responding to a U.S. president and the sudden pressure of time, lead to the question of collaboration in *Hawaii's Story by Hawaii's Queen*. Evidence indicates that the manuscript, in response to McKinley's speed, was completed just three months after the treaty was made official, then quickly edited and produced. By late January 1898, seven months after the treaty went to Congress and less than four months after reaching its Boston publisher, the book was in print. It is hard to imagine this rate of progress without other persons committed to the project. This is especially the case with works of political resistance, whose editors consider possibilities of lawsuits, the taste of the reading public, and other related matters. Certainly Lili'uokalani was the only person who could generate the mass of detail that the autobiography provides about the lives of ali'i in Hawai'i. But other parts of the book, especially the catastrophe narrative, are constructed on more than personal memories. Letters by diplomats, federal documents, and newspaper articles had to be located rapidly, examined, copied and critiqued. Advisers, secretaries, editors, and publisher all had roles to fill. Consulting and collaborating must have been especially important because her papers were confiscated when Lili'uokalani was arrested in January 1895. Writing about that experience, the narrator describes being led away from her residence and later being informed that the building was searched twice without a warrant:

> ... all the papers in my desk, or in my safe, my diaries, the petitions I had received from my people,—all things of that nature which could be found were swept into a bag, and carried off by the chief justice in person. My husband's private papers were also included in those taken from me.
> To this day, the only document which has been returned to me is my will.

Lili‘uokalani. *Hawai‘i State Archives*

Never since have I been able to find the private papers of my husband nor those of mine that had been kept by me for use or reference, and which had no relation to political events.

After Mr. Judd [the chief justice] had left my house ... militiamen ransacked it again from garret to cellar. Not an article was left undisturbed. Before Mr. Judd had finished they had begun their work, and there was no trifle left unturned to see what might be hidden beneath. Every drawer of desk, table, or bureau was wrenched out, turned upside down, the contents pulled over on the floors, and left in confusion there.

Having overhauled the rooms without other result than the abstraction of many memorandums of no use to any person besides myself, the men turned their attention to the cellar, in hopes possibly of unearthing an arsenal of firearms and munitions of war. Here they undermined the foundation to such a degree as to endanger the whole structure, but nothing rewarded their search. The place was then seized, and the government assumed possession; guards were placed on the premises, and no one was allowed to enter. (271–72)[43]

Liliʻuokalani with friends and supporters. *Hawaiʻi State Archives*

Given these circumstances and taking into account the primary sources
that were undoubtedly lost, the achievement of *Hawaii's Story by Hawaii's
Queen* is all the more impressive. Scholars may never know the exact give-
and-take, and the details of the research (perhaps at the Library of Congress) that made it possible for this work to come into being, and some
primary materials are still missing. Lili'uokalani's diary for 1897—written
after the Republic took over her possessions—has never come into the
public domain, and so her private remarks on the writing process while
she was engaged in it do not exist.[44] Nonetheless, to understand the history of Lili'uokalani's efforts, it is important to understand the politicized
contexts that worked to discredit them.

Lorrin A. Thurston, one of the queen's fiercest opponents, claimed to
know how *Hawaii's Story by Hawaii's Queen* came to be written. But as an
aggressive leader of the annexationists, he considered the book to be
extremely dangerous. He did what he could to delegitimate it and prevent
it from ever serving historiographic and revisionary purposes. In his
Memoirs of the Hawaiian Revolution, this grandson of missionaries hoped
to negate Lili'uokalani's personal authorship on two counts.[45] Thurston
names someone else as the author and then "proves" Lili'uokalani was
incapable of writing her own autobiography. The author, he insists, is the
American journalist Julius Palmer, who was the queen's personal secretary
in 1897. Palmer, a reporter who collected his own articles on Hawai'i for
a book that Lili'uokalani's relatives published, did have a role in the project.[46] In point of fact, Lili'uokalani openly refers to Palmer and informs her
readers that he attended to her "correspondence and other business" until
August 1897. Biographer Helena Allen adds that the two of them talked
about the manuscript regularly, with Lili'uokalani arguing for a philosophical and cultural autobiography and Palmer for a straightforward presentation of events. The give-and-take between them is evident in the text,
which incorporates elements of both approaches in ingenious ways. Allen
assumes there was a collaborative relationship and that Palmer was the
"literary disciplinarian" who "daily urged [Lili'uokalani on] the prosaic
work of *Hawaii's Story.*" Despite her thinking that cultural differences (meaning sections of Lili'uokalani's drafts) were sometimes edited out, Allen
insists that "in no way can the book be said to have been 'ghostwritten.'"[47]

It is important to realize further that Thurston's remarks come out of
a long history of animosity toward Lili'uokalani. They conveniently ignore
the fact that as a late-Victorian woman, a monarch, and an ali'i, Lili'-
uokalani lived and worked in concert with other persons. She had personal

companions and professional aides, some traveling with her from home and others becoming part of her temporary suite. These people carried out her instructions and advised her as she lobbied, entertained, wrote, met politicians, and generally made herself a known figure in Washington. Even though she may have started on the autobiography before arriving in the United States, once there she worked with Palmer on a continuing basis. In addition, her Boston relatives, Sara and William Lee, of the publishing firm Lee and Shepard carefully read and edited her manuscript. None of this assistance is surprising, especially with the burden of finishing the book in time for it to make a difference in the national debates.

Research strongly supports Lili'uokalani's active participation and writing. Given her status even after abdication, the queen herself was not likely to type the hundreds of manuscript pages being generated. She probably dictated some material and shared whatever personal notes she still had in her possession, thereby introducing levels of possible intervention by aides and transcribers. But for Thurston to argue that Palmer actually wrote the book, first, because he was loyal to Lili'uokalani and, second, because she "personally was incapable of using such clear-cut English as that published" is insupportable—based on Thurston's scanty evidence and on additional archival evidence as well. With invective driving his judgments, Thurston accuses Palmer of excessive loyalty to Lili'uokalani and calls this a trait that makes him "a lick-spittle person" deceitful enough to author the book. Thurston then turns to the queen's diaries for proof that she could not have composed her own autobiography; he proclaims that "the English of the book, as compared with that of the diary, is evidence of my statement" (180). In no way does this constitute evidence. The style of a genre that is meant to be entirely private is not comparable to the style of another genre, which is meant to be entirely public. As Felicity A. Nussbaum writes, "Diary is the thing itself, not a failed version of autobiography."[48] What Thurston chooses not to say in his memoir is that he knows the difference between public and private text. After all, he reaches his conclusion by reading the diaries, which were never meant for an audience. Taken from Lili'uokalani's private safe, they were used against her during the trial by the prosecution. In time and in an effort to protect her private writings, the queen felt it was necessary to devise her own code, in which the letters of the Hawaiian alphabet corresponded to specific numbers. Nor does Thurston explain what anyone who sees the actual diaries understands; most of the volumes are very small in size, and their compactness encourages clipped, elliptical constructions and a compressed prose style.[49] Finally, he avoids comparing the autobiography to Liliʻuokalani's letters, private as well as public. Many of these letters have survived, and their style is, in fact, as gracious and dignified as the writing in *Hawaii's Story by Hawaii's Queen*.

There is much research to be done, and the dynamics of consulting, editing, and collaboration may never be fully known. However, Liliʻuokalani unquestionably maintained control over the manuscript and stayed in contact with her editor and publisher, who respected her comments on the proposed changes. A series of unpublished letters on both sides of the correspondence indicate an active exchange with recognition, again on both sides, that to be part of the international debate over annexation, the book had to strike a certain tone and remain balanced between history and anecdotes, Polynesian tradition and contemporary events.[50] Sara Lee was a cautious reader, dividing the continuous typescript into sections and apparently coming up with titles for the chapters.[51] She also aimed for a moderate tone, and paragraphs marked for deletion on the typescript confirm the comment in *Hawaii's Story* that, concerned about libel, the publisher refused to print the biographical sketches of the annexationists that Liliʻuokalani had prepared. Ironically, one of these deleted sections is meant to alert readers to Thurston as a man "absolutely without scruples" and so "determined to win at any cost" that "he never troubles himself about any question of honesty, the word does not stand in his way."

In committing her life to text, in sharing multitudinous details that no one else could know, and in engaging in a mediating process that made publication feasible under catastrophic conditions, Liliʻuokalani knew that she had to protect her work. Her editor, progressing speedily to have the book published before Congress convened, wrote to say that obtaining a copyright in Liliʻuokalani's name was proving difficult. Editorial work could not continue until hearing further which options would be most preferable. With a history of losses and still living in Washington, D.C., Liliʻuokalani was adamant that a solution be found, and she responded:

Dear Cousin William,

. . . I notice you say that you did not think it was necessary to take out a copyright in this country because you do not think any party would interfere by republishing without my consent.

My dear Cousin. You are too pure, to [*sic*] good and so is Cousin Sara;

both of you are too noble to believe that there are people so mean, so low as to take what was not theirs ... You good people of Boston could not believe one half the assertions made in my Diary but all I said I would not be afraid to say in their presence ... I have given my consent to those alterations because dear Cousins, I would please you, and it does not matter much after all if you did alter it. Your advice is for my good and I yield to you...

Your affectionate Cousin,
Liliuokalani[52]

This response not only points to the queen's insistence that nothing more be stolen from her but to an editorial relationship inflected by family ties, good will, legal necessities, and editorial and time constraints, to say nothing of race and social protocols. Our understanding of the editorial and production process will change as present-day and future scholars study the primary materials in the context of the few crucial months that stepped up the writing process and hastened every stage of production. What is extremely unlikely to change is the power of this autobiography, which Lili'uokalani's political adversary—long after Hawai'i had become a U.S. territory—worked so hard to defuse.

The most powerful section of Lili'uokalani's book may well be its elaborate series of appendixes, on which Thurston remains silent and which evolves from a recasting of historical events into a subversive discourse that exhibits indigenous history, culture, and stability. Seven appendixes, spanning thirty-four pages, address the catastrophe by constructing a textual heteroglossia that *re*contextualizes information already provided in both the crisis and catastrophe narrations. The approaches for readers are nearly inexhaustible, because the network of discourses compels multiple explorations and reading strategies. Some of the appendixes have subsections, and almost all of them incorporate different styles and have other genres inserted in them. For example, the second appendix, with the most elaborate arrangement of voices, creates a political dialogue in the form of a letter that Lili'uokalani sent to the United States.[53] Embedded in the letter are historical narratives, letters to U.S. presidents, commentaries on the letters, and quoted texts of protest documents. These interior discourses are complex, and because they operate recursively, they exert centrifugal pressure against the framing discourse. To counter that pressure a number of passages function as a metatext, outlining and summarizing the very points that have just been made. Whether the texts are read separately, linearly, or as a series of intersecting references, the dynamics are charged and the judgments are emphatically against U.S. expansionism in the Pacific. Configuring its content differently from the narrations in the book proper and creating new dialogical tensions, the appendix enriches the book while it protects and archives its author's historiographic records and viewpoints.

Although the appendixes recursively present material from the text, it is significant that they avoid doing this for the material that is strictly autobiographical. Indeed, references to the protagonist's life are absorbed entirely into the political and evidentiary registers of the heteroglossia. The queen may be mentioned in a letter or formal document or as a participant in an event, but personal details are given no textual presence whatsoever. Their omission confirms the careful planning that is behind this project even while its writing process remains tethered to external events. It also corroborates the strategy of using autobiography appealingly and coherently as a pretext that makes subversive activity possible, going far beyond personal concerns. As Owana Ka'ohelelani writes, Hawaiians "are motivated to achieve for the group rather than themselves. Our answer to the 'American Dream' [in its earlier form, annexation] is not the survival of individuals but the survival of the species."[54] This concern for the general over the specific occurs throughout *Hawaii's Story by Hawaii's Queen*, which uses its Western autobiographical paradigm merely as the opening act of a drama whose middle acts are loosely linked to it and whose final act is not at all dependent on it.

As the autobiographical paradigm moves into the background, a new mode of life writing suddenly and dramatically comes onto center stage—in the format of Native genealogies. Occurring in the last three appendixes, the change is startling because it is virtually the first time in the book that the lives of Hawaiians are positioned entirely in their own contexts. The important role that the genealogies play is unmistakable; it is established and reiterated in patterns that reveal a cultural richness that is off limits to most non-Hawaiians. Genealogies are narratives, and Polynesian narratives, as Judith Binney explains, are restrictive in the way that they maintain boundaries apart from Western epistemologies. Interested in their own people and leaders, genealogies are stories of filiation and social relatedness.[55] Coming at the very end of the volume, the genealogies do not interact with the narrative materials in the first few appendixes. The social order and continuities that the genealogies project have nothing to do with Western-based events, be they crisis-driven or catastrophic.

APPENDIX E.

ARRANGED BY LILIUOKALANI.

No. 1.

GENEALOGY OF LILIUOKALANI.

ON HER MOTHER'S (KEOHOKALOLE) SIDE.

Three sisters . . . {
1. IKUAANA.
2. UMIULAIKAAHUMANU.
3. UMIAENAKU.

Father.	Mother.	Child.
Ahu a I.	Umiulaikaahumanu	{ Heulu
Ku a Nuuanu	"	{ Kamakaimoku
Heulu	Ikuaana	{ Keawe-a-Heulu
"	Moana	} Hakau
Keawe-a-Heulu	Ululani	{ Keohohiwa / Naihe
Kepookalani	Keohohiwa	Aikanaka
Aikanaka	Kamaeokalani	Keohokalole
Kapaakea	Keohokalole	{ Kaliokalani / Kalakaua / Liliuokalani / Anna Kaiulani / Kaiminaauao / Miriam Likelike / Leleiohcku W. P.
Cleghorn, A. S.	Likelike	Victoria Kaiulani

NOTE. — Keawe-a-Heulu was chief warrior and councillor of Kamehameha I. Ululani, his wife, was the most celebrated poetess in her day. Their daughter Keohohiwa married Kepookalani, my great-grandfather, first cousin of Kamehameha I. Her brother Naihe married Kapiolani, the celebrated queen who defied the goddess Pele. Naihe was one of the councillors to Kamehameha I., and chief orator of the council. Kamehameha's councillors were Keawe-a-Heulu, his son Naihe, and their cousins Kameeiamoku and Keeaumoku.

AUTHORITY. — C. Kanaina, A. Fornander, and others.

GENEALOGY OF LILIUOKALANI

ON HER FATHER'S (KAPAAKEA) SIDE.

KEAWEIKEKAHIALIIOKAMOKU. KING OF HAWAII.

Father.	Mother.	Child.
Keaweikekahialiiokamoku	(1st wife) Lonoma Ikanaka	Ka I–i mamao, *alias* Kalaninui Iamamao
Kalaninui Iamamao	Kaolanialii	Alapaiwahine
Kepookalani	Alapaiwahine	Kamanawa
Kamanawa	Kamokuiki	Kapaakea
Kapaakea	Keohokalole	Kaliokalani James. Kalakaua Liliuokalani Anna Kaiulani Kaiminaauao Miriam Likelike Leleiohoku, W. P.
Archibald Scott Cleghorn	Likelike	Victoria Kawekiu Lunalilo Kalaninuiahilapalapa Kaiulani

NOTE. — Liliuokalani's great grandmother, Alapaiwahine, is the same person given in the history of the "Tradition of Creation." Her husband, Kepookalani, was first cousin to Kamehameha I.

Appendix E

No. 1.

GENEALOGY OF KAMEHAMEHA I.

Three sisters . . . $\begin{cases} \text{1. Ikuaana.} \\ \text{2. Umiulaikaahumanu.} \\ \text{3. Umiaenaku.} \end{cases}$

Father.	*Mother.*	*Child.*
Ahu a I.	Umiulaikaahumanu (brother)	Heulu.
Ku a Nuuanu	" (sister)	Kamakaimoku.
Keeaumokun Nui	Kamakaimoku	Keoua.
Keoua Kalanikupuapa	Kekuiapoiwa II.	Kamehameha I.

NOTE. — The relationship of the two families on my mother's side. Heulu, my ancestor, and Kamakaimoku were brother and sister. Keawe-a-Heulu, my ancestor, and Keoua, father of Kamehameha I., were first cousins. Keohohiwa, my great-grandmother, and Kamehameha I., were second cousins.

Kamehameha I. m. his aunt	Peleuli	Kahoanoku.
Kahoanoku	Wahinepio Kahakuakoi	Kekauonohi.

Kekauonohi was grand-daughter of Kamehameha I., and the same who adopted my sister Anna Kaiulani.

Appendix E

GENEALOGY OF KEPOOKALANI,

THE GREAT—GRANDFATHER OF LILIUOKALANI.

	Father.	Mother.	Child
Three brothers. {	Haae a Mahi m. (1st wife)	Kalelemauliokalani	{ 1. Kamakaeheukuli } 2. Haalou } Four sisters.
	Haae a Mahi m. (2d wife)	Kekelaokalani	3. Kekuiapoiwa II.
Twins. [	Kamanawa (2d husband of)	"	4. Peleuli
	Kameeiamoku	Kamakaeheukuli	Kepookalani
	Kekaulike	Haalou	Namahaua
	Keoua Kalanikupua (1st wife)	Kamakaeheukuli	Kalaimamahu or Hoapilikane
	(2d wife)	Kekuiaoiwpa II.	Kamehameha I.
	Kamehameha I. (marries his aunt)	Peleuli	Kinau Kahoanoku
	Kinau Kahoanoku	Wahinepio	Kekauonohi.

NOTES. — Haae a Mahi and Kameeiamoku and Kamanawa were brothers, of one father and different mothers. The two latter brothers were twins, and called " The Royal Twins of Keeaumoku." They are also mentioned in history by the early missionaries or historians.

The above genealogy is most perplexing. Kepookalani (my great-grand-father), Namahana, and Kamehameha I., were first cousins. Kepookalani and Kalaimamahu were brothers by the same mother. Kalaimamahu and Kamehameha I. were brothers by the same father. Kepookalani's mother was the oldest of the four sisters, and the third sister was mother of Kamehameha I.

Haae a Mahi, Kameeiamoku, and Kamanawa were half brothers by their mother to the grandfather of Kamehameha I.

Kepookalani being first cousin to Kamehameha I., my grandfather Kamanawa I., son of Kepookalani, becomes second cousin to Kamehameha I. The latter Kamanawa was named for the first.

The intermingling of the two families is not only from his mother's, but also by his father's side, and is both from my mother's as well as my father's side.

You will recognize Kekauonohi's name as the grand-daughter of Kamehameha I., and the same who adopted my younger sister, Anna Kaiulani.

Kalanikauleleiaiwi is the name of Haae's mother, also Kameeiamoku and Kamanawa. Kepookalani's mother was sister to Kamehameha I.'s mother.

Kepookalani's first wife was Keohohiwa, their child was Aikanaka; his second wife was Alapaiwahine, and Kamanawa was the child of that marriage. My father and mother were first cousins.

Keapo o Kepookalani was brother of Kamehameha I. and had no children. He was called Keliionaikai on account of his kindness to the people of Hana, Maui.

AUTHORITY. — Fornander and Kekuanaoa.

APPENDIX G.

BY LILIUOKALANI.

No. 1.

GENEALOGY OF MRS. BERNICE PAUAHI BISHOP.

Father.	Mother.	Child.
Heulu	Moana	Hakau
Kanaina	Hakau	Hao
Hao	Kailipakalua	Luahine
Kaoleioku	Luahine	Konia
Paki	Konia	Bernice Pauahi Bishop

NOTE.— It was from the above that Mrs. Bishop won her position in Kanaina's property.

AUTHORITY. — Fornander's History, p. 193; Kekuanaoa's Book, p. 8; Kanaina's Book.

No. 2.

GENEALOGY OF QUEEN EMMA.

Heulu	Kahihiokalani	Kalaniwahineuli
Kalaniopuu (2d wife)	Kalaniwahineuli	Kalaipaihala
Kalaipaihala	Kalikokalani	Kaoanaeha
John Young (Olohana)	Kaoanaeha	Fanny Kekela
Naea	Fanny Kekela	Emma Kaleleonalani

AUTHORITY. — Fornander, p. 204; Kaunahi, and Kanaina's Book.

Lilikalā Kameʻeleihiwa cites three characteristics of Hawaiian genealogy, all of them evident in the genealogical appendixes and all of them intended by the author. Genealogies "define our *Lāhui* (nation) as an entity distinct from the waves of foreigners," and they "*are* the Hawaiian concept of time and they order the space around us." They are also "an unbroken chain that links those alive today to the primeval life forces— to the *mana* (spiritual power) that first emerged with the beginning of the world."[56]

The historical moments, implied stories, different voices and lives that constitute the heteroglossia of the genealogies are substantively different from those found in the earlier appendixes. The indigenous material generates its own set of interrelations from numerous sources and sites, but the information is not embedded according to chronology or hierarchical arrangements. This suggests there is no single, encompassing discourse or genealogy that contains and establishes the sequences of the others. Rather, there are three discrete appendixes labeled "E," "F," and "G" (see figures). Each section consists of a number of genealogical charts, most of which develop laterally from the maternal to the paternal side and geographically from one island to another, then horizontally to the families of other female aliʻi who are Liliʻuokalani's contemporaries. Presumably the lists within each genealogy are arranged sequentially, but because there are few internal dates, chronology is subordinate to the overall scheme. The genealogies have a plenitude of data, but Liliʻuokalani seals off from foreign readers the histories and individual biographies that lie behind them. This allows her to do what Kameʻeleihiwa describes: to declare her nation as a distinct entity, to exhibit Hawaiian time and space as integrative and expansive, and to draw an unbroken chain from the past to the present, all the while shutting down full accessibility. It should also be said that this material is restricted in the sense that it bars editorial intervention and mediation. No non-Hawaiian close to the project was in a position to advise changes or correct Liliʻuokalani. In fact, a single sheet in her own handwriting of one of the genealogies survives as evidence of her meticulous attention to the indigenous narratives that conclude the autobiography.

Liliʻuokalani's presence as a part, and a small part, of this capacious narrative-history-collective biography underscores the way that she metamorphically develops over the course of the book. Beginning as an autobiographical protagonist, she passes through the intermediate stage of an enunciating and argumentative "I" until reaching her most culturally meaningful identity, the one in which she is materially absent, characterologically subordinate, and verbally silent but present in her desired and unchanging genealogical position, where power is signified by an encompassing social relatedness. According to Kameʻeleihiwa,

> in Hawaiian, the past is referred to as *Ka wā mamua*, or "the time in front or before." Whereas the future, when thought of at all, is *Ka wā mahope*, or "the time which comes after or behind." It is as if the Hawaiian stands firmly in the present, with his back to the future, and his eyes fixed upon the past, seeking historical answers for present-day dilemmas. Such an orientation is to the Hawaiian an eminently practical one, for the future is always unknown, whereas the past is rich in glory and knowledge.[57]

Liliʻuokalani's orientation is indeed practical; it situates her firmly in the present of her writing time and allows her to look back and guide her readers to do likewise—so when they all look forward they will see a Hawaiian nation, not a territory of the United States.[58]

Hawaii's Story by Hawaii's Queen first shows its author working autobiographically inside a bildungsroman paradigm, where a leisurely pace is possible as long as the crisis continues. It then shows the author abandoning the paradigm when conditions of catastrophe make necessary a more compact and urgent approach. Finally, it shows her turning to an indigenous form of narrative in order to pay tribute to her own rich past. The narrative piece that is missing, however, is the denouement of the U.S. congressional vote on annexation. One reason is that it has no place in the appendixes that draw the book into Hawaiian epistemology. Another reason has to do with what H. Porter Abbott calls the "turbulence" of autobiography relative to the historical moment of the book's composition.[59] The turbulence caused by the historical catastrophe of June 1897 was at its height when the book was published in early 1898; consequently, Liliʻuokalani's work was able to participate in the debates but could not include the outcome. Addressing the American people in her own apparent voice and pleading for their opposition to annexation, the author can do no more, and in the final chapter, "Hawaiian Autonomy," she comes to a stop: "Here, at least for the present, I rest my pen" (373). A few months after she put down her pen, supporters of the treaty were forced to admit defeat, with the two-thirds majority required for approving it no longer possible. McKinley's treaty proposal proved unsuccessful, had to be tabled, and never was voted on.[60] There were many contributing factors, including the Spanish-American War, fighting in the Philippines, and competing ideologies in America of nationalism, expansionism, immigration, and race.[61] Stirred into this volatile mix were the protest petitions from Hawaiian resistance groups with tens of thousands of signatures constituting over 90 percent of the Native population and, of course, the queen's own impressive testimony.[62] When Hawaii became a territory, it happened only by a majority vote in the Senate, which is all that is necessary for a joint resolution. This was introduced in May 1898 to replace the treaty proposal. The House of Representatives passed the resolution 209 to 91 on June 15, and the Senate voted a few weeks later, in early July. Forty-two senators voted in favor, twenty-one against, and twenty-six did not vote. The fate of Hawai'i rested on fewer than half the members of the Senate and on an inappropriate and illegal mechanism for annexation.[63]

Realizing the obstacle of a two-thirds majority had been pushed aside, Lili'uokalani could only wait in her Washington, D.C., residence for the official congressional votes to be released.[64] She had done everything possible to make her case, and few autobiographers have ever had a more ambitious purpose and such a narrow time period for carrying it out. What is remarkable about *Hawaii's Story by Hawaii's Queen* is its responsiveness, its ability to alter content, structure, and approaches as the need arose and crisis exploded into catastrophe. Lili'uokalani was especially skillful in connecting her life writing to life performing. Her autobiography thus illustrates that realistic self-imagery is simply good imagery, the result of strategy, compromise, and recognizing that carefully selected episodes and first-person enunciations offer convincing illusions of verisimilitude. When the autobiographical subject seems most plausible to its intended readers, it is operating tropologically and is ambiguously, if not tenuously, connected to the author. Conversely, when self-imagery seems remote from the narrating "I," when it is merely an entry in a diagram of births and marriages, it comes closer to the woman who lives, and views her life, on a plane that does not utterly align itself with the text that bears her name.

Of all the women in this study, Lili'uokalani works from the most extreme point of marginalization to the most centered target imaginable, right to a U.S. president. The vast distance to be covered results in a book that is a series of autobiographical, narrational, and dialogical balancing acts between conventional and resistant images and viewpoints. The unexpected event that pushes the autobiography into a catastrophe narrative is indicative of the diverse external pressures that affect all the women discussed in the chapters that follow. *Hawaii's Story by Hawaii's Queen* may be the most extreme case study in which the autobiographical subject is a medium for other materials, arguments, actions, and goals. Perhaps that is why the author writes herself into an indigenous location in time and space inaccessible to most of her readers. If so, it is a magnificent gesture that signals her desire to be someone somewhere that no American event— be it annexation, overthrow, territorialization, or even statehood—can trespass.

CHAPTER TWO

Autobiographical Fiction as Testimony

H.D's *The Gift*

RITICS AGREE THAT World War I was personally and creatively devastating for H.D. Though she had established herself in British literary circles after leaving America in 1911, her life changed drastically when England declared war on Germany in 1914, and a series of personal tragedies connected with the war inevitably impacted her work. Her husband, the British poet Richard Aldington, volunteered to serve in the military, and two tours of duty in the trenches in France left him suffering from shell shock.[1] Her older brother, who enlisted as soon as America entered the war, was killed in France in 1918, and in less than six months her father was also dead. In 1915 H.D. had a stillborn daughter, and she always believed that the infant's death was related to the "shock and repercussions of war news."[2] Her marriage deteriorated, with infidelities on both sides. In 1919 H.D. gave birth to a daughter; Aldington refused to accept the child, and the relationship effectively came to an end. Even after the war H.D. found it difficult to write. While managing to publish some of her work, she left numerous manuscripts unfinished and discarded others. She also left instructions that certain manuscripts dating from this period be destroyed. Susan Stanford Friedman traces H.D. through the aftermath of World War I and concludes that by the 1930s she had reached "an aesthetic dead end."[3] Friedman further argues that although the postwar novels are useful in understanding the author's fragile psychology, their experimentalism, in the form of "distressed and fragmented discourses," offers ample evidence that H.D. was artistically blocked.[4]

While World War I was destructive to H.D.'s creativity, surprisingly, World War II had the opposite effect. In the earlier war H.D. was removed from the front lines of battle on the European Continent and thus personally protected from harm at the same time that members of her family were in the center of combat. In the later war, as Germany seemed ready to invade Great Britain in 1940, she deliberately chose not to return to America, where, for a second time, she would be at a safe distance from military action.[5] She had strong loyalties to Britain, where her first book was published, and saw proximity to the war as a test of her courage as well as a form of moral support for her adopted country.[6] The decision to remain in London, though the city was likely to be a major target for bombs, also grounded her emotionally and artistically. It served, in a larger sense, as a rehabilitative measure to her insulation—despite her personal tragedies—precipitated by the First World War.

In *Within the Walls*, which she began shortly before the Battle of Britain in 1940 and to which she returned after the most sustained period of bombing was over, H.D. reflects on her different positions relative to the two wars. Suggesting that she has experienced a "personal miracle of readjustment," she writes, "1941, by an easy trick, could be resolved to 1914. Then all those post-war years of Lethe or stagnation, did not matter."[7] Reversing the last numbers of these dates was a symbolic gesture, but in rejecting the first postwar period H.D. was asserting a new resilience and a sense of expectation for the second postwar period.[8] Real change would not take place for a number of years, for the worst of the war was still to come, but by mid-1941 while writing this part of *Within the Walls*, H.D. was also drafting the early chapters of *The Gift* and overcoming her creative block. Bryher (Annie Winifred Ellerman), who became H.D.'s companion and support, confirms that one of the differences between the two wars was a shared recognition that everyone was at risk. In *The Days of Mars: A Memoir, 1940–1946*, Bryher credits this sense of community—among the civilians and between the civilian and military populations—for making World War II easier to bear. "We were all 'in it,'" she explains, "and there was not the dreadful gap between soldiers and civilians that had caused so much stress in 1914."[9] The difference also helped make it possible for H.D. to write *The Gift* and then to begin her most productive decades of work in both poetry and prose.[10]

Critics acknowledge that *The Gift*, written during the air attacks over London and posthumously published forty years later, in 1982, marks an

important juncture in H.D.'s career.[11] Studies by Friedman and Rachel
Blau DuPlessis in the 1980s and 1990s firmly established the book's importance and the role of psychoanalysis, myth, spiritualism, and H.D.'s Moravian history, all operating within the context of World War II.[12] It is
impossible to study *The Gift* without recognizing these connections. However, there has also been a tendency to generalize the references to the
bombing and thus to give the impression that the battle over London,
throughout the war, was a series of daily, uninterrupted attacks occurring
in a pattern that did not qualitatively change over time. Even when the
arguments are specifically based on the war, recent studies do not distinguish between the important stages of the fighting. Henke, in *Shattered
Subjects*, generalizes the situation as "civilian life under siege."[13] In a discussion of H.D. and the Blitz in *The World Wars through the Female Gaze*,
Jean Gallagher goes further, noting a change in 1944 when Germany introduced pilotless V-1 bombs and targeted London. Her examination of violence and visuality is insightful, but it does not pinpoint ways in which
new, unpredictable forms of violence—such as the V-1 bombs—determined the form and content of *The Gift*.[14]

In fact, analyses that use broad characterizations of the Blitz misrep-
resent *The Gift* as a crisis narrative because they fail to investigate the
specific context of catastrophe, which led H.D. to write in spurts. If we
were to assume that she wrote most of the book during the intense, uninterrupted months of bombing, we would be forced to limit her writing
time to late 1940. And this is not accurate. H.D. did not complete the manuscript until the end of 1944, and the continuous pounding of London
lasted from early September through early November 1940. Within this
limited period Germany launched almost eighty raids on the capital,
attacking nearly every night with an average of two hundred planes.[15] Certainly major attacks on the city took place through May 1941 but never
again on such a regular or predictable basis, and historians have always
pointed this out. Henry Pelling, in *Britain and the Second World War*, cites
six heavy raids and two lighter ones over London from mid-November
1940 through mid-January 1941 as a stark contrast with the number that
had occurred in the previous few months. Angus Calder, in *The People's
War: Britain 1939–1945*, writes that bad weather in January 1941 limited
Germany to only two major attacks and "three other sizable attacks" on
London with three major raids in February 1941. From mid-February
through mid-May, seven large raids were directed at London. Then the
city was again very gravely hit. On May 10, 1941, the "last and worst night

of the London Blitz," nearly fifteen hundred people were killed, eighteen hundred seriously injured, and over two thousand fires were started.[16] The intensity of the May 10 raid convinced many people that there would be one more devastating blow to "finish off" London. But it never came. In other words, the intermittent air attacks from late 1940 through 1941, coinciding with H.D.'s first concentrated period of drafting *The Gift*, indicate that it was catastrophe, far more than crisis, which most powerfully triggered her creativity. My approach, which distinguishes crisis from catastrophe in H.D.'s response to the war, clarifies the relation between her autobiographical fiction and very specific, changing material circumstances.[17]

Crises extend continuously over time, but catastrophes are sudden and inconsistent. They, too, may be prolonged, but when this occurs the catastrophes stop at some point and begin again in unpredictable and erratic ways without stabilizing into a discernible pattern. H.D., like everyone else in London in the fall of 1940, experienced that wave of bombing on civilian areas as an unrelenting assault, fully characterizing the elements of a shared crisis. In fact, as an ongoing battle against the larger context of the global war, the 1940 Blitz could be viewed as a crisis within a larger crisis. The accounts of this period by survivors and historians typically refer to how effectively the population adapted to the situation and rallied, carrying on as much as possible with daily life.[18]

While historians may attribute Londoners' resistance *during* 1940 to their ability to accommodate to the continuing crisis, they link the city's resistance *after* 1940 to its citizens' efficient responding to the *noncontinuous* nature of the raids.[19] The dates of composition that H.D. specifically provides inside of her text, 1941, 1943, and 1944, correspond to such periods of irregular, noncontinuous attacks, all of them followed by intervals of calm.[20] In 1942, a year that she does *not* cite as crucial to the project and a period in which she was more actively working on poetry, the most significant battles were taking place in locations remote from London.[21] In fact, after a major raid on the capital in the summer of 1941, another major attack did not take place until January 1943. This later attack corresponds exactly to H.D.'s second intense period of writing *The Gift*. As an external context, the attack jolted H.D. back to her manuscript. Turned into text, it is also the subject—"my first raid after the interval"—with which chapter 7 opens and to which it bears witness. In the lulls between the attacks—when it was the cities in the southeast and north that were targeted—Londoners recuperated quickly and prepared for the next phase of bombing. They also endured the anxiety of not knowing when, where, or even if a next phase would occur.[22] In periods characterized by this same kind of uncertainty and instability, where she could tentatively feel out of danger even though she realized that she might actually be *in* danger, H.D. wrote *The Gift*.

Catastrophe—in the form of random, erratic, violent threat to life and body—impedes *The Gift* at the same time that it also drives it. The text bears witness to immediate trauma, but unlike most testimonies, it does not strive to reproduce the event throughout or to create a continuous narrative. Instead, it performs the emotions and sense of disequilibrium that the catastrophe sets off and enacts patterns of interruption and fragmentation.[23] Bearing witness to catastrophe, the prose exhibits a high degree of anxiety, and it does so intermittently in response to catastrophe rather than continuously in response to ongoing crisis.[24] Through displaced images, the experience of instability and of alternately feeling safe and vulnerable infiltrates family scenes from H.D.'s childhood. Potentially idyllic memories, filtered through the experience of random violence, become unsettled and unsettling, reflecting the author's unease. The narrator alludes to death, to actual bodies, and sometimes to female bodies in the midst of conversations or scenes from half a century earlier. The memories seem generally to progress according to time, but little attention is given to chronology. Striking images, associational flow, and an actively searching gaze are far more important in linking together the fragments of memory as they come into consciousness.[25] Explicitly referring in a 1941 letter to the uncertainties of the post-1940 period, H.D. attributes much of what she suddenly remembers to the shocks of living through the intermittent bombing raids. They leave her emotionally and psychologically on edge but not creatively blocked, with "just time to draw such a deep breath ... and say 'I am alive'" and then say it further in her writing. [26] H.D. composed much of *The Gift* during such "breathing" spaces, writing at intervals over the course of nearly five years. Her autobiographical writing thus transcends self-representation and serves as a strategy of survival, a way to contend with wartime developments at their least predictable and most volatile moments.[27]

Recognizing that the manuscript was written primarily during three distinct air strikes in 1941, 1943, and 1944 also restructures the way that we see the book. We approach *The Gift* as the author produced it, at intervals over time, not simply as readers progressing through seven chapters and a substantial "Notes" section.[28] From this perspective the book has three related but separate discourses, each one with its own style and subject matter and each one using different tropes to reflect its material circumstances. The first and longest discourse was written primarily in 1941. Extending from chapters 1 through 6, it reflects the months of erratic bombing soon after the fall 1940 crisis of nightly raids.[29] Its tropes suggest extreme instability and uncertainty, and the prose is fragmented and elusive. Memories of family scenes turn surreal, overlaid with images of death, fire, and random perils. The narrating voice is inconsistent, abruptly shifting out of its predominant first-person mode; most often it enunciates as the woman and author H.D., but sometimes it performs in the voice of "Hilda," the child (H.D.'s actual name). As the focus of the witnessing activity is displaced onto recollected scenes from childhood in America, the chapters are implicitly argumentative and dialogic in their relation to the war. Chapter 7 is the book's second discourse, written in 1943 when, after more than a year, renewed bombing drove H.D. back to the unfinished manuscript. Entitled "Morning Star," it is notably different from all the preceding chapters. It directly and immediately informs us of its witnessing function because it establishes itself as testimony of the bombing attack of January 1943 *before* it shifts into recollected scenes of childhood. More explicit than the preceding material, this chapter clarifies the suggestive correspondences between the past and present and shows further how life writing functions tropologically as argument, social commentary, and testimony. The third discourse, which is the section entitled "Notes," remained unfinished until mid-1944. Nearly one-third the total length of the seven autobiographical chapters, this section is discursive, long, and explicative, rich with genealogical information and details from H.D.'s research on religion, myth, and history. Radically different from the rest of the book, it constitutes still another form of testimony. In addition, "Notes" bears witness to events of mid-1944. This section of the book points to a double catalyst driving the end of *The Gift*: Germany's new weapon, the pilotless V-1 bomber plane, and the D-Day invasion of Normandy. Responding to the V-1, or "buzzbomb," which was completely unanticipated by the general population, and then to the Allied victories from June 6, 1944 on, H.D. evolves out of the role of autobiographical narrator and subject. Foreseeing an end to the war but once again personally at risk, she now adopts the multiple roles of editor, researcher, and historian, effectively closing off and distancing herself from her autobiographical project. The portrait she draws of herself, in the act of literally ending her book, serves in a larger capacity as her final reflecting trope for a war whose end is also in sight.

Like other life writing texts set into motion by catastrophe, *The Gift*
uses self-representation for metonymic purposes. As tropes, memories
participate in the act of bearing witness—indirectly in images, references,
changes in voice and perspective, and in a shifting relationship between the
narrator and her autobiographical self. In the pages that follow, I discuss
how H.D. makes *The Gift* perform as testimony *through* a substitutive
discourse of autobiographical and family memories, which symbolically

H.D. during the Second World War. *Courtesy of New Directions and Yale University,*
Collection of American Literature, Beinecke Rare Book and Manuscript Library

reflects the conflicts of present time. I also examine how H.D., by lyrically fashioning those memories into her own imaginative vision, uses them tropologically to counter a world at war. In chapter 5 she tries to reconstruct a story told to her by her grandmother half a century earlier of peace between the Moravians, who settled in Pennsylvania, and a group of Native Americans, a story that H.D. wholly forgot until wartime violence shattered it back into memory. Whereas chapter 5 dramatically presents the grandmother in a trance, sharing obscure fragments of the event, I show how H.D., returning in 1943 to the same story and treating it in chapter 7, refashions it for testimonial purposes as well as a substitutive trope for her own imagined visions of peace.[30]

CATASTROPHE AND TESTIMONY

Shoshana Felman and Dori Laub's approach in *Testimony: Crises of Witnessing in Literature, Psychoanalysis, and History* is particularly applicable to *The Gift*. It helps us to realize how powerfully H.D.'s childhood in Pennsylvania functions as a displaced site for catastrophic experience and

German flying bomb descending near Drury Lane, London. *Imperial War Museum (HU636)*

Plume of the Aldwych Flying Bomb. *Imperial War Museum (HU638)*

protest. Examining poetry and fiction which, like *The Gift*, are not primarily considered to be testimony literature, Felman and Laub discuss ways in which biography and history, emerging through "subterranean" devices such as displacement, allusions, transference, allegory, and formal structure, are "reinscribed, translated, radically rethought and fundamentally worked over."[31] Explaining that the "empirical context needs not just to be *known*, but to be *read*; to be read in conjunction with, and as part of, the reading of the text," the authors argue for reading modes that expose

> how the basic and legitimate critical demand for *contextualization of the text* itself needs to be complemented, simultaneously, by the less familiar and yet necessary work of *textualization of the context*; and how this shuttle movement or this shuttle reading in the critic's work—the very *tension between textualization and contextualization*—might yield new avenues of insight, both into the texts at stake and into their context—the political, historical, and biographical realities with which the texts are dynamically involved and within which their particular creative possibilities are themselves inscribed.[32]

In other words, elements of testimony come forth when readers fluidly move between the text and the events surrounding the writing of the text, assessing each one relative to the other throughout the reading process. Context is not merely a background but, as it functions for H.D., a crucial, internal dimension of the text.

Reading *The Gift* for the interrelations of text and context helps situate H.D.'s late-nineteenth-century childhood in America in twentieth-century London. The recovery of memories, some forgotten for half a century, takes place in the form of scenes and dialogues, which burst into consciousness in what the author calls "flashes of flash-backs" (42). H.D. had undergone analysis with Freud in the 1930s and believed that without psychoanalysis she "would hardly have found the clue or the bridge between the child-life, the memories of the peaceful Bethlehem [Pennsylvania] and the orgy of destruction, later to be witnessed and lived through in London."[33] But the self-exploration that occurs in this text, along with scenes of maternal transference, of paternal power, and a general psychoanalytic framework, is also attributable to the external threats that H.D. was witnessing.[34] According to her own explanation after the war had ended: "That outer threat and constant reminder of death, drove me inward, almost forced me to compensate, by memories of another world, an actual world where there had been security and comfort."[35] The key word here is "almost." It stops us from concluding that in *The Gift* childhood recollections are simply an escape from, or a full-scale substitution for, wartime London. It points instead to a complex symbiosis between the two time frames. The immediate catastrophe triggers forgotten and repressed memories into consciousness; then turned into narrative, the memories function reflectively and indirectly as tropes for the catastrophe itself. As a result, the two time frames relativize each other.

Many of the scenes from childhood that comprise the six chapters of the 1941 discourse are shot through with violence or permeated with a sense of anxiety. In the opening paragraphs, where H.D. introduces her parents and grandparents, repeated references to violence and death interrupt the narrative, creating out of her memories a trope for the violence of the war. The child, Hilda (H.D.'s autobiographical protagonist), is preoccupied with death. She wonders at its randomness and looks for reasons why it strikes when it does. The adult narrator is preoccupied with the same subject, and memories inevitably veer in that direction. The child thinking about death is thus a metaphor for the adult author responding through literature to the catastrophe that surrounds her and using memories of her life as an expressive and stabilizing response to the bombing. The images of death that interrupt the flow of the narrative, on the level of text, enact the effects of the intermittent terror that interrupted and altered H.D.'s life at the time of writing.

One particular image in *The Gift* that intrudes at the very start becomes in itself a trope for the troping of violence that connects present time with the act of remembering the past. Chapter 1 begins with a reference to a little girl burning to death. This same image recurs at intervals and blocks the progression of the narrative. While introducing the members of the Doolittle and maternal Wolle family, the narrator suddenly asserts: "There was a girl who was burnt to death at the Seminary, as they called the old school where our grandfather was Principal."[36] She immediately moves on to her parents and grandparents, but the memory of the burning girl returns in the midst of the descriptions, enacting tropologically and narratologically the connection of the past to the present bombing and threats of fire: "But the girl who was burnt to death, was burnt to death in a crinoline. The Christmas-tree was lighted at the end of one of the long halls and the girl's ruffles or ribbons caught fire and she was in a great hoop." When the narrator switches our attention to a photograph of the women in the family, the image suddenly and incongruously asserts itself again: "But the girl in the crinoline wasn't a relation, she was just one of the many girls at the Seminary when Papalie was there and she screamed and Papalie rushed to her and Papalie wrapped a rug around her but she is shrieking and they can not tear off her clothes because of the hoop" (35). The change of tense at the end has a jolting effect. While allowing the image to function in the remote past, it also drives the image grammatically into the narrator's frame of reference, thus hinging an explicitly described scene onto something allusive in present time.

This connection is made explicit in a later chapter, when H.D. is describing her reaction to the unexpected bombing raids as the "very worst terrors" and returns to the image of the burning child: "I could think in terms of one girl in a crinoline, I could not visualize civilisation other than a Christmas-tree that had caught fire" (215). The anonymous child is only one of many death-and-fire, burning-star, falling-sky images in the first discourse that come both inside and outside of the childhood story.[37] These recurring references operate as unifying devices in an otherwise discordant and disjunctive narrative. They suggest that for H.D. memory is less a recuperative act than a narrative strategy to describe and displace the unpredictable violence going on around her. Through their metonymic purpose, these images further make *The Gift* a testimony to global victimization. As H.D. reconstructs her life, filtering it through catastrophe, she transforms the act of autobiography into a text of cultural and historical import.

Many readings of the book interpret the repeated imagery and fragmented memories through a psychoanalytic framework, but *The Gift's* discordant technique is also H.D.'s particular form of historical testimony. Independent accounts stress that the attacks over London between 1941 and 1944 were in some sense more harrowing than in the fall of 1940 because they occurred irregularly, not every night, and were varied in intensity. Calder even calls mid-November 1940 through mid-January 1941 a period of "respite," with half a dozen heavy raids and various lighter ones. Though "respite" may overstate the situation, the British newspapers also remark that the longer intervals between strikes created a noticeable change from the earlier crisis period. On January 10, 1941, for example, the *Times* described raids over the city occurring after a lull of three nights. On January 30 it noted that the most recent attack was the first one in ten nights; on March 10 the paper called attention to what had been the heaviest air attack in a number of weeks. Calder outlines a second irregular pattern from mid-February through mid-May 1941, when very serious bombing temporarily resumed. Then another pattern began with quick, surprise attacks throughout the country, including "tip-and-run" raids by fire bombers that came in low in order to harass and terrify civilians.[38] These smaller and less regular poundings may have offered London some measure of relief, but there were always emergencies that mitigated it. In two isolated nights of bombing in April 1941, for example, more than 140,000 houses in London were damaged or destroyed and more than two thousand citizens were killed.[39] The calm periods were so uncertain they must have been nearly as straining as the actual violence, and this paradox is reflected in the imagery and structural tensions throughout the chapters.

The tensions that H.D. lived with produced structural disjunctions in her book, and these made it feasible for the first publisher, New Directions, to produce an abridged edition in 1982 without providing editorial commentary on the changes. Since H.D. did not publish the book in her lifetime, a posthumous edition, even a version one-third shorter than the original typescript, was valuable. However, the purpose of this first edition was to make the book conform to the "familiar marketable genre, the memoir of childhood," and this significantly changed the nature of the original text.[40] The autobiographical protagonist occupies a larger portion of the abridged text than she does in H.D.'s typescript, and the publisher failed to call attention to this. The abridged edition remains stylistically disjunctive, but again less so than H.D. intended it to be. As the only edition available for fifteen years apart from the manuscript materials at Yale University, the New Directions paperback was widely read. Though it undoubtedly helped during the 1980s to expand her reputation as a major writer of prose as well as of poetry, it was, in substantial ways, not the book that H.D. had written. Indeed, the only clue to the extensive editing was a remark by Perdita Schaffner, H.D.'s daughter, in the introduction that the manuscript has been improved by "judicious" cutting.[41] Scholars such as DuPlessis have thought otherwise, and over the years some of the excluded material appeared in journals, including the missing second chapter, "Fortune Teller." To read the "Notes" section critics had to use the ninety-page typescript version at Yale.[42] Finally in 1998 the complete text was published by the University Press of Florida, expertly edited and annotated by Jane Augustine. As Augustine explains in her introduction, this edition is the full-length version of *The Gift*, "complete as [H.D.] wrote it and wanted it read" (1). From this point on, all critical discussions need to recognize that the widely available 1982 edition is the product of heavy-handed cutting, probably to make the book accessible to a large readership. It is, regrettably, an inaccurate reflection of the author's wishes.[43]

The restored *The Gift* should rightfully supersede the earlier version. It carries out H.D.'s original testimonial purposes with many additional references to the war, and, indeed, it looks much more like a war memoir, though always in creative ways. From a contextual and biographical perspective, the once-excised sections are vital, for they enable us to see the book even more convincingly as a catastrophe narrative. Restored passages explicitly describe the impact of a life-threatening environment on the author's psychic process, which is to trigger repressed memories to surface. The most substantial change, along with the addition of the original chapter 2, is certainly the inclusion of the "Notes" section. Confirming the responsiveness of text-and-context, part of this final section hinges itself referentially to events that take place in 1944. The connection helps to reveal a book that is primarily historical despite its other dimensions. Augustine describes the unabridged edition as being a religious quest, giving "access to an all-important secret—the way to end war" (3). DuPlessis characterizes it as a spiritual prophecy, which incorporates history, religion, and meditation and life writing. From my own perspective, *The Gift* contains all of these elements, but like the other texts by women in this study, it responds to and narratively performs catastrophic experience. It moves through various modes and genres, exploring, fictionalizing, and compressing them to fit into moments of narrative recovery. The volume's original, more diffuse structure is a performative response to catastrophe, one that stresses its archival and testimonial functions.

The complete text recasts the role of childhood memoir because the reinstated sections are primarily fiction, history, and observations of life under extreme wartime stress. This means that *The Gift*'s testimonial functions relative to catastrophe become all the more visible.[44] Specifically, the 1998 text structurally reinscribes context into text by repeatedly evoking the unpredictability of the author's situation. We can see, for example, to a much greater extent the way that most chapters break the design of the chapter that precedes it. In fact, each chapter tends to open in a different style or genre from the next. The structure of the book is thus made discontinuous and dramatic, with segments coming in and out like shards of narrative materials. Chapter 1, entitled "Dark Room," starts with family genealogy and then switches to a series of recollected childhood fragments presented through the author's first-person narrator. Chapter 2, "Fortune Teller," opens unexpectedly with H.D. omnisciently allegorizing a biographical fiction of her mother as a young woman. Chapter 3, "The Dream," starts out in a new vein with personal meditation on the nature of mythology and dreams and only then shifts over to memories of the Doolittle household. It jumps back to the author's present time when Hilda wants to know what "nightmare" means. A series of images-as-explanations ensues, but when it ends with examples of dead children, we can see that the narrative has troped far across from the Doolittles' living room into H.D.'s contemporary enunciating time and site and drawn substitutive images of her fears. The images are heavily weighted in their own narrative location, but as distant references to London's nightmare of severe nighttime raids, they displace and reinscribe the author's material context.

One of the most important changes occurs when the second chapter, "The Fortune-Teller," is reinstated in its entirety in the new edition. Not integral to the autobiographical design per se, it is a biographical fiction or, as indicated in the later "Notes" section, a "reconstructed reverie" (232). The central figure of the story is H.D.'s mother, Helen Eugenia Wolle, "child of a long line of musicians" and a romantic and marriageable woman in her twenties. An epigraph from *As You Like It* establishes a pastoral atmosphere for the story, which takes place on Bethlehem's lush riverbank. The characters include a cousin who wishes to marry Helen, and the plot will eventually take the couple to a fortune-teller. But because the fiction is inevitably hinged to H.D.'s writing time, ominous and anomalous images shoot through the pages, including furnace fires, flames streaking the sky, bushes that somehow ignite, a black rose, and fears of destruction by fire. As a complete chapter, "Fortune Teller" has more power than any single trope, and it develops allegorically in suggesting the subtextual presence of a different protagonist, namely H.D., and a different script involving war-ravaged London. In fact, the story evolves out from a pastoral into a cautionary fable, warning of danger and violations to the female body. The biographical protagonist is apprehensive that something external will harm or crush her, and this fear is projected onto images that subvert the idyllic mood and romantic direction of the story. Helen creates her own scenes of entrapment, including one of a trap door under her feet, another trap door that "would snap shut over her head and she would fall and fall" (68), leading her to fear a vague presence threatening pursuit and abduction. In the context of Helen Wolle's female body and the story of getting her fortune told, the unexpected image of rape functions as a metonymic marker for invasion and victimization: "raped, yes ... by the darkness, by Dis by Death." *Like* H.D. and a projection *of* H.D., the biographical protagonist is temporarily safe but intuits a danger, one that has appeared before and will come back. In images and allusions that are enigmatic in the 1870s story, the narrative refers to identifiable details of the *other* story, the wartime story of 1941 London. A "hidden spring" will give way, "something in the air" will turn stars to black patches in the sky, and, as a result, stones and bricks will give way.

Chapter 4, "Because One Is Happy," with its initial passages restored, also bears witness to catastrophe through its structure and imagistic allusions, concentrating on a single image that functions like a vortex. The image is the object capable of wounding and killing. This is rendered explicitly in the chapter's original first paragraph, because it refers to the author's current situation and describes the most recent source of potential death: "There was a time-bomb that had neatly nosed its way under the pavement edge, less than two minutes' walk from my door. At night, with carefully hooded flares, a party of the London demolition squad, prodded and poked; delicately, they inserted little wires or tubes or blades of steel and disemboweled the monster" (109). Compared to a submarine in its sleekness and a shark in its destructive tendencies, the bomb metamorphoses into the imagined monsters of the childhood narrative that follows. The tropological relation between the bomb in one narrative place and monsters in another narrative place comments on the 1941 war context. Without it, the chapter occurs solely in the distant autobiographical past and begins in medias res, during an art lesson in school. Using the earlier edition for which this was the case, readings of the chapter have been almost exclusively psychoanalytical.[45] With the complete text now in place, we can see how the chapter also was meant to be historically and catastrophically based, with all of the monster images spinning out centrifugally from the time bomb discovered close to H.D.'s doorway. The bomb is not merely a catalytic agent for the rush of memories, but a subject for representation as the childhood story develops the monster tropology. In one scene Hilda watches a serpent take over her parents' bedroom; in another she sees a monster in the guise of "a sick, horrible woman" who turns into a python. On a boat with other children, Hilda is frightened that the live crabs are growing larger as she looks at them and will consume her. Finally, the narrator presents the struggle between herself as a little girl and a second snake so vividly that the line blurs between actual and imaginary threats. The creature bites Hilda on the side of her mouth and the wound to her body seems literal and "real," despite the impossibility. In the context of historical testimony that works through displacement, these "real" snakes are effective war tropes, likewise pointing to very real, but inconceivable, acts of violence. Hilda fears she will die but survives, tropologically reflecting a future time in her life when, as a woman in midlife, she will again survive external monsters.

As critics often note, the imagery in "Because One Is Happy" has Freudian and psychoanalytical dimensions, but with the original opening pages added, the cultural and testimonial dimensions become more visible. The pages realign the chapter's place in the overall structure because the material no longer plunges right into the narrative of childhood. Instead, chapter 4 participates in the book's pattern of discontinuity and, like the preceding chapters, begins in a different genre or style before shifting into childhood recollections. In a personal essayist mode, the opening description of the time bomb functions dualistically. The bomb is a symbol of violated private space and a literal agent of death, as well as a narrative trigger for the short political critique that follows. All of this restored material keeps the chapter focused on present-time catastrophe longer than the abridged edition does. This is because the narrator does not view the conflict strictly in individualist or even national terms and, in the new paragraphs, rejects the argument of "nation against nation," despite being subjected to German air attacks.[46] The represented woman is just "one of thousands and thousands who are equally facing a fact, the possibility, at any given second, of complete physical annihilation" (109). Consequently, the personal details that reflect on larger occurrences are metonymic of what the narrator calls "world-calamity."

Once the contextual/textual reciprocity that fuels *The Gift* is clarified, we can see how this reciprocity works as a crucial part of the fully restored chapter. For example, H.D. certainly wants readers to realize that she is caught in "the grip of vital terror" with planes flying overhead. It is when her body becomes frozen with terror that her mind is ready to switch into the emotional and psychic state from which she composes her chapters. In a direct statement on the public and testimonial aspects of the book, and one that appears only in the 1998 edition, she thinks about all the nights of chaos:

> If my mind at those moments had one regret, it was that I might not be able to bear witness to this truth, I might be annihilated before I had time

to bear witness. I wanted to say, "when things become unbearable, a door swings open or a window." Dying men see through that window smiling with their sphinx-secret unrevealed. Indeed, there is no personal secret; terror or danger shared opens the door wide. (111)

These words both explain and perform the process of textualizing context, and what "swings" into view is a testimony where public and private realms converge. A shared catastrophe opens the individual's "door" and the exposed secrets acquire social signification. The most important convergence of past and present, public and private, is alluded to by the "sphinx-secret." It is the grandmother's secret, which "Mamalie" tries to share with Hilda, concerning a declaration of peace between their Moravian ancestors in Pennsylvania and a group of Native Americans, long established and occupying the same territory.

Much of *The Gift* turns on the victimization of bodies, which is, after all, the defining trauma of war. However, the female body, a trope operating throughout the book for other vulnerable bodies, becomes an active agent in the historical struggle against catastrophe, and this is emphasized in the way that Mamalie's body transmits ancestral history. The process is acted out in chapter 5, appropriately entitled "The Secret." The restored passages are extremely important, for they are most frequently historical and because they are based on H.D.'s research on her Moravian heritage, they clarify the fragments of Mamalie's testimony. In contrast to chapter 4, where most of the restored material is at the beginning, here it is intermittent and throughout, thereby enriching the remembered scene over and over until the chapter ends. The additional passages also emphasize H.D.'s intentions to show the female body with the agency to *know* history, not suffer it passively, and to take on an important role in *making* history. This purpose is illustrated in "The Secret" when the female body is the testifying medium of little-known events and effectually creates history by bringing those events out from obscurity.[47] Contextually as an action and textually as a message, Mamalie's testimony is an alternate history and a dialogic text set against the other chapters that reflect primarily death and violation. The narrator's recollections involve a single night in childhood when her maternal grandmother, in a trancelike state, turned her granddaughter into a second-person listener as an integral part of the testimony process. Specifically, the older woman relayed events between the Native Americans and her ancestors, which resulted in a time of peace. The agreement was formalized on a small island called Wunden Eiland, or Island of the Wounds.[48] Two women, one Native American and one Moravian, formalized the peace agreement by taking on each other's names, thus tropologically and symbolically becoming each other.

> Morning Star was the Indian princess who was the wife of Paxnous, who was baptized by the Moravians. She was really baptized, it seems, but Paxnous was not baptized but the Indians took Anna von Pahlen into their mysteries in exchange for Morning Star; I mean, Anna was Morning Star in their mysteries and Morning Star (who had another ordinary Indian name like White-cloud or Fragrant-grass or one of those other names) was Angelica which was another name of Anna von Pahlen, who was really Mrs. John Christopher Frederick Cammerhof, but I like to think of her as Anna von Pahlen. (171)

Unlike many other recollections, the night in which Mamalie shared this information with Hilda is not fragmented but extends across thirty pages for the duration of chapter 5. While the grandmother's speech is somewhat disjointed, the long presentation of the scene emphasizes the testimony's pivotal role and allows its dialogic and gendered characteristics to develop fully.

The historical testimony, centered on women who performed actively in the cultural reconciliation, is transmitted through a female perspective and is embodied in a female materiality. It also stresses the marginalized status, vis-à-vis history, of the two participants—an old woman and a little girl not yet ten years old. The intimate and domestic details drive home the point that Leslie Adelson makes throughout *Making Bodies, Making History*. "Bodies guard their secrets well and divulge them at every turn," despite the body being a "well-kept secret in the history of Western civilization."[49] Corporeal, feminine, and domestic images set the stage for the testimony: a frail grandmother under her patchwork quilt, her hair gathered in a lace night cap; a candle-lit room strewn with handkerchiefs, sachets, and female clothing; and Hilda in a nightdress, feeling her identity diffusing into the dead female relatives by whose names Mamalie addresses her. These details situate the Moravians' alternate history in a feminine space while linking it further to other histories and bodies excluded from cultural master narratives. These bodies, similarly powerless, invisible, and marginalized, are made to suffer the effects of catastrophe anonymously. The words that attest to this, coming from within the female body, are not subject to conscious control. The grandmother testifies only when her mind is quiescent and her body takes over, pushing the words out of her. This brings us back to Felman's observation that when testimony assumes a "subterranean" form, its power lies in its suggestive possibilities and implications. Hilda does not hear a "completed statement" or "totalizable account of those events," but she witnesses the activity of testimony "in process and in trial," which brings history into the realm of action and present time.[50]

The emphasis on women's active engagement and their potential to generate alternate histories makes "The Secret," in Augustine's words, a "keystone" chapter. Female witnessing activity begins to construct a metanarrative, projecting a vision of unity, not aggression. Richly textured, the grandmother's speech is a heteroglossia of knowledge and historical sources. Mamalie bears witness in her own voice primarily when recalling herself as a young woman, discovering the parchment on which the peace agreement was recorded a century earlier. She speaks beyond herself, though, to become the author's trope—and oral source—of genealogical and religious research. This is confirmed with the restoration of many historical passages throughout the chapter. They give detailed information about Moravianism in Bohemia and America, offer summaries of its leaders, present short dramas between its members, and supply background on theology and religious symbolism. Much of this material is interpolated as chunks of erudite historical research that are slipped into the grandmother's subjective account and *performed as her own words*. However, while these elements give the testimony-as-metanarrative a strong presence in *The Gift*, it is an *attempt* at remembrance more than a successful sharing of knowledge. In fact, the narrator testifies to its blocked transmission: "Mamalie is talking like something in a book and I do not very much understand what she is saying" (156). She pleads for more information, "Mamalie, Mamalie, Mamalie, what were you saying?" and is left to wonder if "it was just that I was dreaming something, because I was afraid a shooting-star might swish out of the sky and fall on the house and burn us all up" (176). The dialogic and pacifist arguments throughout the grandmother's testimony remain highly allusive and, in terms of being effectual in H.D.'s responding to catastrophe, not yet privileged discourse.

The grandmother's testimony may well be the most important chapter of *The Gift*, but it does not recast our view of the preceding chapters, nor does it have a positive impact on the events and symbolism of chapter 6 ("What It Was"). To affect the autobiographical story and transform the catastrophe narrative, the testimony needs to become what Agnes Heller, in theorizing different perceptions of history, designates as "past-present" time. The child, Hilda, fails to understand the story as more than fragments of a remote and obscure time and does not draw them into an encompassing "past-present." In Heller's view, past history, as opposed to the "past-present," stays outside the scope of our lives. Its events fail to threaten or deeply impress us because we perceive them as being unrelated to us: "We have neither pragmatic nor practical relation to them." But the "past-present" is the past made usable. The older "symbols and values have become meaningful," and their story become ours, with the potential both to "threaten us or fill us with hopes."[51] So, as we retell the story, we turn remote history into "past-present" time (145). Since Hilda does not grasp the testimony in terms that are coherent to her, she cannot be identified as what Laub calls the "'co-owner' of the narrated events."[52] In addition, her grandmother, as the testifying agent, closes up before the listener ("Wait Mamalie, there are a thousand questions that I want to ask you") can make the necessary connections. Not only does the child's narrative fail to transform past history into relevant "past-present" perceptions, it represses both the story and the witnessing situation. The declarations of peace exchanged at Wunden Eiland do not function dialogically as an alternative to the catastrophe occurring on the wounded island of Great Britain or across a global landscape. The grandmother's witnessing fades into the background; chapter 5 ends with a return to catastrophe as the narrator locates herself in the midst of yet another air attack. She hears the planes, anticipates the fire, and suddenly, "*the Storm of Death* is storming in my ears now" (182).

The autobiographical chapter that follows is as preoccupied with death as the chapters that precede "The Secret," and it is especially focused on bodily wounding. The text of chapter 6 is not substantially different in the complete edition; but because it follows an expanded and more historicized chapter 5, the chapter's regression back into violence seems more dramatic than in the earlier, abridged edition. The violence takes the form of random injury, thereby reflecting, yet again, the conditions of catastrophe. Remembering the day that Charles Doolittle appeared at the door with a mysterious head wound, the narrator describes washing the blood away and wondering about her father's dazed state of mind. Like other parts of *The Gift*, this chapter lends itself to psychoanalytic interpretations. But from the perspective of H.D.'s writing time and site, it most patently suggests the continuing threat of injury that all Londoners faced through accident and impersonal disaster.[53] Entitled "What It Was," the chapter ends with a question as Hilda, in response to her father's head wound, asks what a concussion is. The child's unanswered question is metonymic of the larger questions concerning war and the absence of logic to account for mass destruction. Making its point through irony, "What It Was" does not explain specifically "what it was" that causes the injury and is characterized by scenes of urgency and tension. The chapter fails to offer resolution because dramatically and tropologically it continues the 1941 drama of violence, wounding, and death.

CATASTROPHE AND THE AUTHORITY OF TESTIMONY

The only section expressly written in and directly about events in 1943, chapter 7 breaks the pattern of indirection of the first six chapters simply by presenting and declaring itself to be undisguised testimony. This important narrational change corresponds to an unanticipated change in the air war, when London was seriously attacked for the first time in a year and a half. Established at the beginning of the chapter, the cause-and-effect relationship is crucial. For the only time in the text of the seven chapters, a specific, contemporary date appears—January 17, 1943, when, according to the narrator, "all the terrors that I had so carefully held in leash during the great fires and the terrible bombing of London, would now break loose because we hadn't had any big raids for some time and we had forgotten how to act" (209). Both the date and the details adhere to accounts in the newspapers. RAF planes had attacked Berlin, and Germany retaliated, choosing parts of southern England and London for its main targets. The headline in the January 18 issue of the *Times*, "Four Night Raiders Destroyed/Weak Retaliation for Berlin Attack," played down the episode, perhaps because the raids were just as likely to stop immediately as to be continuous. The newspapers did, however, stress the intensity of the raid, with horrendous noise coming from the new anti-aircraft gun, "a tornado of sound seldom heard even in the last great raid on London."[54] The raiders flew into the capital at very high speeds, and some dropped incendiaries along a pathway following the Thames River. These were probably the same planes H.D. heard close to her flat in Chelsea coming "over our roof-tops," "just where one was sitting" in "this particular flat in a once pleasant part of London" (220) and whose noise level she could hardly bear. Unlike the newspapers, though, H.D.'s rendering does not downplay the fear experienced by citizens believing that this is the raid that would finally kill them. "This," she declares, "is my last place, my last little room ... my last habitation," adding the probable manner of her death: "I could visualize the very worst terrors, I could see myself caught in the fall of bricks and I would be pinned down under a great beam, helpless. Many had been. I would be burned to death" (215).

Entitled "Morning Star," chapter 7 distances itself from the rest of the book, for it promotes and *enacts* the unity that is proposed tropologically in chapter 5. Drafted much later than the preceding chapters and in a different atmosphere of heightened, renewed fear, it changes the narrative approach in bearing witness.[55] In this section tropes and other modes of displacement and distantiation play a much less noticeable role. Immediate, almost straightforward recounting becomes the dominant approach, and, for the first time in *The Gift*, there is a chapter almost entirely focused on the author's present life. This is not to say that the tropes of the autobiographical material drop out of the narrative. What does happen is that the narrator folds the tropological imagery into her text, allowing it to infuse her descriptive, present-tense observations with a sense of calm and symbolic/historic resonance. The tropes are thus transformed, and the most important difference is that they are integrated into the wartime testimony, not substituted for it. As part of the texture of the witnessing narrative, they are resurrected and recreated according to Heller's idea of past-present time. The history of Moravian pacifism is assimilated and *used* by the narrator, who grasps its contemporary relevance in confronting her own catastrophic experience of nations at war: "I saw, I understood ... a memory of my grandmother's or her grandmother's" (212; ellipsis in original). In other words, the effort to literalize the narrative and have it serve recognizably as testimony is achieved when history, once separate from the narrator's wartime commentaries and confined to enigmatic flashbacks of the childhood story, is used for immediate and proximate purposes.

The shock of this raid drives H.D. back to her project after a long absence. It also alters the narrative, and in creating what effectively is a second discourse, it internalizes January 17, 1943. Because its testimony of events progresses clearly and sequentially through each wave of the attack, we can look back to the first discourse and recognize its modes of disassociation through a sharper line of vision. As a result, the fragments and flashbacks appear to be less elusive and less private. This change is also due to the nature of the 1943 raid and the narrator's reaction. The intermittent attacks in 1941 created, even during the lulls, an expectation that future bombing would occur, and London maintained a state of readiness.

But in the long period without a serious attack, citizens returned to their ordinary routines, and H.D. characterizes herself as one among them who had lost her "protective colouration" (215). The 1943 raid finds her extremely vulnerable, and the *excess* of shock and emotion has a distinctly different effect than the shock and emotion to which she had nearly become accustomed.[56] It leads to a state of calm. The narrator insists, despite previous comments stating otherwise, that she has *not* been afraid and that "the terror and the tension and the *disassociation* must come to an end" (221; emphasis added). She carries out rhetorically an act of courage, which emotionally will keep her fixed to present time. Without fear, there is less need to shield herself by shifting psychically and mnemonically into a childhood time frame. There is also less need to have autobiography serve as a displaced testimony, at least not in the same manner as the chapters of the first discourse.

The denial of fear has important repercussions for the narrative that chapter 7 produces. The triggering device switching the narrator into the past is a reaction to fear, and without that emotion she loses "my trick of getting out, of being out of it." The "trick," a process of "burning" in her brain, which works spontaneously to transform her fears of death into substitutive images, has burned itself out.[57] With no reactive mechanism to catapult her back into the autobiographical narrative or into what Henke views as authorial fantasies and Morris as myth and sacred history, a more straightforward approach is possible. In direct contrast to the temporal disjunctions of the previous chapters, this chapter concentrates on a single day in the author's present life. For the first time in *The Gift* there are many references to H.D.'s adult life and to her partner, Bryher, with whom she shared the Chelsea flat. In fact, with many passages restored, the chapter becomes an intimate scene of two women surviving a catastrophe. Their interaction on January 17, 1943, is a consistent structural frame, with their dialogue hinged to each of the three distinct waves of oncoming planes. Bryher is explicitly named and, in the added material, intimately described as sitting opposite H.D. "with her face collected, ears set close to her head, the short-cropped head." The restored passages stress Bryher's importance to H.D. ("What she said was oracular and always had been"), and they clarify the proximity of the thundering bombs, of the response from the mobile-guns in the nearby park, and the fact that the women are together: "Now that I saw that Bryher was accepting the fury, we could accept the thing together. We had accepted many things together but this last trial, this last acceptance, might still be the last" (216). This textualization of Bryher, with restored comments on the neighborhood and friends "scattered over different parts of this huge and battle-scarred town of London" (221), is significant. It clarifies that as a living and reactive text, *The Gift* undergoes a change. In the complete edition we witness more than in the abridged edition a narrative-in-process. It moves out of the genre in which it began, a narrative of childhood, and sheds its figurative and distantiating layers. It moves the author's contemporary experience, which has always been intermittently present, into the foreground, rendering the details as an immediate and recognizable testimony of catastrophe. With the text of childhood left behind in the narrative distance, the testimony is made vivid through the domestic details involved in withstanding extraordinary conditions.

Memory continues to play a role, not as a bridge that leads away from present time but one that, in drawing the past closer, gives chapter 7 heightened significance. "Wrested from its then-and-there to be planted in the here-and-now," the memory loses its disassociative qualities and remoteness.[58] Rather than being based, as DuPlessis writes, on "free association among semi-related, semi-detached memories," the memories are absorbed into the testimony and made inseparable from it.[59] Their larger context never slips from view because the narrator's voice, time, and location ground them structurally and conceptually. The narrator-in-the-act-of-giving-testimony internalizes her grandmother in the very same act, and this gives her access, and the ability, to assimilate her grandmother's images and allusions. From the standpoint of catastrophe life writing, it is chapter 7 ("Morning Star") and not "The Secret" that is the crucial chapter of *The Gift*. Its clarity and integration of past into present give it more authority than the earlier chapters while the catastrophe of January 17, 1943, causes H.D. finally to cross the "chasm that divides time from time-out-of-time." Beyond the chasm there is no separate time, no disparate shards of memory. There is, instead, a recollecting of words and sounds synthesizing with one another beautifully. The humming of a choir, the speech of the Moravian woman who facilitated peace, phrases in unfamiliar voices and languages—all come out, held together in present time. The memories accumulate and "gather sound": "Harken to us, sings the great choir of the strange voices that speak in a strange bird-like staccato rhythm *but I know what they are saying* though they are speaking Indian dialects. The two voices answer one another and the sound of Anna von Pahlen's voice as she reads the writing on the strip of paper from the woven basket that Cammerhof has just handed her, is pure and silver and clear like a silver-trumpet" (223; emphasis added). Rather than listening to her grandmother's fragmented recollections of distant history and trying to decipher their meanings, H.D. hears, sees, and recovers the history for herself. It is H.D. who bears witness and gives testimony of a past that becomes spiritually a part of herself and linguistically a part of *her own text*. The rhythms and chords then converge in the intentionally spare dialogue that concludes the chapter: "'It's the all-clear,' says Bryher. 'Yes,' I say." In effect, chapter 7 illustrates and performs the process of surviving catastrophe as the effect of blending history into present time, absorbing other testimony, other witnesses, and other unlikely instances of peace. The gift is knowledge transmitted and experienced as living history.

CATASTROPHE, HISTORY, AND CLOSURE

Now that the "Notes" section has been published, it, too, alters *The Gift* and confirms the book's overall purpose as testimony, which progresses *through* the genre of autobiographical fiction and expands outward. H.D. planned this section as her closing discourse, but there is no trace of it in the New Directions edition. Most readers were unaware that the "Notes" existed and assumed, logically, that "Morning Star" was the final chapter. Without this section, however, H.D.'s intentions for *The Gift* are severely distorted. The book seems to end in the story of the author's life and therefore to emphasize the autobiographical and personal discourse. But with the addition of the "Notes," we can recognize even from its general outline why H.D. characterized the manuscript as "autobiographical, almost."[60] The trajectory of *The Gift* is *away* from unified self-representation, and the complete text is more than the story of either its autobiographical protagonist or narrator. With the original closing section in place, the role of personalized narrative is reduced and that of history increased. In time scholars will undoubtedly focus on the specific interrelations of the individual notes and the rest of the book, but even from a comprehensive perspective it is clear that the "Notes" provides religious histories, biographical summaries, family genealogy, and much more. Explicative and discursive, the section corroborates *The Gift* as a medium for transmitting history. It makes public and shareable the Moravian/Native American interaction that otherwise would be lost and enlarges our sense of cultural scripts and possibilities. Finally, the "Notes" creates an encompassing "past-present" consciousness.

Although this section was begun in 1940, it required a catastrophe to end it. Like the previous air attacks that activated intense writing, the strike in mid-1944 came in the form of bombs, but it involved a different type of threat—Germany's new weapon, the V-1 bomb. Called "flying bombs" or "buzzbombs" by the British, these rained down on the capital in June 1944 and took Londoners by surprise, including H.D., still struggling on the "Notes" at that time.[61] In fact, she had sent off the manuscript months earlier to her friend, Norman Holmes Pearson, without this section because its completion had seemed so remote."[62] When the V-1 bombs struck—in daytime and haphazardly—a new form of terror was introduced, and as violence had done in the past, it pushed H.D. into a concentrated period of writing. The British newspapers called the V-1 a "machine of chance"; pilotless and jet propelled, it was estimated to carry one ton of explosives. The unprecedented nature of the destruction forced many citizens to migrate to other parts of the country.[63] "It was as impersonal as a plague," wrote Evelyn Waugh, "as though the city were infested with enormous, venomous insects."[64] Bryher writes that H.D. "faced the first and most terrifying night alone" and witnessed in the weeks that followed "some of the heaviest civilian casualties of the war."[65] The impact of this phase of the war on the evolution of the book is unmistakable. The catastrophe is drawn into the text and, in fact, marks off the writing that predates the flying bombs from that which comes afterward. H.D. writes: "The earth wobbles as it goes round the sun. Indeed, it wobbles very much and in strange fashion. This is June 29, 1944 and I started these notes or biographical memories back in the early days of the Battle of Britain, way back in the early forties. That is a long time ago. Now, this minute, the flying-bomb is on the way—now this minute, there is a distant crash and we are safe for this minute" (254). While it took over four years to draft the first half of this section, the precipitous and late phase of the bombing created its final momentum.[66] After June 1944 it took just seven months to produce almost the same amount of text and to finish the project.[67]

Unlike the earlier chapters, the material drafted after June 1944 is not driven solely by catastrophe but also by the prospects for peace. H.D.'s immediate situation was precarious, but the larger context gave room for hope. This is because H.D. was writing very soon after D-Day. The Allies had crossed the English Channel on June 6 and positioned almost a million soldiers along the coast of France. Though it would take another year for victory to be declared in Europe, the effect of the Normandy invasion was immediate, and an end to the fighting was now conceivable.[68] With these developments mitigating the flying bomb alerts in London, the second half of the "Notes" reflects the larger context of the war, particularly in what is missing from it. There are no additional references to the V-1 bombs and no heightened sense of anxiety. Nor are there references to the V-2 bomb, which began to hit London in early September. More powerful than the V-1, it was an actual rocket that gave no warning of its arrival and fell on London at intervals over the next few months. Yet once H.D. was triggered back into writing by something *in addition* to catastrophe, namely the long-range possibility for peace, she worked rapidly toward closure.

The text written after D-Day also contains a new kind of self-portrait, one that projects authority and control. The portrait emerges in the midst of the historical material and depends on our reading the "Notes" just as the author intended—as *The Gift*'s eighth and final chapter. Augustine explains three functions for the "Notes," and these support the full restoration of the section: to explain names and places, to foreground Moravian history and theology, and to enlarge the scope of the book to take in the "creative processes and the interrelations of this memoir with [H.D.'s] other writings of the wartime period" (15). None of these, however, is accomplished in the manner of traditional footnotes. H.D.'s "Notes" is structured to be read through as a separate chapter with its own internal structure and momentum, and since all the previous chapters lack numbered footnotes, the "Notes" does not function as an ongoing reference guide. Its explanatory passages rely only on underlined phrases to refer back to the chapters, and this device fails to direct us to their exact location. The "Notes," therefore, is clearly not intended to be a secondary discourse but a primary element in the author's catastrophe-driven project. Like every other chapter, it is a discrete, yet mutually related segment that bears witness to wartime violence. Unlike every other chapter, however, its second half is a response to peace as well as to catastrophe, and this gives the "Notes" even greater cultural and testimonial significance.

The self-portrait that emerges from the historical material in the "Notes" is not representationally comprehensive but sharply delineated as a portrait of a writer. The portrait depicts H.D. in the process of ending *The Gift*, and this self-representation is both literal and tropological. It literally describes the completion of the manuscript as it is taking place, and it figuratively reflects the new conditions that are making the completion possible. H.D. refers to the long process of composition and her relationship to the autobiographical protagonist, Hilda: "In assembling these chapters of *The Gift* during, before and after the worst days of the 1941 London Blitz, I let the story tell itself or the child tell it for me. Things

that I had thought I had forgotten came to light in the course of the narrative." She characterizes herself as an editor who is critically assessing her
manuscript and methodology:

> I tried to keep "myself" out of this, and if the sub-conscious bubbled up
> with some unexpected finding from the depth, I accepted this finding as part
> of the texture of the narrative and have so far, in going over these chapters
> (to-day is July 2nd 1944) changed very little. Instead of tidying up the body
> of the narrative, I thought it better to let things stand as they were (as the
> story was written under stress of danger and great emotion) and where indi-
> cated, confirm certain statements or enlarge on them in these Notes. (257)

In this revealing passage, H.D. distances herself from the autobiographical
protagonist of the previous chapters and is soon referring to herself through
the third-person voice as "the Editor." She is most interested in recording
herself in the act of writing and, with closure imminent, is in a position
to draw back from the heightened emotionality of earlier parts of *The Gift*.

The more the narrative focuses on its own production, especially on its
own final stages, the more literal it becomes. The need to rely on displaced
images and substitutive conflicts is less pressing, for the author is no
longer experiencing or expressing her external conditions as intolerable.
This contrasts with the 1943 discourse, which is a deliberate effort to prove
that "one's mind and body could endure the very worst that life had to
offer" and, when forced into "the uttermost depth of subconscious terror,"
to be able to "rise again" (219). The 1944 discourse of the "Notes" is composed and self-consciously dispassionate. Indeed, the decision to take on
the identity of "Editor" for the benefit of an implied reader suggests an
orientation toward the future and H.D.'s active, productive role in it. Even
when writing in the midst of the earliest and most frightening of the V-1
raids, the author chooses not to focus obsessively on the danger. Remarking, for instance, that she can hear one of the bombs directly overhead,
she is not diverted from her writing and simply returns to her ongoing
historical commentary.

Life writing texts that call attention to various stages of their own development can create a picture of the working writer that does not actually
correspond to what the author was doing. In the case of *The Gift*, however, we know that H.D. was finally completing her manuscript. If even in
its broad outline only, the last part of the "Notes" is biographically accurate. But the literalized discourse, of one woman completing her "almost

autobiographical" book, *is* an illusion in another sense, because the portrait, at the same time, is tropological. The final self-portrait stands in for something larger, because *The Gift* continues to bear witness even when it seems to be focusing on itself. The portrait of the author at work is an "image," and the more literal and developed the image, the more powerfully it serves the tropological design of *The Gift* as cultural testimony. H.D. does not write directly about a cessation of conflict, but she certainly illustrates the effects of the realistic prospects for peace. She therefore uses herself, in her closing self-representation, as a metonymic device and metaphor. The image of being able to complete her book signifies a global condition in which the materializing and literalizing of this very image becomes possible.

The compositional and textual history of *The Gift* spans almost sixty years, a duration in which literature as testimony has come to occupy a central place in our collective consciousness. Pulled out from the catastrophe of war, this midcentury testimony enabled H.D. to accomplish what we now identify as part of the genre—using both recollection and creativity in order to merge the personal and the cultural dimensions of bearing witness. H.D. wrote herself out of a creative stalemate that began with the First World War. She generated in addition to *The Gift* the poetry of *Trilogy,* the sketches of *Within the Walls,* and a draft of *Tribute to Freud.* Despite her psychological fragility, she continued to write until she died in 1961, producing some of her finest work, including *Helen in Egypt, End to Torment,* and *Hermetic Definition.* [69] In choosing to remain in London and witness the bombing of her adopted city, H.D. recast personal experience into public testimony, channeling what she saw through autobiographical, memoirist, fictional, and historical presentation.

Elie Wiesel wrote in 1977 that "our generation invented a new literature, that of testimony."[70] Since then, our generation has learned that this literature, in recording crises and catastrophes from around the globe, is not reducible to a single form. Nor is it always recognizable, at least initially. *The Gift* dramatically illustrates how testimony changes itself, perhaps more than any other literary genre, because it works from, and adapts to, the exigencies of each particular situation. If the discourses that comprise *The Gift* recall, invent, and re-imagine the author's personal battle to regain her expressive and literary voice, they also reflect on and historicize some of the most catastrophic years of the twentieth century. Felman makes the point that "texts that testify do not simply *report facts* but, in different ways, encounter—and make us encounter—*strangeness*."[71] Applied to H.D.'s autobiographical fiction, this comment points to each major stage of its testifying activity. The sections on childhood, which comprise the first discourse, force readers to encounter discontinuities and ruptured narrative as a textual reflection of living through the intermittent raids of 1941. The second discourse is more recognizable as testimony, but it, too, creates an encounter with "strangeness," for the "facts" of the January 17, 1943, surprise attack are amalgamated into sounds and phrases that cross the space between centuries, geography, and generations. As *The Gift's* third discourse, the "Notes" forces another experience of strangeness, first, because the "facts" themselves have been obscured for so long and, second, because they are foregrounded as the primary text of the chapter rather than provided as ancillary details. In each encounter, the mode of giving testimony is different from our expectations and, after the first discourse, different from the section we have just read.

In responding to catastrophe, the other women in this study confronted a single event or development. Whether a Congressional vote, a destroyed home and ruined manuscript, a stroke associated with historical memories, or a physical coma, the catastrophe was identifiable and specific even though its effects were profound and long-lasting. Lili'uokalani knew who her opponents were as well as their strategies and power. Banti wrote in response to the fighting in Florence that took place in the first week of August 1944. Weil relived (perhaps hallucinated) the Holocaust through the aggressive treatment of foreign doctors after her late-life stroke. And at the very least Allende could fight the catastrophe of her daughter's illness with an army of physicians, therapists, family members, and hope. The catastrophe that H.D. faced was different. It lasted for a long period of time; but since it did not extend continuously, it failed to revert to a crisis. Even when the air strikes appeared to stop, eventually they began all over again. As a result, repetition—not often associated with catastrophe—became an integral part of the experience. The structure and content of *The Gift*, particularly with all the chapters restored as H.D. originally wrote them, reflect this difference, with reinscribed memories and reiterated imagery and patterns forming a catastrophe redux. The autobiographical fiction thus performs catastrophe while it responds to catastrophe, repeatedly suggesting ways in which the author's personal body and London's collective body were at risk, with death an imminent, but unpredictable possibility.

CHAPTER THREE

Biographical Fiction as Autobiographical Palimpsest

Anna Banti's *Artemisia*

L IVING IN FLORENCE during the Second World War, Anna Banti managed to pursue her intellectual interests despite the hardships that the long crises of war inevitably produce.[1] Although she could not have failed to be affected by events, evidence suggests that she stayed a course with her creative work. She published a collection of short stories in 1940, the year Italy joined the war against Britain and France. Two more works were in print by 1942, when Italy was struggling against Britain in North Africa and Italy, and Germany was occupying southern France.[2] As the Allied campaign was advancing up the Italian peninsula toward Rome and Florence in 1944, she was also able to draft a manuscript of *Artemisia*, a biographical fiction of the Renaissance painter Artemisia Gentileschi, which eventually became her most famous book.[3]

Artemisia was a compelling biographical subject for Banti.[4] They both strove to be respected as women in artistic professions dominated by men. Moreover, both were working within contexts of crisis. Although their lives were in no way strictly parallel, these two women experienced and survived devastating violence over which they had very little control, Banti in World War II and Artemisia in the horrific circumstances of her personal life. Both lived with instability and were vulnerable to threatening circumstances in volatile times characterized by prolonged conflicts. Historical records show that as the only daughter of the renowned painter, Orazio Gentileschi, Artemisia was raped at the age of fourteen by her art teacher and her father's friend, Agostino Tassi.[5] From that point on her future was ruined, for the violation made her unsuitable for an appropriate marriage. The injuries done to her in private became public in 1612 in

Rome when her father accused Tassi of raping Artemisia and brought a lawsuit against him. Artemisia is documented as having suffered physical examinations by midwives and torture with a "sibille," or fingerscrew and ropes. And while she had to endure these tests of veracity, her defendant was merely instructed to say the truth, and he denied all responsibility. Artemisia also became a target of vilification and, admitting to repeated violations, was publicly mocked as a whore. After a trial that lasted for months, a husband was found for her, but they lived as a couple for a limited period of time, with Artemisia eventually settling in Naples, raising her daughter alone, and establishing an independent, creative life for herself.[6] Artemisia emerged from the ruins of her adolescence to create heroic portraits of women from the Old Testament and classical mythology and is considered today by art historians to be "the most creative and most significant woman artist of the premodern era."[7]

Banti appears, however, not to have recognized the parallels between her biographical subject and herself, even in the broadest sense of ongoing violence. In the introduction to the book that was published in 1947, she explains that her earliest concerns for this manuscript were its literary characteristics and language, particularly relative to other works of prose being published in Italy at the time. Her strategies in combining fiction and history were intended solely to bring to life the figure of Artemisia Gentileschi and give her artwork the visibility it deserved. Regardless of any common elements in their lives, Banti, who was an art scholar as well as a creative writer, was drawn to Artemisia for being both extraordinarily talented and little known (2). In most ways, then, this wartime project was unrelated to the crisis of war, serving more as a respite from ongoing events of the Italian campaign than as an acknowledgment or expression of those events.

Crisis, however, was transformed into catastrophe in a few crucial days in the summer of 1944 when the war became a direct threat for Banti and the other citizens of Florence.[8] As a consequence, Banti's relationship to her biographical subject was dramatically altered. The confrontation between German and Allied forces advanced to the area around the city and led the Germans to dynamite nearly all the bridges and to order 150,000 people to evacuate their homes.[9] In the battle that took place during the first week of August, neighborhoods were demolished, citizens were made homeless, and the city was left in mass confusion. Banti's house was reduced to rubble, and, in it, the manuscript for her book was destroyed. The *Artemisia* that exists today is a second version of the pages that the author had earlier drafted and nearly finished by mid-1944. Entirely re-written, it now acknowledges the catastrophe of war. The book also expresses the author's grief for those who were victims of the violence, including her own incarnation of Artemisia. In her introduction Banti emphasizes how the transition from a state of extended crisis into catas-trophe forced her to reconceptualize the project. She warns readers that since the rewritten *Artemisia* accomplishes autobiographical purposes that go beyond her previous biographical intentions, the book just partially recovers the original text, for "this time the aim of the narrative was to preserve only the commemorative form of the unfinished story and ... the writing of it became bound up, instinctively, with personal emotions too imperious to be ignored or betrayed." Further suggesting that she does not see the published version as wholly biographical, she believes that "the reader is owed a little information about the life of Artemisia Gentileschi, one of the most talented female artists, and one of the few, recorded by history," and thus provides a short précis of the artist's life before embark-ing on the first chapter (2). The narrative that follows actually foregrounds the circumstances that influenced Banti's decisions in reshaping the orig-inal material and in making substantive additions while repositioning her personal voice vis-à-vis the biographical storyline. The experience of the war permeates the book as the narration, in its second version, recognizes the broad connections between the author and her biographical charac-ter. Banti's self-references may converge on only a single location and nar-row time frame, but the references are extremely important. They ground the biographical material and link the biographical characters to the wartime catastrophe the author suffered from and through which she was forced to recompose her manuscript.

The change from crisis to catastrophe in the author's circumstances infiltrates the biographical discourse of *Artemisia*, creating a complicated and multileveled text. The complexities that derive from Banti's working in the midst of sudden disaster also turn the book into the kind of life writing that my larger study explores—women's self-representation dis-tinctively formed by catastrophe and, at the same time, made extremely difficult by it. Catastrophe motivates and contaminates the writing process of the book, and readers are able to trace the ways that Banti establishes a dual presence for herself—as an author struggling to write and as a nar-rator struggling to resurrect a historical character. She projects herself intersubjectively and intertextually through the common elements of gen-der and calamitous experience. This helps her to form a close relationship

with her Renaissance protagonist in a mutual context of violence, violation, as well as resistance through art, with both women creating female
portraiture that shows their subjects in acts of resistance or countervio-
lence. For the second *Artemisia*, resistance through art is enacted as the
author's working of memory, and memory, of course, leads right into
autobiographical processes. This chapter therefore studies *Artemisia* as a
biographical fiction that transforms itself into autobiography.[10]

Artemisia structures itself in three primary ways: as a bildungsroman of
the life of the artist; as a self-referential wartime discourse for Banti; and
in the form of interstitial passages where the two women, the "character"
and the "author," come together in a mediating and supportive space. I
will examine specifically the ways that Banti configures her biographical
fiction so as to perform this relationship between author and character.

Ponte Vecchio, Florence, August 1944, after the German retreat. *Imperial War Museum*
(NA17682)

I will demonstrate how she portrays Artemisia biographically as a woman and an artist struggling to produce artwork in a context of violence. In the process of her narrative, Banti discourses in her own voice on the creative challenges of writing in a similar context and performs discursive interchanges between herself and her imagined subject on the difficulties of the creative process because of this context.[11] These metatextual passages, in addition to the sections where Artemisia is allowed to narrate her own story, finally confirm the importance of the autobiographical conditions, imperatives, and textual operations. The different narrative structures also point to the most unusual feature of *Artemisia* relative to its self-representational status. This feature is the textual performance of

New Zealand troops in Florence, August 1944. *Imperial War Museum (NA17762)*

memory returning and functioning despite conditions inimical to sustained concentration. The biographical discourse remains entirely dependent on both the author's experience of catastrophe and on the narrational situation of the author gaining strength as her voice relates that experience and recalls (and changes) the details of the earlier manuscript. This means that conceptually, and from the perspective of intentionality, the two women are effectively one and the same. Implicit when not explicit, and below the surface when not itself visible, Banti's catastrophe is Artemisia's autobiographical palimpsest; it underlies the pages where it does not appear and controls the terms that make possible the detailed accounting of the biographical story.

Like other books in this study, *Artemisia* unfolds as a series of shared and partial stories tropologically related to one another. The historical Artemisia could be seen as a substitutive image for Banti, especially since the latter imagines her subject in full maturity as a woman who lived by her art even when she felt vanquished by circumstances and certain of death. The tropological correspondences through characterization are often suggestive, because the hardships that Artemisia faced, among them rape and the disgrace of a public trial, were very different from those that Banti faced in 1944.[12] But the tropes in *Artemisia* work in many ways. The writing "I" comes to see the figure of Artemisia as a metonymic object, functioning as something other than a whole person—rather as a name, a project, and an object toward which memory strives and goes beyond.[13] A governing metaphor for the tropological and metonymical functions of the book is, in fact, Artemisia's most famous painting, her own self-portrait of 1630, wonderfully entitled for Banti's purposes *Self-Portrait as the Allegory of Painting*.[14] Artemisia painted herself in the act of painting herself, but significantly she left the canvas in the painting without any image. Replete with possibilities, the blank canvas is the trope that signifies all of the self-representational tropes that power this book. It is a name that captures the spirit of the text, a "thing" inside the story, the final artistic triumph Banti gives to Artemisia, and also a sign outside of the story that has multiple meanings and extensions. It points to an author who, like her subject, creates portraiture that is suggestively both singular and plural, which calls attention to the female body, the represented body, and the interpreting and controlling gaze, all of which this chapter examines.

More than an exact sum of its parts, *Artemisia* is ultimately a narrative engaged in a larger cultural memorization, which means that consciously or otherwise it performs aspects of both the past and the present to make them relevant and public.[15] It seeks to remember one individual manuscript destroyed by war, and expands it tropologically to other, larger things and human lives also destroyed by war. While the "I," grounded in present time, realistically declares the impossibility of retrieval, she partially succeeds, for writing about what cannot be retrieved is surely one way of retrieving it. Banti's autobiographical catastrophe narrative extends its motifs and discourses to perform beyond themselves and to imagine what can be remembered as a strategy of protest, memorization, and healing.

CATASTROPHE AND THE MAKING OF NARRATIVE

Discussions of Banti's most famous literary work tend to emphasize *Artemisia* as a biographical fiction at the expense of its autobiographical dimensions. Critics who consider the authorial self-references to be secondary, or who do not consider them at all, concentrate for the most part on Banti's story of Artemisia. Developing along the lines of a bildungsroman, this story portrays a woman in history who was successful despite the violence of her early personal life and the cultural sanctions that worked against her social rehabilitation and integration.[16] Valeria Finucci appreciates the biographical details for the way that they make important feminist changes to the *kunstlerroman* tradition and consequently she has no reason even to mention the autobiographical references.[17] JoAnn Cannon acknowledges the role that the autobiographical references play in the book, noting importantly that the Renaissance story opens in the last days of the Italian Resistance movement in the struggle to liberate Florence from Nazi occupation.[18] But she remains chiefly interested in the book as a biographical fiction. This leaves her to downplay the autobiographical functions to which life writing critics would give more weight, arguing instead that Banti "powerfully underscores the supreme importance of the artist's story by favoring it over the tragic events of the Resistance." In contrast to these critics, Deborah Heller examines *Artemisia* as "something other than a simple documentary reconstruction" and as a book that is "more personal, more imaginative, and more arbitrary" than a bildungsroman.[19] She looks at the dialogues of the female characters and the metafictional aspects of the material, yet she does not stress the autobiographical dimensions and finally puts *Artemisia* into novelistic rather than life writing traditions. My chapter argues from a different premise. It starts with the hypothesis that even though she allows the biographical material to occupy a major portion of the book, Banti is equally concerned with her own representation. Because she stops short of giving the bildungsroman complete autonomy, Banti draws attention to the embedded nature of Artemisia's discourse as well as its dependence on her emotions and memory in a time of extreme pressures. Her own situation is the controlling focus of *Artemisia,* even when the self-representation lies below the surface of the developing fiction.

In my view, the Second World War drives the fiction, exposing readers to the author's experience and compelling them *not* to forget it as they read. They cannot forget, because the reconceptualized Artemisia is a highly visible device for enabling Banti to come to terms with the tragedy. The text actually memorializes parts of the author's experience by lifting them out of their contemporary site and reusing them in the historical discourse. This takes place in the childhood vignettes in the early pages of the bildungsroman, which Banti imaginatively invents for Artemisia, because there is little historical data on her very early years. Banti presents her with a friend whom she names Cecilia Nari, but the source for this character is apparently a little girl Banti knew about and worried over during the war. The portrait of Cecilia is a tribute to this child and, by implication, to all innocent victims who miraculously survive widespread destruction. Banti describes in her own voice her fear that this "real" child, an orphan and a paralytic, is a casualty of the fighting—that is, until she sees the same girl struggling to keep pace with a procession of refugees seeking food. As a symbolic form of remembrance, the narrative transformation of the child into a fictional character allows her to be reborn. The character Cecilia is given her eyes and mouth, even the same physical disability, and "that is why," explains the authorial voice, "I hold her [Cecilia] dear" (6). Realistically, though, Banti knows that the future is uncertain in the wake of catastrophe, especially for those who are least able to protect themselves. Her script for Cecilia reflects this knowledge. It gives her just one more year to live and, by insisting on the child's death, stays committed to representing the drama and the irreversible effects of war.

Artemisia in these early episodes is also autobiographically suggestive. Her perseverance and worldliness reflect the disposition of an adult who has withstood misfortune far more than a ten-year-old girl with the privileges of social class and a well-known family name. Even if Artemisia's toughness anticipates the kind of woman she will become after she is raped, the qualities that Banti gives her indicate a pattern in the book of reciprocal movements and traits shared by the author and her characters.

For example, Artemisia is a child preoccupied with violence. Telling Cecilia about her father's artwork, she is drawn to scenes of physical brutality. She describes Orazio's current portrait of Saint Sebastian and, mesmerized by its depiction of pain and martyrdom, recounts the wounds on the saint's body, the arrows, and the running blood. Artemisia adds that the male model was purposely wounded and bled in order to be completely convincing as the saint: "'Yes, real blood,' she specifies shamelessly, spurred on by the amazement in [Cecilia's] blue eyes, 'whoever's modeling for Saint Sebastian has to put up with being hurt,'" almost as if she intuits that blood will one day come to define her as well (8). For Artemisia it will be virginal blood, functioning as what Sidonie Smith calls "the metonymic marker of 'woman,'" determining all aspects of her future and enforcing a life of social martyrdom.[20] This kind of interaction between the two children seems inappropriate for the context and certainly lacks adequate motivation at this stage within the bildungsroman. It is understandable, though, in a more generalized way for the author who is *outside* of the bildungsroman. Seeing Florence ravaged and its inhabitants injured and homeless, she is displacing her knowledge of catastrophe onto her figure of Artemisia. Once Artemisia is portrayed with characteristics of the author, she becomes a tropological device that serves autobiographical purposes more than as a protagonist in her own right. In confirmation of this, Banti admits that since she and her character are so tightly bound to each other, it is impossible for the revised narrative to be in any sense objective. In fact, she admits that if Artemisia "was expecting more, above all a logical, calm account, a carefully considered interpretation of her actions, [this is] the very thing that I can no longer give her, for she is too close to me. Having her follow me so closely means that she distorts the images and memories I have of her" (20).

As the exchange between Cecilia and Artemisia demonstrates, the tropological relationship between the author and her Renaissance character is suggestive. However, the reciprocal relationship between the modern and Renaissance discourse is more direct. The movement from one to the other occurs frequently in the early parts of the book to establish a pattern of reciprocity and interconnections. One of the most vivid instances occurs in the beginning of *Artemisia* as Banti describes conditions on the day following the worst of the fighting. Responding to the heat and the sun and disbelieving the extent of the damage ("this time yesterday Florence and all her stones were solid, everything that they sheltered was intact"), Banti seeks relief from the blasted-out landscape (13).[21]

She closes her eyes as a gesture of self-protection, but her eyelids transform themselves into an interior screen that simply exhibits a different
landscape of death—Cecilia's funeral.

> I am shocked by the impetus with which I am carried beyond the limits my
> memory allows me, beyond the bounds of the story.... She died a year later.
> To be precise, in the year 1611, in the month of April. *I specify this, half
> closing my eyes against the sun which is red under my eyelids, like the flames
> of the torches at her quiet funeral, which, to tell the truth, was not really all
> that quiet....* Artemisia cannot take in the fact of Cecilia's death.... (12–13;
> emphasis added)

In other words, the trope that represents her rewriting of the first manuscript compels the author to represent herself as literally seeing, and thus
giving in to, the power of her remembered story. Even when Banti is not
consciously thinking about the manuscript, her psyche seems to be pro-
cessing it, causing sudden shifts between her and her characters and
between her autobiographical context and the biographical fiction. In this
instance, the sun's heat causes the author to "see" the burning torches that
belong to the ceremony of Cecilia's funeral and then to pick up on the
visual clue and describe the funeral. Some of the words the author attributes to Artemisia at the funeral seem just as easily her own, and this has
the effect of making them and their discourses converge. Similar instances
of reciprocal movement involving representation, self-representation, and
enunciating sources occur frequently in the early pages of the book. In
every case, however, they stress the focal position of August 1944 while
pointing to the refusal of memory to leave it entirely behind for biographical storytelling.[22]

Banti's representation of her own wartime situation is just as compelling as her representation of Artemisia's life. In fact, the most startling
portrayals of Artemisia are actually inside of Banti's discourse. Delaying
her character's involvement in the Renaissance story, Banti first makes the
artist an important presence within the contemporary time frame as a
source of consolation. Artemisia initially may be nothing more than a
voice, but she is a soothing voice that calms Banti at the very moment she
realizes the extent of the damage done to Florence. Artemisia's words, "Do
not cry," are the opening words of the book, and they are addressed to
Banti, who is portrayed doubled over in anguish and shaking with tears
at the "reality of the terrors of a night during which the German mines

one after the other shook the earth's crust" (4). The voice quickly develops into a more palpable presence. A woman materializes, someone dazed by the bombing: "Silently she moans, like a Medusa among her snakes, and once again she is supine, crushed in a white sleep of dust, turning her head to one side like a woman in death searching for her last breath" (13). The figure gains definition. She metamorphoses into a companion who finds shelter along with Banti in the Boboli Gardens. Although she helps Banti withstand the tragedy of "death that is all around us," Artemisia, in a more encompassing way, is also a repository for the author's anger and recognition of loss: "In the dark, in the brutal roar of war, Artemisia's face, underneath my tightly closed eyelids, becomes inflamed like a hot-tempered woman's. I could reach out and touch it; in the middle of her forehead I can see the vertical line that she had from an early age and which deepened as she grew older. She begins to scream into my ear like a furious sleepwalker; she has the jarring voice and mangled accent of a lower-class girl from the Borgo, the wornout but inexhaustible means by which the destitute express and justify themselves" (14).

Artemisia is also the device through which Banti endures her own isolation. When, for example, the author returns to her street, she describes taking Artemisia along. Together, the two grieve that "in this place there once existed, and since a few days ago no longer exists, the house in which I had so easily placed her and heard her confession: now she is obliged to help me find the house again and with it her activities" (40–41). Finding (or imaginatively projecting) Artemisia in the communal areas where people gather to shield themselves from the stray firing of machine guns (16), Banti is, at the very least, not alone and admits that she is adapting her biographical character for her own purposes and reconceiving the Renaissance artist according to the urgencies of present time. When "cursed night is upon us once more" and Banti suffers from insomnia, she has Artemisia stay awake with her. She spares Artemisia no amount of grief, making her perform whatever supportive tasks become necessary in the autobiographical discourse and, consequently, preventing the artist from moving back into her own "life" and her own discrete biographical narrative. Those tasks may be painful reminders that the manuscript has just been destroyed and, in a textual sense, that Artemisia does not *have* a life any longer. The initial stages of her rebirth take place in Banti's *self*-representational passages, which give Artemisia preliminary identities that are particularly useful to her author. Banti borrows her biographical protagonist for her own representational purposes until she feels strong enough to release her into a literary arrangement that more closely resembles the original biographical fiction.

But the biographical story develops in spurts, its very formation a trope for the problems of artistic activity in times of catastrophe. Banti acknowledges these problems by composing Artemisia as highly erratic, a character migrating from one textual site to the other as a reflection of Banti's instability and disequilibrium. Banti starts her out in the twentieth century but does not keep her there, for Artemisia has autobiographical imperatives of her own. As if trying to avoid the distraction from present circumstances that a biographical fiction would present, Banti also gives her potential protagonist a disruptive, rebellious personality, forming a woman who argues vehemently for her independence. She demands from the author an identity closer to what she had in the first manuscript:

> "Fourteen years old," she goes on to stress in a tearful voice, with the last light of day, now a different Artemisia, a wronged and dignified young woman. It does not matter to her that I am getting over my distress at having lost her. She vaunts the fact that she exists independently of me and she all but takes it upon herself to walk one step ahead of me when the sunny path along which I am walking turns a corner into the shade.... Her language is soft, modulated, drawn from all sorts of experiences, experiences of telling an everlasting story which, from being painful, can turn into pathetic boasting for the benefit of a friend. "Fourteen years old! I tried to defend myself, but to no avail. He had promised to marry me, he promised it right up to the end, the traitor, to thwart me of my revenge...." Unsteadily she follows the troubled remembrance of what I had written, of what I had tried to guess or sacrifice to the accuracy of her story. (15–16)

As the passage demonstrates, Artemisia wants back her story and alternates between aggressively demanding it to boasting about the pain she has experienced. She goes so far as to recite lines from the first manuscript as a way to replant them into the author's memory and present consciousness. Before long she is instructing Banti on which specific episodes from the lost manuscript and lost life should be retold.

In the process of developing from a voice into a more substantive figure, Artemisia uses one strategy and then another in her efforts to persuade Banti to remember and retextualize the seventeenth-century narrative. She tries, for example, to appeal to Banti's sentiments by reverting back into the guise of Artemisia, the little girl: "'Tell about the walk.' She is the child pulling at the adult's sleeve, asking for her favorite story; she is the accused who never tires of calling on the sole witness in her favor" (19). However, the cajoling and persuasion also tire Banti out and cause her to remark that "once again she [Artemisia] tries to step over the irreparable, to go against the current, to undo the event [the destruction of herself] with an explanation; and she will not allow me to arrange her words." Time and again Banti merges the two discourses. Artemisia makes a request, and Banti yields. If the details she comes up with fail to be acceptable, Artemisia becomes "a stubborn, scrupulous conscience to which I grow accustomed as to sleeping on the ground. It is no longer our conversations that bind me, as in the early days, but a sort of contract legally drawn up between lawyer and client, and which I must honor" (33). Banti therefore gives her "client" the space to describe in her own voice one of Tassi's many betrayals, but Artemisia's first-person testimony turns out to be short, for Banti reclaims narrative control, insisting that Artemisia's words are exactly what she herself wrote in the former manuscript. Clearly, Banti struggles with narrative continuity and thus shifts and blends a variety of textual elements. As this occurs, two ongoing problems are manifest. Memory, under pressure, is shown to be fragile and unpredictable, because it is subject to outside influences; and writing in the midst of widespread suffering is exposed as an ethical issue, leading Banti to question her own motivation and goals.

Still at the early stages of being recollected into a biographical protagonist, Artemisia has another function within the autobiographical discourse. She serves as a witness to the disaster, someone who makes it possible for the author to describe whatever she can. Much has been written on the role of witnessing in the processes that transform private or cultural experiences of trauma into public narratives. According to Dori Laub, a second-person witness, who listens to a first person recollecting the trauma, allows the experience to be "re-externalized" and go out into the open. This happens "when one can articulate and *transmit* the story, literally transfer it to another outside oneself and then take it back again, inside." [23] Laub's discussion of the relationship of witnessing and testimony applies to *Artemisia* in an unusual way, because Artemisia serves in a double capacity as a witness. Since she witnesses the catastrophe itself, she corroborates and amends Banti's version. And since Banti composes the text soon after the event, Artemisia is also present to witness the narrative-making process. Most analyses of witnessing are concerned primarily with this latter function, since the narrating of trauma tends to take place long after the catastrophe or trauma. This means that the second-person role is more passive than Artemisia's, carried out by a silent listener, a recorder, a therapist, or, in the case of World War II survivors, often a historian or facilitator. The relationship between teller and listener that Banti constructs is not passive. Dynamic and contestatory, it belies the distinctions between inside and outside that Laub describes, for Artemisia is both inside and outside of the author. In some ways she is dead and other ways alive, a product of history but also a subjective, imagined subject. Though she is certainly a protagonist, the project transforms her into something larger than a single character with her own story. These collapsed borders amplify and problematize Artemisia's witnessing operations. As a victim (in one form) of the catastrophe, she is the narrative's subject. However, as a survivor (in another form), she is a witness to the events, and as a constant companion to Banti, she is integral to the actual making of the catastrophe narrative and an active agent responsible for its development and dynamic structure.

Ethical questions about her project pose a dilemma for the author and contribute to the correspondences and fluctuations between discourses. On the one hand, she feels guilty for committing herself to rewriting a biographical story that has no overt connections to the war. On the other hand, connecting it to the war involves exploiting Artemisia's life and changing it to serve a twentieth-century story that is much more violent. Still, with the compulsion to turn experience into narrative stronger than both reservations, Banti incorporates these tensions into the text, often indirectly through Artemisia. She, too, has choices involving the issue of guilt, which do not offer her freedom or viable choices. Women of her century rarely had meaningful alternatives. Thus, she can "choose" a lonely exile in Florence or be a pariah in Rome; she can marry the person her father designates before Orazio leaves the country or be utterly without masculine protection. Tassi offered one of the most deceptive choices. She recounts that after abusing her over a period of time, he promised marriage with a ring to signify their engagement. But the ostensible solution was a sham, and Artemisia is as penned in by her guilt as Banti is by hers. In order to marry, she would have to say publicly that Tassi was not the first man to have her. Consenting to this lie would allow the charges against him to be dropped and he would be free to become her husband. If she chooses the other alternative and insists on the truth—that Tassi violated her innocence—the charges against him would stand and there would be no marriage. Either decision involves moral inconsistencies and pressures between public and private expectations that are wholly unsatisfactory and leave her to think, "If they are treating [me] like this, they must be right: a stain has always marked [me] out to the eyes of others" (25). Artemisia does not choose between two bad possibilities but allows events to take their course, and when Banti gives her the chance, the situation becomes one more trauma that she turns into narrative. Certainly the form of guilt that the two women experience is far from identical, but the difficulty of overcoming it is much the same, and the conflict between the individual's needs and public expectations encumbers both women.

Ethical questions are further worked out in the interstitial passages, which offer space for debates on the intersections of memory, creativity, narrative, and social responsibility and catastrophe. As brief as a sentence or two, or reaching a few pages, these passages show the author intent on expanding personal testimony—her own and Artemisia's—out to cultural and historical arenas. These passages also show her acutely aware of the difficulties and contradictions in carrying out this task. For example, in the segment that follows the author makes a point of shifting the responsibility for narrative away from herself and onto Artemisia. This enables Banti to suggest that *Artemisia* is a cooperative enterprise over which she only has partial control. Artemisia, who also bears responsibility, is more decisive than Banti over the course of action they should follow. Having lived a productive life despite the guilt imposed on her by the public, the artist is less susceptible to the obstacles that encumber Banti. Precluded in history from a woman's conventional life because of rape, and losing a literary existence because of the destroyed manuscript, Artemisia is not about to sacrifice a third opportunity, regardless of how much or how little it resembles her life of four centuries ago. If necessary, the text implies, she will merge her story into the autobiographical account, remember what Banti cannot, and ensure, without being weighted down by guilt, that she has a future existence. Experienced in catastrophe and in moving beyond the limitations that others enforce, she is more willing to accept risk than Banti. She thus forces her way into the text by pushing herself inside of the author's body. While merely a tropological embodiment of the desire to write and a character in limbo at the edge of her own discourse, Artemisia is "real" and potent enough to cause physical pain.

In the courtyard of the Palazzo Pitti the human cicadas are screeching: already it is midday, it has been light for eight hours, the South Africans [part of the Allied forces] have been here for six and the women have been kissing them, as we could see from the broken windows of the Palatine gallery, our refuge. In the burning sun an overpowering nausea attacked those standing watching. With an unforgiveable lack of tolerance I banish Artemisia in her dismay and regret: I am ashamed of the persistence with which I have kept her here all morning in the midst of war. But I know that I will relapse into my madness, *and already I can feel her grinding through clenched jaws, as though my own* (12; emphasis added).

The subject of the biographical fiction is here arguing the cause of her own characterization through a strategy of corporeal assault rather than rhetoric. This means that the author is pitting herself against Artemisia in distinctly physical terms that are also dialogical. In effect, she is setting forth her conflicting ideas about auto/biographical, fictional, and cultural priorities by displacing them onto action and oppositional reaction. Allowed to behave on her own volition, Artemisia is brazen enough to stop Banti in midsentence by creating internal pressure and pain. To find relief, the narrator will have to eject Artemisia out in the open, so to speak, give her latitude to exercise some freedom, and, presumably, develop into the protagonist of her own biographical account.

The reciprocal activity of the autobiographical and biographical characters illustrates Banti's hope that her guilt over *Artemisia* will eventually resolve itself. From a wider angle, it also brings into view Kristeva's idea that certain types of identifying practices take place through a form of fusion. According to Kristeva, the metaphorical object (or person) and the subject, moving toward each other, begin to incorporate or assimilate each other's traits. In the world, fusion is a psychological concept or theoretical construct that is particularly useful during psychoanalysis. In a literary world, especially one that is testing out subjective processes and formations, fusion can be creatively achieved, and this is what happens in *Artemisia*. To be sure, the desire to write, as exemplified in the above passage, seems tropologically displaced *away* from Banti, transferred to Artemisia, and thus shown to be external and disassociated from the author. The reluctance to write is externalized again as Banti banishes Artemisia out of her presence. Fusion is nonetheless achieved with Artemisia's reciprocal action that forestalls Banti's apparent distancing of her. A trope for all aspects of *Artemisia*, Artemisia forcibly reinternalizes herself, merging into Banti's bone structure and entering her active consciousness. Banti will have no choice but to remember her biographical character back into text and develop text into story. Guilt diminishes as a pressing concern, for without viable choices and alternatives, the idea of free will is irrelevant.

This exchange, like others similar to it, shows that responsibility for constructive action is ultimately with the central "I," who paradoxically strives toward decentralization and intersubjective relationality. Therefore, the drama between Banti and Artemisia does not yield discrete identifying spaces. Banti, the writer, may use tropes to displace and dramatize her ethical dilemma, yet she is the person who creates them and determines how they mutually engage, and she is the person in whom all the tropes converge. This suggests that even though disassociation of the narrator and the biographical subject takes place rhetorically, in other ways the gap is not there: Artemisia can be resurrected only if someone revives her, and with Banti expressing ambivalence, Artemisia's prodding, cajoling, persuading, yelling into her ear, and grinding into her jaw are all Banti's conflicts externally projected. As a woman in a war-torn community where social obligations should come first, the author inscribes her misgivings through the psychic battles she sets up, but in going even this far she creates a narrative of two women transactionally moving toward fusion. Their palimpsestic nature means that distinctions between self and other, literal and figurative, inside and outside become inconsequential and thus allow the authorial "I" to trace how private memories, with imbricated layers of discourses, expand themselves outward.

However, in the most basic of ways, namely plot, *Artemisia* appears to move away from fusion as it gradually concentrates on its biographical subject. As the Renaissance story progresses through the first half of the book, Artemisia is richly developed in her own time and setting, maturing into an accomplished artist. Banti relies generally on a third-person voice and, when she stays within the boundaries of a bildungsroman, presents what happens to her protagonist in the years after the rape trial. She locates her in Florence, where Artemisia is less hampered than in Rome by her reputation as a fallen woman. There and in Naples she paints women from classical mythology and the Bible and finishes the portraits for which the historical Artemisia is well known, of Lucretia, another victim of rape, and Judith beheading her enemy, Holofernes.[24] Though Banti follows the historical record and includes the marriage to Antonio Stiattesi, she characterizes the relationship as unproductive. The couple lives in makeshift cellars with the entire Stiattesi family, whose members subsist by peddling and dealing. Artemisia languishes in this environment and neglects her artwork, but in time she abandons the family and leaves her dull, but attentive husband behind. The most compelling episodes are always those in which the narrator writes her protagonist as artistically productive, finding creative outlets for her private rage. Painting her canvases of female heroines is the only activity that allows her to feel powerful, with her revenge achieved and "her lasting shame in Rome atoned for" (48).

Regardless of the extent to which the biographical sections are developed, they are never presented as independent from Banti. In fact, Artemisia and Banti seem merely to reverse their position vis-à-vis the primary discourse. In the opening pages of the book where the author's misfortune dominates, Artemisia is situated at the borders of the modern discourse. As the artist's story occupies more of the text, it is Banti who remains at the edges of the bildungsroman, working the narrative seams. Her metatextual comments are precisely what make it impossible for readers to forget that Artemisia is always larger than herself. She remains a metonymic figure, not only incorporating parts of Banti but also representing and exhibiting the difficulties of self-representation under extreme pressure. She evinces the refusal of memory to be wiped out by catastrophe and signifies the process of recording a specific moment in history for future generations. Performing these functions at the same time, the activity that constitutes "Artemisia" is the successful collaboration of the autobiographical persona and the biographical protagonist. The ways in which together they energize the text would seem to indicate that the rest of the book will use similar collaborative methods to produce additional intersubjective and intertextual self-representations. In other words, there is every reason to expect that *Artemisia* will continue to be the author's dynamic response to catastrophe.

REVERSING THE NARRATIVE

The second half of *Artemisia* is startling, however, for the absence of active collaboration. It transforms itself into a rather slow-paced biographical fiction in the form of a bildungsroman with minimal authorial commentary or argumentative discussion. There are few traces of autobiographical material and very little evidence that *Artemisia* continues as the kind of writing that Michael M. J. Fischer calls "autobiographically figured."[25] The book *is* autobiographically figured, but no longer in the sense of a catastrophe narrative. Its structure reverses itself, moving away from dual voices vying for expression to a single, controlling voice intent on developing a traditional biographical discourse. In the process the dynamics that pervade the first part of the book disappear and the resistant "I" backs off.

The chief reasons for the lack of collaboration and reversion to a single-voiced presentation may well relate to the political and social changes that brought an end to the catastrophe in Italy and the rest of Europe. One year after Florence was under siege, the rewriting project appears to have reached a midway point. Banti's personal voice comments on the literary progress made relative to the amount of time that has passed, "now that the ruins have been ruins for a year" and "the immunities granted by war" ended (111, 108). With those who were killed in the catastrophe "resting in their final graves," 1945 was a very different context for survivors. Catastrophe was no longer the overwhelming threat it had been during the previous year. German forces in Italy had surrendered, and Italian partisans had captured Mussolini. The final battles were over, and victory in Europe was made official on May 8, 1945. Conditions for those who outlived the war belonged more to crisis than catastrophe, and a period of ongoing assessment and reconstruction was starting. Relief over the end of catastrophe was countered as the concentration camps were exposed, the genocide of millions of victims was ascertained, and the war crime trials were started. The use of atomic bombs, ending the war in the Pacific, also had to be confronted, thereby expanding discussions of mass destruction to even more inconceivable levels. With all these developments—yet her own survival no longer in question—Banti was less compelled to write about her own circumstances. Many of the remaining pages of the biographical fiction are thus deliberately unhinged from the authorial context. Once severed from contemporary references, dialogues, and the cultural task of commemoration, these pages also lose vitality and seem lifeless in comparison to the earlier segments.

The time necessary to rewrite *Artemisia* prolonged the text beyond the limits of a catastrophe narrative and extended it over into crisis. Crisis narratives do not necessarily center on the writer's present time, and, predictably, the postwar sections of Banti's manuscript shift off from present time and make use of past tense constructions. Not based on shock and sudden occurrences, crisis narratives often lack the particularized tensions of catastrophe narratives. *Artemisia*'s postwar sections have a tired persistence to them that does not exist in the sections written during the war. Artemisia-as-protagonist continues faintly to suggest the author, but her "postwar" identity enacts, rather than resists, problematic Western conventions of female representation, and the text does not have the energy to counter them. The book starts to exhibit the disturbing traits that Barbara Kosta critiques in women's traditional histories: instead of enacting "narratives of independence and autonomy," they become "melancholic testimonies of 'damaged' self-images and loss."[26] Once the text reverses its dynamic design, it concerns itself with Artemisia's wounded sense of self and seems reflective of the moral accounting and disillusionment that are integral to a postwar sensibility.

The interstitial passages remaining in the postwar sections serve purposes that actually reverse the roles they served in the wartime sections. The most revealing are the few pages that Banti constructs in her own voice, where she justifies the new direction that her text is about to take. The imperative that drove her to begin *Artemisia* through a series of interacting voices and to situate her historical character "in my own time" is gone. Without this imperative, she will devote the rest of the narrative to a single discourse. The narrating voice works at length to set forth the argument for making such a drastic change:

> Artemisia's obstinacy in making me remember her, my own obstinacy in remembering her according to my whims, in emotional fits and starts, is becoming a game, maybe a cruel game. I was betrayed by the urgency with which I saw her, yes really saw, that she expected from me, after my grief at having lost her and the trepidation of finding her again so very much alive, that inexhaustible surge of stubborn hope of someone who continues to nurse the incurably ill. I had grown accustomed, through contradicting her and even teasing her a little, to situating her in my own time, to feeling her standing behind me, present. I was certain that she understood and needed me. I was in the habit of preparing small surprises for her, interpretations that were the opposite of what the record of her life had suggested to me; and I believed that she enjoyed it, given the fact that she had been lost.... Only today do I realize that I lacked respect in her regard and that what I longingly took to be her consent has been, for a long time now, her absence. (108)

The passage acknowledges the cost of reconstructing the manuscript while external conditions were still volatile. The effort led Banti to write herself in as a major character and to sacrifice her biographical subject. As a reassessment of the project, these sentences harshly judge the earlier dialogues and label them a game. They also insist that the empathetic bond of author and character is an illusion and sign of self-indulgence. In the

end, the sentences simply reject the idea of autobiographical and biographical writing as a collaborative effort.

The seriousness of reversing the book's dynamic causes Banti deliberately to emphasize her decision to focus on biography. First she takes up
considerable space rationalizing her change of plan, suggestively linking
the shift to the postwar environment. Then she dramatizes the change by
returning to tropological devices and completely turning around their
earlier functions. In the segments written during the war, tropes illustrate
the relationality of all aspects of the autobiographical and biographical
discourses, giving characters and events significance beyond themselves.
Tropological representation is now used for arguing the opposing case for
nonrelationality and singularity. After the author decides in the passage
just quoted that merging the artist's life with her own is a sign of disre-
spect, she supports her stance by having Artemisia tropologically perform
the very same decision. She imagines her character in the act of physically
shielding herself from further intimacy and becoming inaccessible to the
person who has remembered her into a position of feminist strength.
With a straightforward and aggressive defense, Artemisia is depicted in
the act of blinding the author. She shines a light at Banti to block any
close-range vision and moves far off into the past. Banti is left describing
the action as if it objectively took place: "She has merged once more into
the distant light of three centuries ago, a light which she shines full into
my face, blinding me: the speed with which the images of her life followed
each other and merged together wavers, coagulates into pictures of a lunar
magic lantern, cold, flat pictures" (109). Stopped instantly from seeing
images of the artist's life in configurations that have previously been clear,
the author is prevented here from transferring them over into a literary
form. In addition, Banti writes this passage so that Artemisia controls the
argument for severing the discourses while her own persona represents
the counterposition for intersecting them.

To make the decision for a biographical emphasis even stronger, the
author dramatizes herself using secondary strategies for remaining on
intimate terms with her character. Banti represents herself bodily attempting to move Artemisia into a different position, then provoking Artemisia
into changing her mind and allowing their "joint collaboration, active and
shared," to stay on course. When the exchange is over, it is again the artist
who wins. She retreats into silence, which looks as though it is *her* own
new goal rather than Banti's, and she locates herself far off from the
author, "immeasurably distant, light years away" (110). Banti presents one

final tropological action, and that is to bury the protagonist and confirm her own determination to change the direction of what remains of the manuscript. She finds two grave sites for Artemisia, "the real and the fictitious." This signals the narrator's victory, which, ironically, is her definitive losing of the argument.

Declaring a limited role for herself, Banti turns her own voice into that of a third-person narrator of a distant biographical fiction. Ideally, this change should give the biographical character more freedom and opportunities for development. It could also allow Artemisia to reflect some small degree of optimism in the author, writing to a future of peace and reconciliation. This does not happen. The narrator relies on descriptions of passivity and weakness while her vantage point becomes so remote that the portrayal of Artemisia is barely recognizable as the woman from the earlier sections. No longer portrayed as rebellious, the biographical character does not, for example, scream into Banti's ear to make her point or insist on a particular interpretation. She is instead three centuries away and treated as a distant personage. Rather than celebrate the apex of her protagonist's career, the narrator seems intent on undermining it. She has the artist concentrate on how her life is three-quarters over and in taking account of her past finds "the sum total beats dismally: nothing" (130). She analyzes Artemisia as a woman who is isolated and exhausted and focusing exclusively on her losses. She now has an unloving daughter old enough to be married and whose dowry she cannot afford. Her father, Orazio, abandoned her, preferring to be a famous painter in the British Royal Court, and she still craves his paternalistic approval. Then there is the peddler she married and left years ago but waxes sentimental over as if she is a character in a romance novel.[27] If splitting Artemisia off from the author's self-representation is a vehicle to acknowledge the end of a catastrophic time and free Banti to focus on her biographical subject, it is both a high price to pay and a decision that sacrifices the feminist integrity of its subject.

The narrative moves chronologically and methodically, all the while exposing the difficulties of Banti's decision to shift over to a biographical mode. Consciously or otherwise, its episodes subvert the normative story the book has argued itself into telling. The descriptions of Artemisia's travels do not integrate the protagonist into society as they would in a conventional bildungsroman, nor do they put "alternate visions in its place" as Rita Felski explains women's bildungsromane will do through feminist themes and values.[28] This part of the book has created difficulties for critics trying to explain its modus operandi. Heller, for instance, calls it a "beautifully imagined odyssey." But in a text concerned with life writing ethics and with women's subjugation, the word "odyssey" seems out of place. Caracciolo, who translated the English edition of *Artemisia*, searches for positive effects in this long biographical section. She believes that Banti's additions to what has been historically verified about Artemisia's trip to England give coherence to the plot and psychological motivation to the protagonist. Yet from a life writing standpoint, the travel episodes have an opposite effect. They backfire as a literary convention for showing the protagonist's maturing process, and the psychology they reveal is not that of a woman who has painted heroine after heroine in positions of strength. Artemisia's experiences from Italy by boat, through France by carriage, across the English Channel to London to join her father, Orazio, to work for the British Court all fail to renew her vitality. [29] Even when she is in London the narrative is very slow to allow her a burst of creativity, making her dote on her father instead and perform domestic chores for him. This new version of Artemisia as a woman who cleans for Orazio and does needlework actually makes a case *against* separating life writing discourses from one another. It shows biographical writing as suggestively autobiographical in times of both crisis and catastrophe, revealing, in a phrase by Carol Hanbery MacKay, "the autobiographer within the act of writing biography."[30] We "may not learn very much about the facts that constituted her life," as MacKay says about "autobiographical biography." But we recognize what MacKay calls source points in the text that are clues to understanding "a creative writer coming to terms not only with her biographer's task but with herself." This is what takes place in *Artemisia*. The source points that expose Banti's presence are the biographical episodes themselves, which undermine their stated purpose and lead the author to reassess her own position.

REVITALIZING THE NARRATIVE

From a life writing perspective, the most significant development in *Artemisia* is the way that self-representation comes to revitalize the text. This takes place as Artemisia begins to paint, effectively reversing her biographical characterization and shattering the pattern of the bildungsroman. She accomplishes this *in spite of* the biographical text, which has kept her inactive even while acknowledging her potential, saying, "If she wanted, she could take on this world, assail and conquer it; but she does not want to" (195). Artemisia returns to the task of painting a self-portrait that she abandoned earlier when she was portrayed as creatively blocked and unable to envision an appropriate image for herself. The biographical narration quickly ended that scene, as if giving up on its female subject. In fact, it misinterprets Artemisia's lack of action as unproductive and fails to notice that the pose in which it leaves her is absolutely identical to the one that the "real" Artemisia selected in painting her brilliant *Self-Portrait as the Allegory of Painting*.[31] This is the work of art for which Artemisia remains most famous, where she depicts herself in the moment just before she begins to paint, instrument in hand and her body in front of the blank canvas. The third-person narrator describes Artemisia in exactly this way, as an artist deep in thought, with her "black hair gathered in a careless knot, falling down over the neck and ears" and a single lock falling "from the temple, unraveling down over the cheek and hiding the ear" (195). Artemisia's head is angled over the left shoulder in a similar way, with only part of her face visible. But the narration moves to another scene, apparently not sensing that Artemisia is on the brink of representing herself so that she can survive beyond the stultifying portrait that has developed throughout this part of the book.

It would be tempting to conclude that Artemisia rebels against the biographical discourse and, hence, against the author's plans for her. Yet it is always Banti who controls the narrative and Banti who allows Artemisia to paint herself into a position of strength ostensibly without help from the biographical narrator. As a result, it is more accurate to say that the text tropologically uses Artemisia to reflect Banti's ideas on representation as they undergo change. Artemisia's return to the unfinished self-portrait reflects the author's final decision concerning biographical and autobiographical writing. The decision is that the two life writing forms are inseparable and integral to each other's very existence. Completing the project is, to use MacKay's term, a source point through which Banti admits to the necessary intersections of life writing modes. Artemisia seems to be in the process of painting her own self-portrait, that is, until she stares right at it and discovers another woman in the space where she expects to see herself. The figure is the artist, Annella de Rosa, a minor character from an earlier section covering Artemisia's years in Naples: "So now Annella has been resurrected *by chance*, Annella who would barely be thirty years old if she had not been felled by a man's dagger and left

Self-Portrait as the Allegory of Painting, or *La Pittura* by Artemisia Gentileschi. *Courtesy of The Royal Collection,* © *Her Majesty Queen Elizabeth*

on the ground to bleed to death, as white as a Lucretia, a Cleopatra"
(196–97; emphasis added).[32]

The revelation that Artemisia draws Annella, who is from *our* perspective Artemisia, has important thematic implications within the story. It
underscores the relationality of women, particularly those who have experienced collective or personal catastrophes. Years after the two women meet
each other, Artemisia discovers the terrible results of not recognizing or
acting on her knowledge. She had made gestures of friendship to Annella,
who rejected them because she realized that the famous Artemisia merely
wanted to appear generous in public as the supporter of a lesser-known
woman artist. Artemisia comes to understand that had she been sincere,
she would have known for certain that Annella, too, suffered from male
abuse and she might have prevented Annella from being stabbed to death
by a husband in a jealous rage.[33] When Artemisia paints Annella without
being conscious of it, Banti is allowing Artemisia to expiate for her behavior by performing a biographical and artistic tribute as well as acknowledging women's responsibility for one another. In a thematic sense, *Artemisia*
commemorates women who experience persecution and violence, returning them to life historically and imaginatively through, as Carol Lazzaro-
Weis traces it, Banti's effort to negate "the defeat and erasure of female
creativity."[34]

Beyond theme, the self-portrait is *Artemisia*'s most powerful use of
metonymy. The portrait calls attention to the female body as a substitute
for the culminating argument of the ongoing ethical discussion of how
to represent women's lives. The body that materializes on the canvas is a
rebuttal to what thus far has been the last "word" in the debate, Artemisia's blinding the author so that the story converges on just a single
protagonist. The body in the self-portrait is a convincing counterargu-
ment, for it is more than a single female figure. It is a site where women's
bodies converge and blend, suggesting traces of one another, like images
in a palimpsest. Artemisia's body in the self-portrait of the text is Annella's
body in the biographical discourse. And Annella's body is identical to
Artemisia's body in the 1630 *Self-Portrait*, the actual painting that has survived into our own century. The narrator takes note of the merging: "To
bump into her like this, to stand in her way. Pinned down by the truth
of a shoulder, an arm, a hand, the thumb of which is slipped through
the hole in a palette, Annella cannot escape" (196). Seeing Annella's body
where we expect the historical Artemisia's body, we must see Artemisia
where we locate Annella. In other words, our gaze breaks down because

our expectations are exposed as unreliable. The gaze sees as much as it is cued in to see and is left with a collection of women's bodies, between one unfinished story and another, one character and another, and one representational form and another. Separating the female subject from the female object becomes impossible because there is too much instability and cross-identification. A final fact, that some art historians suspect the figure in *Self-Portrait as the Allegory of Painting* is not Artemisia but indeed another woman, is beyond the scope of this discussion. Still, merely knowing that the controversy exists adds exponentially to the debate on identification relative to portraiture and self-portraiture and autobiographical and biographical practices.[35]

The self-portrait—as an object inside the plot and a trope that amplifies metonymically far beyond itself—makes a claim for life writing that is mutable and open both to historiographic and metaphoric representation. Pressured by external circumstances to move along different tracks, the book converges on a single moment, action, and "thing," thereby transforming *Artemisia* and pointing to this claim. The autobiographical first-person voice is not only freed to reenter the text but to bring back the twentieth-century context and reaffirm the legitimacy of shifting perspectives and personae. The "I" voice acknowledges all this, now that she lets herself hear "the dusty breathing of centuries, our own and Artemisia's combined" (197), and for most of the remaining pages she intersects memories, imagined events, and present-time references. She even cites, for the very first time, an autobiographical episode that is earlier than 1944, one that corroborates the transformative role of the famous self-portrait. It is a Sunday in 1939, the location a royal castle in England crowded with weekend visitors. Most of the paintings on view are far from extraordinary, just "a few goddesses, a few useless saints covered with the dirt of centuries," and another few pictures of royalty and knights (198). But "higher up, hanging above the portraits of queens and warriors," Banti notices the canvas of "a sulky young woman [who] continues to paint as though she were alive; and underneath, in official letters, was written a name that was legible: Artemisia Gentileschi." The narrator then switches back to her own writing time and place. She wants to confirm that the canvas she recollects really is Artemisia's self-portrait:

Artemisia Gentileschi. I can assure you of this, affirm it in good faith on this page written by the light of a wartime candle. And in the air, the air at my back, the winter air of the year nineteen hundred and forty-five, there is not a breath of assent; nor do I need to swear it in letters of blood, Artemisia! . . .

How laboriously those English Sunday visitors spelled out her name. And just as laboriously did those others who, on numerous occasions in sixteen hundred and forty, forty-five, year after year, repeated, reread that foreign name, every time the painting was put up, taken down, exhibited, scorned, praised, rediscovered. The truth was that people liked the subject of the portrait: a young woman who paints, a woman from the south of Italy, with that untidy black hair, someone you feel you could approach freely. *The Art of Painting* was the title given to it one day by the custodians of the royal palaces. "Self-portrait by Artemisia Gentileschi," declared the inevitable descendant of . . . a keen archivist. Perhaps he was inspired by Annella's revenge, sullen Annella who did not have time to travel, only to die young, and who slips once more out of Artemisia's hand. And with this torrid brunette's face was confirmed the reputation of Artemisia's scandalous youth. . . . Thus it was repeatedly written, even in English. But Artemisia's hand is strong and Annella cannot free herself. Whether it is a self-portrait or not, a woman who paints in sixteen hundred and forty is very courageous, and this counts for Annella and for at least a hundred others, right up to the present. "It counts for you too," she concludes, by the light of a candle, in this room rendered gloomy by war, a short sharp sound. A book has been closed, suddenly. (198–99)

In this crucial passage, the autobiographical voice does not finally reconcile the ambiguities of representation or choose one modality over another. She gladly accepts the fluidity of relational representation, the impact of history over time, and she feels comforted by the ways in which the portrait allows disparate victims across centuries and cultures to coalesce and confirm each other's existence.[36]

Artemisia in the final pages of the book may well be Banti's attempt to satirize and discredit the biographical paradigm for not living up to its promise of faithful representation. The conclusion deploys the customary props, chronology, an episodic structure, a journey, and a protagonist trying to understand herself and her experiences. However, she does not match the woman in the passage above, a version of Artemisia with enough agency to make a difference three hundred years after her death.[37] According to Banti's last phase of the bildungsroman, after Orazio dies in London Artemisia grieves uncontrollably. She travels back to Italy, consumed by grief for the man who alternately nurtured and rejected her. She presumes, contrary to the evidence of her artistic triumph, that nothing is left for her but dying, that her obligation is to die, and that it is about to happen at any moment, in each new location where she journeys. Cannon describes this melodramatic behavior as Artemisia languishing while she "imagines her own death in a dozen dramatic scenarios."[38] If her character is implausible and the denouement unconvincing, it is because the author seems to take one last opportunity to expose the bildungsroman as moribund. The narration itself, impatient with the task of containing Artemisia inside of this pattern, counts the versions of death that Artemisia imagines "at least" thirty before she leaves England and many more once she is en route to Italy. Everything about this section indicates that the protagonist no longer fits the conventional narrative scheme, especially when used in isolation from other schemes and techniques. The final pages configure Artemisia into a shadow of her earlier self, violating what we sense is appropriate for this remarkable woman. They also contradict the argument that all parts of the book have made for life writing frameworks capacious enough to reflect the life writing conditions that pressure the text's development.

The insufficiencies of the paradigm are further linked to an author trying to write in a time of catastrophe and then in the aftermath of crisis. Faced with a dual task of recovering one story through memory while recording the substance of her own wartime experience, Banti alters the form and function of the original manuscript. The implications of the changes lead her to comment metatextually on her revision as it unfolds. Her narrator questions the desire to write during a tragedy, but simply in doing so puts the process in motion. She relies initially on dialogues and interactive personae but shifts to more traditional modes when the catastrophe appears over. When traditional modes seem too distant from her present-time priorities, she experiments with other approaches. For much of the text, the autobiographical voice writes over, across, and through the women it seeks to memorialize, confirming Sharon O'Brien's description of biographical work as "a meeting of two spirits, the subject's and the biographer's, at a particular moment of time."[39] Scholars have little biographical information on Artemisia from her return to Italy to the end of her life in the mid-1660s.[40] The author thus leaves her protagonist with an uncertain future only *in the story of her own life*. Artemisia may be certain she is about to die, but she is given no melodramatic death scene.

Instead, Banti keeps her in limbo, noting that her appetite, a trope for much more than the desire for food, has become "demanding and immortal" (214). In the discourse of Banti's life, which is the larger text entitled *Artemisia*, the protagonist has a good chance for survival, for immortality, in fact. The argument for her central role in Western art is here, thirty years before feminist art historians in the 1970s began to make the same case. The argument for her life as inspirational is here too, established by Banti remembering and recontextualizing Artemisia in her own autobiographical response to the catastrophic effects of war.

Biblical Renarratization as Autobiographical Intertext

Grete Weil's *The Bride Price: A Novel*

ORN IN 1906 to an assimilated Jewish family living near Munich, Grete Weil was taught nothing that might have prepared her for the crisis of surviving the Nazi regime that progressively dominated the world in which she was raised. She had a privileged childhood and a good education, concentrating on German literature and attending schools in Frankfurt, Berlin, and Munich. Judaism and Jewish culture were rarely discussed in the home or at school, and like many European Jews before the Second World War who privileged nationality over religion, she considered herself a German citizen.[1] She married Edgar Weil, who was Jewish, in 1932, and when he was arrested and detained for a number of weeks, the irrelevance of her personal views in the face of Nazi ideology was undeniable. The 1935 Nuremberg Laws forced Jews to reconceptualize their self-definitions, and, realizing the dangers of staying in Germany, the couple fled to Amsterdam and were relatively safe until the Germans invaded Holland. Unable to find another country of exile, the couple remained in Amsterdam and went into hiding. Edgar Weil was nonetheless arrested in 1941. He was deported to the Mauthausen concentration camp and killed there three months later. Stranded in Amsterdam and eventually fearing for her own life, Grete Weil went into hiding in 1943 until the end of the war. Contrary to the vast majority of wartime Jewish survivors, however, she traveled back to Germany as soon as she could, fully aware of the anomaly of deciding to return to "the land of my murderers."[2] Living in Germany from 1947 until her death in 1999 and insisting that she never wished to be anywhere else, Weil acknowledged her Jewish identity because she was treated as a Jew, and for no reason beyond that.

Grete Weil. © by Herlinde Koelbl, courtesy of David R. Godine, Publisher, Inc.

Weil's autobiographical work, *The Bride Price*, emerges as testimony less of the events of the author's life than of the difficulties of maintaining a dual and problematic sense of self in the face of world destruction.[3] Unlike Banti and H.D., whose life writing texts bore witness to the ongoing devastation of the war itself, the crisis for Weil was not only the "fact" of the Holocaust but the pressures of identifying herself as both Jewish and German in the face of that fact. This sense of duality is manifested in the structure of *The Bride Price*. As autobiographical writing, it achieves its purpose by juxtaposing the author's personal history to the Old Testament story of Michal, the daughter of King Saul and the first wife of David. Michal's story, as *The Bride Price* represents it, does not strictly parallel the author's struggle with identity but rather enacts a complex web of dualistic tensions. These entangled strands reflect the quality of life suffered by Weil in her inability to respond comprehensively to the global horror in which, as both a German and a Jew, she was implicated.

The generic designation of "novel," prominently displayed on the cover and title page of *The Bride Price*, would seem, however, to indicate that efforts to approach Weil's 1988 text as autobiographical writing are misguided. Reviewers of the book, taking their cues right from the subtitle, stressed the fictional story over the personal account. Edith Milton, for one, placed the text in the tradition of revisionist fiction such as Jean Rhys's *Wide Sargasso Sea* and then called the book's life writing segments "brief essays" that sound "a contemporary counterpoint to the central story."[4] Even the jacket copy of the 1992 English translation by John Barrett declares *The Bride Price* to be a work of fiction. The first paragraph of the jacket copy affirms that the book is not just a novel, but a "strikingly original novel." The originality, it says, is due to the book's constitutive rhetoric, which consists of "two narratives—one a moving recreation of a Biblical story, and the other a haunting testimony of her [Weil's] own experiences as a survivor of the Holocaust." *The Bride Price* is a particularly original novel because of the structural and rhetorical effects of the author's personal, *non*-novelistic, autobiographical testimony (of eight short chapters) on the thirteen fictional chapters. With this, readers are expected to consider Weil's youth in Germany, her twelve years of exile, the Nazis' murder of her husband in 1941, her hasty return after the war, her lifelong ambivalence toward Judaism, and her struggle with old age and debilitation as all subordinate to the more developed and encompassing second narrative.

To be sure, the biblical narrative comprises more pages than the auto-biographical sections and is dramatically recounted with action, characters, and chronological progression. And the book's title, *The Bride Price,* refers directly to this second narrative, which is an imaginative reconstruction of the story of King David, from his youth as a shepherd and musician through his transformation to warrior, hero, and aging king. The first-person enunciating voice, which is just one of the author's innovations, belongs to Michal, who married David before he devoted his life to creating a single nation-state of Israel with himself as its ruler. Michal is one of the most confounding and forgotten women of the Old Testament.[5] Appearing only briefly in the story of David in 1 and 2 Samuel and referred to once in 1 Chronicles, she is noted for loving David early in her life (1 Samuel) and despising him later in her life (1 Chronicles).[6] Weil invokes her own version of Michal, who was Saul's oldest royal daughter as well as David's reward for vanquishing Goliath.[7] She is the object of an additional "bride price" that David must provide—cited in the Bible as one hundred foreskins taken from Goliath's warriors, which, as Michal can never forget, David raised to two hundred. Michal's renarratization of biblical materials, with her ostensible corrections and reinterpretations, powerfully critiques bloodshed and militarism, especially when they are justified collectively because they fulfill nationalistic purposes and are presumed to warrant divine approval.

The problem in viewing *The Bride Price* as a novel is that it leaves crucial issues unaddressed. To assume that the novel is the privileged genre is to eliminate the autobiographical tensions that are source and motivation behind *The Bride Price.* Weil's repeated and provocative remarks on her simultaneous attraction to and disaffiliation from her ancestral religion and community become the elements of dramatic *story*telling. The loyalties that changed the course of her life and led her to return to Germany are no more significant than any other details Weil has imaginatively thought up and placed into the renarrativized episodes from the Bible. If Weil utilizes the most painful events of her life merely to serve novelistic purposes, then the issues most vital to the text are diminished, or can be read even as fiction. We move into a position in which we may fail to realize the seriousness of the questions that operate self-consciously throughout all of the chapters, the thirteen biblical as well as the eight personal ones.

By recognizing that life writing, specifically autobiography, is indeed the main trajectory of *The Bride Price,* we are faced with questions more immediate to the twentieth century than those just the biblical story by itself would elicit. Preoccupied with the contradictions between nationalism and religion, Weil implicitly and explicitly poses questions that explore the difficulties of her own case history. What does it mean for a person to insist on national identity after fleeing that country and being pursued in exile? What do the terms "Jew" and "Jewish" signify to a woman with no belief in the God of the Old Testament and no stake in the success of a post-Holocaust Jewish nation, yet whose husband was murdered because he was Jewish?[8] What is the connection of a personal illness like the one Weil suffers to collective victimization? Why does Weil so patently call attention to her late-life stroke and make it instrumental in her unfinished writing? Finally, how do we explain, from the perspective of this study, the complex relationship of the "novel" with the author's intermittent comments *about* that novel with her changing and dramatically different self-perceptions that are separate from the novel? On the one hand, Weil feels closer to her roots and asserts she has become more Jewish since beginning her Old Testament project. "Yes," she writes, "surely, something has started that was not there before" (128). On the other hand, she admits that "being Jewish is a fact, but I'm not successful in giving it any content," meaning, in effect, that she has addressed the lack of content largely by inventing her protagonist (51). As a result, the larger question, also relevant to the women studied in these pages, concerns the relationship of life writing to distantiating and adjunct genres. Does the generic designation of fiction, so patently invoked by Weil on her title page, problematize the autobiographical elements to the extent that it has the effect of neutralizing them?

It seems clear that the answer is no, and that the power of the text, to the extent that it does perform as a novel, is the underlying reason for it. As an imagined speaker, Michal cannot contain the author, who has written her into a detailed existence and who comments metatextually on her fictional counterpart. While their voices may "intertwine," as the jacket copy declares, a closer examination shows that the two narrators do not specifically engage in dialogue with each other as, for example, Banti and her character do in *Artemisia* and as Allende, throughout *Paula*, wishes her daughter was physically able to do. It is Michal who is the embedded, actually the intertextual, speaker and Michal's discourse, despite its greater length, that is ancillary—certainly not Weil's. In this light, the author's autobiographical chapters are not small segments of narrative enfolded within Michal's more elaborate first-person chapters; Michal functions, in a sustained way, as a tropological projection and as a suggestive characterization of "Grete." All of Michal's memories become a kind of landscape through which Weil displays, however obliquely and allusively, the contradictions of her own life, her political views, and her personal values.

Once we acknowledge that the primary narrative is not the biblical fiction but the contemporary autobiographical testimony that intersects with it, *The Bride Price,* at least initially, comes under the rubric of crisis autobiography. It is a powerful instance of life writing that projects back into personal and collective history while still remaining responsive to ongoing, present-time conditions. Like the other authors treated in this study, Weil positions her life within the context of a continuous state of overwhelming conflict. However, as a crisis, the Holocaust created another related context for Weil more abstract and philosophical than those surrounding the other women; and this condition is reflected in the dual structure of her narrative. Langer emphasizes in *Holocaust Testimonies* that the process for survivors of remembering and recording often fails because events have not receded into a past. They remain intensely immediate, grounded in what he calls an obsessive "insomniac faculty."[9] Weil did not suffer as a victim of the concentration camps, but in parts of the book she imagines herself as just such a victim, and her text has an obsessive and dramatic immediacy similar to what Langer describes; grief and anxieties related to the past lose none of their intensity, tormenting her as much in her old age as they did half a century earlier. In fact, the experience of victimization and the inability to forget, which we have come to associate with survivors, are precisely what drive *The Bride Price.* The author's insomniac memory, manifested in her ongoing problems with sleeplessness, is not attributable only to her history of persecution. It is also the effect of her continuing belief that, because of her loyalty and love for German culture, she should not have suffered as she did (saying, in another context, "that's bad, but I can't get it, not me" [56]). Unable to move off from this point, Weil fails to use a smooth, progressive narrative structure for presenting her own memories, which are static and fixed on the contradiction. She does, however, adopt a developmental structure for her intertext, which offers a more successful space for telling a "long, complicated, sad story to the end" (58). Michal has little existence apart from Weil, so in reminding readers that "I, Michal" must sit alone in the shade of olive trees with no one to witness her statements, she is always the author engaged in self-representation. The movement out of herself, then back across to herself—through the intertextual dynamics of her chapters—enables Weil to explore aspects of her own difficult history without becoming mired in them and immobilized by them.

Also in contrast to the women who write directly and in detail about themselves in times of crisis, when Weil bifurcates her story into two unconnected histories, she describes her life relative to the immediate, ongoing crisis and, at the same time, displaces her experience onto a fictionalized and historical heroine. The originality of *The Bride Price* as autobiographical writing, then, comes from a structure where fiction and memory intersect under Weil's direction in order to "tell" Weil's life. Not even Banti's double structure of autobiography and biographical fiction is as bifurcated as Weil's, for *The Bride Price* contains neither dialogue nor direct interaction between its two narrators. The mirroring effects in *The Bride Price* therefore operate quite differently from those in Banti's work and, indeed, from other women's self-representations in this study. In Weil's volume, the mirroring effects actually link the author's deconstruction of the traditional bildungsroman design to the representation of unresolved and unresolvable crisis. The other women take the opposite approach to crisis. They go to extreme efforts to construct, rather than deconstruct, a bildungsroman for either their autobiographical or biographical protagonists at least until crisis turns into a catastrophe. Whereas the catastrophes suffered by the other women were directly related to the subjects of their writing, the catastrophe that Weil suffers—a severe stroke and coma—in the midst of her writing was not related to the Holocaust or to the war in even a general sense. Nor was it integral to her ongoing postwar state of crisis. But because Weil *interprets* her illness in terms very much central to the Holocaust, the catastrophe profoundly affects her writing conditions, her self-imaging, the way she viewed the nature of the crisis, and, as a result, her perspectives throughout the remaining chapters of the book.

The Bride Price dialogically performs its tensions through the intertextual exchange of *independent* but interacting generic discourses. Examining dialogical autobiographies and biographies that are built on similar kinds of relations and complexities, Michael Fischer refers to the term "sondages," or "soundings," for its similarity to the exploratory techniques that archeologists use in excavations.[10] He explains that by listening to the voices deep within the structure of such texts, we can find authorial identity "in the interface" between different cultures and traditions. An anthropologist, Fischer focuses on what contemporary life writing reveals about global social changes that outpace the ability of established social theories to account for them. In Weil's case, the predominant theories of

Jewish assimilation—especially of the middle class into European Christian culture and post-Shoah theories concerning a national Jewish state—
are dialogically voiced in prismatic fashion. As Fischer emphasizes, life
writing does not furnish empirical evidence for new theories but is a good
source for ideas on which to base new formulations. Both "autobiographically figured" fiction and dual-voiced biographies provide "sites
for seeing new connections, new articulations of how cultural, social, psychological forces are interacting in the consciousness of writers situated
in various social and cultural loci."[11] The autobiographical *Bride Price* is also
autobiographically figured fiction, and the connections and articulations
that create its dialogic relations are not representative of most Jews who
survived the Second World War. Nonetheless, the dual narrative creates a
powerful two-way perspective on religious, moral, and cultural traditions.

Intersecting her own history dialogically with a story from the Old Testament, Weil implicitly acknowledges her ancestral identity. Her use of
David suggests a desire to participate in widely known Jewish narrative
and historical traditions. Her choice of Michal as her biblical speaker
suggests an active interest in furthering Jewish scholarship and narrative
by adding a new female personage for critical analysis.[12] Not only does
Weil mine this character from fragments, but she creates a voice for her
and a distinctive point of view. She allows Michal to be a rich source of
information and to examine comprehensively various prophets, kings,
wars, royal successions, royal sibling hostilities, and nation building, thus
participating in debates that remain central to Jewish history and religion. But as the book's primary narrator, Weil has complete control over
Michal, whom she also creates as a tropological configuration of herself.
A dialogic mechanism for airing views that Weil does not articulate fully
in her own voice, Michal is the author's "sounding" for exploring and
asserting a dual identity, which derives from conflicting loyalties. Moreover, by transforming Michal's story from its brief, fragmented biblical
version into a fully developed narrative, she also empowers a Jewish
woman who had been rendered by the Bible historically insignificant.[13] By
allowing Michal to articulate her life in her own voice and therefore privilege her point of view, Weil thereby gives Michal narrative control over
David, one of the most revered figures in the Old Testament and for many
a symbol of Israel and Judaism itself. In this way, the author not only contextualizes her own experience in terms of Jewish biblical history, but she
also distances herself from that culture by providing a critique—through
the voice of a previously silenced woman—of the history that defined it.

Correspondences between the two women are ingrained in the text and serve to dramatize the crisis of dual identity exacerbated in previously unimaginable ways for Weil by the Holocaust. Both narrators are portrayed as very old women, widows who never had children and whose husbands were forced to go into exile ("My husband was murdered, Michal's husband got away by a hair's breadth" [35]). Both feel the disabling effects of age and realize they are out of step with the newer generation's ideas on nationalism. Except for a trip to Israel described late in the book, Weil depicts herself as confined to a small apartment where she struggles with insomnia and ruminates on the disasters of her lifetime. Similarly but not identically, Michal—as "she" unfolds her life story—is permitted by Solomon (David's son with Bathsheba) to live out her final years in the royal palace, but she has no agency whatsoever. Limited to inhabiting the narrow space "between houses and garden, garden and house," Michal has enemies who dislike being reminded of the chapters of Jewish history she represents: David before he was a warrior and Israel before it was united with Jerusalem as its capital. In a general sense, as the sole survivor of the Saulide dynasty with everyone else killed in battle or assassinated, she is a cultural symbol of less violent times. Her father's wars look almost pacifist in comparison to the Davidic legacy left to Solomon. Hence, she is also an outcast and a historical anachronism. Both of the book's narrators know that their opinions on nation building create hostile reactions in the community, but their common stance exemplifies a moral imperative to define themselves comprehensively and to sustain a dual sense of self, enabling cultural criticism to take place. Fischer points out that the reflections in autobiographically figured novels tend to be fragmented somewhat like mosaics rather than be systematically aligned, and we can see this throughout the early chapters of *The Bride Price*. Weil recounts in the short autobiographical chapters significant events and moments from her life and then tropes them—or the conflicts they symbolize—onto her narrator's recollected life. Since the fiction creates an impression of distance, the author's criticism is offered more emphatically and lavishly through Michal's narrating segments than in the shorter, terse autobiographical sections.

The specific event that links the two narrators is presented autobiographically by Weil when she describes her first view of Michelangelo's sculpture of David as a picture in a book. She recalls being introduced to David through an artistic image rather than as a historical and biblical figure. As a teenager, she subordinated the bits of knowledge she had about David to the Renaissance view of "the young David, the beautiful, the unconquerable" (4), the hero created by an Italian, who was also a Christian. It took a visit to the Hague, where she saw a contrasting portrait of David by Rembrandt, for her to confront the double identities through which Jews historically have lived as well as been represented by others. David, portrayed by Rembrandt, the Dutch Renaissance Jew, is a small boy, a musician and singer, playing the harp for King Saul. The binaries that will operate in the course of the book are thereby established: soldier and artist, power and weakness, classical and Hebraic, Christian and Jew, the process of living *in* history and the process of *representing* history through narrative forms. Although Weil recalls wanting as early as in adolescence to be strictly German, the desire itself signified the understanding that she was, at the same time, always Jewish; self-representation using one identifying label without the other was as unsuccessful as attempts to synthesize them.[14] She kept the portraits of David side by side on a bedroom wall where they formed, depending on perspective, either two separate images or two halves of an ostensibly unified whole.

These two portraits, and all they represented for Weil, are amplified in Michal's autobiographical narration and, consequently, have autobiographical significance for Weil. She tropes herself into Michal, tropes her husband presumably into Michal's husband, David, and uses Michal's beliefs and ambivalences toward Jewish culture as representational of her own weak faith. This series of displacements provides intersecting tracks for the author to explore the dilemmas of self and self-representation. Specifically, if she can make the daughter and the wife of Jewish kings find a measure of peace in the Old Testament history of war and mass killings, then perhaps "Grete," by extension, can find a comparable compromise. Many questions surround the figure of Michal, but scholars agree that her representation in Samuel and Chronicles is contradictory, and this makes her a particularly effective autobiographical device. Arguably she is the only woman in the Old Testament who declares openly her passion for a man and who actually chooses the person she will marry.[15] Her boldness, though, is countered by obedience to royal authority, and then her obedience is replaced by her rebellion (when Saul wants David killed, Michal betrays her patronymic lineage and schemes to get David into exile). Her defiance is brief, and, obeying her father, she marries again according to Jewish custom.[16] The author liberally uses the tensions displayed by the biblical Michal that bring up duty, loyalty, and desire. Michal's increasingly conflicted attitudes toward all things Jewish allude transculturally to the author's similar difficulties. How, she wonders, can she reconcile duty toward her grandparents' religion with her dislike of its patriarchal subordination of women? What might allow her to think affirmatively about Jewish culture when all her instincts draw her to German literature and language? As mirrored images, or more accurately images at refracting angles, Michal's struggles illuminate the author's loyalty to Germany but also her hatred of the Nazis, her admission of her genealogy and her bitterness at being held accountable for it.

How could Grete (Weil indirectly asks), surrounded by all things Christian, continue to uphold any part of a Jewish identity, when even Michal, immersed in Jewish life from birth on, challenges it? The answer initially would seem to be that she feels compelled to do so. At least in the first few chapters of the book, neither woman renounces her ancestry even though both of them criticize and resist Jewish tradition, and are both sorely tempted toward outright rejection. Indeed, the intersections of the two stories thematize the necessity of living *with* a sense of duality even if it means living in a perpetual condition of crisis. It suggests that living with the binaries without any pretenses that they can be comfortably united is the only possible course of action. Enacted in the dialogics of *The Bride Price* is thus Weil's argument that the highest level of morally responding to a crisis of belief is to acknowledge and endure it. The moral grounding here is to insist on contradiction as a basic condition of survival ("Survival: the single form of resistance left to me" [35]). This applies both to the crisis of the Second World War and then to the postwar years up to the 1980s, when historical perspectives on the Holocaust triggered widespread public debates in Germany. The purpose of the early autobiographical chapters is to state and reiterate Weil's position while the biblical narrator and intertext illustrate, and more elaborately work through, the intricacies and difficulties of maintaining that position despite public and community pressures to do otherwise.

The result of both narrators' inability to resolve the duality of their crisis identities is estrangement from their communities and inevitable isolation. Michal in old age, representing Weil's view of herself in old age, knows full well that she is an unpopular presence in the community. She has no audience, and despite being a rich source of history and a firsthand witness, she is left only to "tell my story to myself" (8). Although Weil's work continues to find a public audience, the readership is small in Germany and smaller in the United States, where three of her volumes, *My Sister, My Antigone, The Bride Price,* and *Last Trolley from Beethovenstraat* were published in translation respectively in 1984, 1991, and 1997.[17] John Barrett, who translated *Last Trolley from Beethovenstraat* and *The Bride Price*, describes some critics' attitudes in Germany toward Weil as coming close to "antipathy," with one reviewer refusing to consider her writings at all.[18] According to Barrett, other Jewish authors returned after the war also to Austria and East Germany, but it was Weil who was singled out and broadly condemned. Presumably the hostility was directed more at her political stance than simply her geographical return. But Weil does not express a sense of a mutual and *shared* context of crisis with other Jewish German women writing in the postwar period. She needs to be assessed separately and on her own terms, because her writing remains "distinct from both German mainstream literature and most Jewish authors."[19]

In the early chapters written before catastrophic illness interrupted the composing process, Weil transfers her own conflicts over Judaism onto Michal's portrayal of David. Michal loves David passionately in the first three biblical chapters because he is a common man willing to risk his own life to fight Goliath and save his people. Weil problematizes this portrayal through Michal's assertion that her brother, Jonathan, came to his aid (stoning the enemy at the same time) and that David would not have succeeded on his own. Her love is tested when David proves himself blithely willing to kill hundreds of others, albeit Philistine enemies, to provide the bride price for marrying her. It is further tested by his transformation into a military leader who sacrifices his soldiers' lives for causes he declares in the name of God. Details from the Old Testament episodes are embellished throughout the book, but for the most part they are treated in ways that clarify Michal's contradictory attitudes, alternating between idealism and skepticism, between love for David and hostility for the kind of heroism he comes to represent. Regardless of how disapproving she becomes, the young Michal loves David when they are together and misses him when he is in exile. She stays apprised of his military conquests and continues to think about him throughout her second marriage and, in fact, does not consummate the marriage because of her faithfulness to him.[20] Years later, when David is politically secure enough to send for the wife of his early youth, she continues to balance her personal feelings for him with her criticism of his policies and politics. Regardless of the historical realities that Michal witnesses, her potential for rebellion or outright dissidence is kept in check.

CATASTROPHE AND RADICAL RE-IMAGING

Although the Holocaust continues to provide the context for the author's life story, the crisis condition instigated by this larger global crisis is in some sense resolved for the text, when Weil describes herself having a major stroke in the midst of the writing process. With the onset of this illness, crisis is suddenly transformed into catastrophe for the remaining chapters of *The Bride Price*. Weil experienced the profound and catastrophic effects of the stroke, which precipitated a coma. Once she returned to consciousness, she found herself in a state of disorientation and disequilibrium. Unaware that she had suffered a medical and neurological breakdown, she interpreted what was happening in a context ingrained in her, namely that of persecution and, suddenly, persecution in the form of a concentration camp victim. She made the literal situation comprehensible by troping it into a scene of actual incarceration and torture. As represented in the middle of the third autobiographical chapter, there was sufficient evidence for her to confuse her medical condition with the historical one. Extreme hunger, isolation, physical restraints on the body, impairment, weakness, pain, and the difficulties of thinking clearly are all symptoms that Holocaust victims repeat in the narratives of their lives. In the immediacy and blurred perceptions of a stroke victim recovering from a coma, Weil interpreted the nightmare circumstances as if she had been seized by the Nazis and tortured by their supposed doctors. Apparently, she even remarked while still unconscious, "I have Auschwitz." Through this catastrophe, and then in her textual treatment of it, Weil resolves the issue of dual identity in an extreme manner. The paragraphs dramatically show her quite suddenly experiencing her life as a Jew and obviously in complete opposition to anything German. This radical shift in her self-representation is, however, a signal of defeat. As a woman who has prided herself on being politically and personally independent, she is, in the role of a Jew, rendered entirely helpless and victimized: "Not a moment's knowledge of the danger. Although everyone who saw me those days claims I was fighting desperately" (54).

At the crucial juncture that marks the point at which the crisis narrative is transformed into catastrophe, the focus is on a hospital scene in which Weil is being treated as a frail, elderly patient. She assesses the situation for her narrative as it was happening; and as her captors force their will on her in brutal and sadistic ways, the tropological implications of the text alter and expand. Transforming the situation into a torture scene in an anonymous room, Weil dramatically casts herself in the role of victim:

> Then I am fed through with a nasogastric tube. When it is put in, it hurts, I resist, grab the hands of the young doctor and announce threateningly: I'll scream so that they even hear me in the street. Just calm yourself Madame, we're only doing what's necessary, says the doctor, shocked.
>
> Since I don't see the necessity, I experience the procedure as a torture. I try to pull out the tube, then they tie my hands fast to the bed and the torture is complete.
>
> Untie me, I beg every nurse who comes in and each one reacts the same way: *Il dottore ha detto no.*
>
> How I hate them. (55)

Weil does not characterize the experience as something *within* her body that manifests its symptoms outwardly. Instead, the illness is something that happens *to* the body, that takes over the body and physically straps it into confinement. It is crucial that there be an apparent and overwhelming external cause, for the event is what robs the author of all that has grounded her sense of being and self-definition for decades: a body resistant to external threats.

In fact, the above description corresponds to a point Elaine Scarry makes in *The Body in Pain* concerning modes of torture, which bears on Weil's interpretation of her own "torture" scene as the nexus between crisis and catastrophe narrations.[21] Scarry notes that one consistent element of torture is the conversion of objects that signify "normal" reality into the very process of torture. The objects of a room become the instruments that inflict pain. A prisoner is handcuffed to the bed otherwise used for sleep or is bludgeoned with a chair, while other parts of the room—walls, doors, anything—have their usual functions perverted into sadistic ones. Scarry explains these conversions as strategies that cause a dissolution of the world of the victim, and this process is precisely what Weil remembers in her own experience. The conversion is ironic, however, because Weil is not, in fact, interpreting an actual torture. She is literalizing what she imagines to be torture, and then setting into motion a chain of nonliteral, metonymic associations that formulate into a central experience of her life. The "experience" of corporeal torture alters Weil. No longer a survivor of the war who evaded persecution, she tropes herself into being a survivor of Nazi torture. Because she perceives the event while it is occurring as "real," it is both literal and tropological, very belatedly transforming her into a different kind of victim, and a different kind of survivor.

The experience and its effects relate to what we now recognize in literature born of the Holocaust. This is a pervasive sense that the calamity is not an illness that can be cured or a trauma from which victims are able to recover. Langer and other historians stress that literature of the Holocaust is concerned not only with physical destruction but also with "the death of the very idea of the self."[22] In his work Langer often quotes from survivors who testify that during the time of their incarceration they did not feel anything in terms of their own individual subjectivity, just the instinct to stay alive. What happens in *The Bride Price* is that the author has a private experience that stands in for (and, through intersecting literal and tropological perceptions, *is*) a concentration camp memory. This forces her similarly to confront the experience of the demise of the self, and in the chapters written after the catastrophe she presents herself subjectively and conceptually as a different woman. Part of the loss involves realizing that the condition will never change; from the perspective of the victim, this kind of illness is chronic and capable of continuing self-infection. "Now, I am convinced," Weil writes, "that I have every conceivable illness within me and that I will soon break out with all of them" (56). Weighted with questions that we associate with the Holocaust, Weil asks why it is *she* who fell sick, then why *she* survived, and whether *she* will ever be able to say the suffering is behind her.[23] She ponders these questions in terms that we also know to be elements of Holocaust testimony and literature, in memories of atrocities that fail to recede into a distant past. Accordingly, the author characterizes herself as a woman "who has not forgotten, cannot forget, and does not want to forget." Implicitly using her own memory of "torture," she shifts into collective memory and, after citing Auschwitz and the "doctor" Mengele, conveys a death scene that converts an object, a wall, into a weapon of torture, as infants are thrown against it while mothers are forced to watch.

Much closer now to being a "real" survivor—through an imagined experience that is nonetheless real enough almost to kill her—Weil returns to her writing with a far more critical perspective and a radical development in her self-representation. She rejects the idea that contrasting national, religious, and moral traditions can co-exist, at least in terms of her own subjectivity. The damage to her body and her weakened cognitive powers change the way she conceives of herself. Devastated by circumstances and made to feel she has no defenses, she witnesses how the self-image she has held on to for decades comes apart. No longer a resister and a rebel, she is a woman unable to carry out the most basic chores of caring for herself; when she returns to her text, she thinks along a different plane because she has been physically changed and defeated. As a result, her fundamental approach to the writing project also changes. The paragraphs describing the torture that halted the project are brief, with their conciseness subtly emphasizing their importance. They demarcate implicitly the end of one segment of the volume and the beginning of another—namely, the end of Weil's long-held double subjectivity in different traditions and cultures and the start of a gradual distantiation from her Jewish sense of self. The experience that might well have caused her to embrace her own people and history has the opposite effect. Resentment over the illness and bitterness that it could ever happen lead Weil to a rejection of her Jewish subjectivity.

Weil's attempt to turn against her Jewishness is enacted in the final chapters, where the Old Testament is turned back on itself and then *against* itself. The biblical narrative starts to use Michal as a channel through which the author articulates her own rejection of all that symbolically made her vulnerable to the suffering imposed on her body. In fact, the author's most visceral remarks are displaced onto her biblical narrator. Michal's auto/biographical accounting of David, the man she loved and married, also goes back on its original purpose. Initially the material seemed to be a tribute to Jewish literature and culture and David a possible surrogate for Weil's deceased husband, but this is not borne out in the postcatastrophe chapters. The narrative content becomes a condemnation of Jewish history and modes of survival, and David is so broadly censured for his military victories that no resemblance between husbands can possibly be drawn. The catastrophe that occurs *outside* of *The Bride Price* is utilized as the definitive event *inside* the text, which pressures it into becoming more aggressive and offensive than defensive, far removed from the precatastrophe efforts to balance identic contradictions. When the authorial "I" describes her postcatastrophe self as newly aggressive and fearful because of recent suffering, she is imbuing a catastrophe that is strictly personal and affecting only her own body with vast political and historical symbolism. This turning point, and what follows because of it, is performed dialogically through the remaining sections of text and the storytelling modes and patterns. Weil attempts to purge herself of all things Jewish and uses her fictional narrator and protagonist, and all of her intertextual and transhistorical material to make the gesture of rejection as emphatic as she possibly can.

After and because of her medical stroke, Weil manifests her identification with Judaism and hatred of the Nazis into a fierce opposition between Michal and David, who, in the text, is now clearly and provocatively associated with Hitler. Because historically David was Jewish, the narrative must acknowledge him, even in his incarnation as "Hitler," as also Jewish and Michal's animosity in the narrative toward him as reenacting Weil's hostility toward Israel and her Jewish heritage. In the most general sense, the act of storytelling thereby becomes a tool for sabotaging the biblical materials, while the dialogic tensions of the narrating acts and narrated stories function as arguments to counteract the earlier arguments.[24] Dagmar C. G. Lorenz suggests this reversal, and her summary of David, attributed to Michal's changing descriptions of him, points to his portrayal as an oxymoronic coupling of the nationalism of the Jewish state with Hitler's Aryan ambitions: "The David presented in Weil's novel is a calculating opportunist and a mass murderer: his sanctimonious speeches show him to be a master of crowd manipulation, and his character traits combine the seducer's sexual allure and the tyrant's brutality. He possesses the intense appeal of a sex symbol, but his frigidity rules out sustained intimacy with him—these very traits have been attributed to Hitler. By way of a Jewish text, Weil probes the roots of genocide, ethnocentrism, and the domination of women."[25] Lorenz takes this analysis even further; Weil's pairing of the two leaders is a strategy to assert that Jewish patriarchal structures must share responsibility for past and present imperialism and genocide and, indeed, that nazism, "rather than beginning in nineteenth-century Germany, started among Jews at the time of David."[26]

The effect of the catastrophe on the narrative is profound ironic reversal. Just when Weil has identified most strongly with victims of the Holocaust and blamed her German heritage, the resulting transformations in the biblical text construct the opposite position from what we would expect. They radicalize Weil into effectively declaring herself "German, only German." Stressing the violence and betrayals that are part of the Old Testament accounts, Michal's memories portray the ambition, the hunger for power, the subjugation of women, and internecine rivalries as elements motivating and corrupting patriarchal rule. A large part of the catastrophe narration recounts the story of David's children by wives other than Michal, who fought and destroyed one another. The account of Tamar, raped by her half-brother, Amnon, exposes how David blindly ruins his daughter in order to appease his son. According to Michal, because David rationalizes the tragedy by saying that Tamar may be partly to blame, he is complicit in her subsequent madness and then in her brother Absalom's act of revenge in killing Amnon. (Michal embellishes the biblical account, saying that Absalom kills not just Amnon but all of the king's sons). Eventually when Absalom gathers military forces against David, loses the battle, and is killed, David's lamentations, handed down through the millennia, fail to gloss over the brutality—the acts of fratricide and intrafamily killings—that made them necessary. Increasingly in this second discourse of *The Bride Price* the biblical intertext is used subversively to undermine its own foundations. The highlighted events are consistently those that end badly and show the evolution of Israel as the product of human slaughter, with the deaths of members of the royal family mirroring the countless numbers of commoners and soldiers who also die. Refracting back to the author's contemporary story, to be "only German" is, by implication, to take a stand against Jewish violence for begetting more violence in its own population and others. The narrator takes her stand and refuses to side with Israel. She critiques the Old Testament for rationalizing a history of crimes committed for a Jewish homeland and reimages herself as decidedly not Jewish: "Oh, if I could only say: I'm a Jew. Jews don't blow things up. But they do. Perhaps this land, promised to them by God, has always made them fighters" (173).

Operating as a second ideological argument for the author, Michal's negative portrait of David reflects tropologically on Weil's feelings on Jewish militarism. The memories no longer center on Michal's passion for David but follow the major Old Testament episodes of the evolution of the Davidic dynasty with a deliberate intent to dismantle them. Whereas 1 Chronicles stresses that David's military triumphs are sacralized by God's intentions for a divinely sanctioned kingdom, Michal has far more radical opinions on the bond between God and Israel. She focuses on the conspiracies and the carnage and doubts the legitimacy of a God that would allow these to take place for any reason whatsoever. After David consolidates power and unites the tribes of Judah, he sends for Michal, who, in the presence of his other wives, observes her husband firsthand after many years.[27] These postcatastrophe chapters elaborate on the brief references to Michal in Samuel and Chronicles, and they endow her with a new role: acerbic commentator on David's ascendance to power. He wars against the Philistines whom he has not already vanquished and makes Hebron his base of operations. When ready to relocate the capital of a united Israel in Jerusalem, he overtakes the city and kills the Jebusites who live there. These are a people that David says are "hostile to us, live there, but," as he insists, "on what their claim to it is based is not known to me. It can be taken from them; even if it will not be easy" (92), eerily alluding to contemporary Israeli and Palestinian animosities. From her vantage point, Michal severely judges her husband as a conqueror no different from other tyrants in history who wage battles and assassinate enemies and former allies, all the while hypocritically invoking God's will. Physically weakened by age, Michal, as Weil creates her, maintains all her intellectual acuity and suffers because she comprehends the larger picture of regional, nationalist, and religious wars. Overwhelmed by memories of "the worst that [she] experienced with David," on one level she certainly has come to despise her long-dead husband. Yet, on other levels, David is integral to her own subjective processes and history, and regardless of how reprehensible she now finds him, Michal still remains preoccupied with memories of him. Always working crosswise through her secondary narrator's memories and assessments, Weil distributes her own contentious political views through voices and subjects that will carry more legitimacy than she as viably and acceptably Jewish. The final result is that the expressed opinions appear somewhat less volatile than they otherwise would, and because the surrogate speaker has a certain amount of latitude, the opinions ultimately command attention.

Nearly all the autobiographical chapters written after Weil's catastrophic and sudden illness work to deconstruct the complexities of identity down to a single unitary German self-representation. As soon as the narrative picks up again, it embarks on this project by establishing the author's legitimacy as a German, very specifically as to how she schemed in order to obtain identity documents right after the war, which allowed entry back into Germany. In her own voice, Weil defends the German point of view, arguing that the Nazis did not have a monopoly on killing. To readers who would still accuse her of betraying millions of victims, including, we have to assume, her husband, she is defiant: "Don't tell me you would suffer from the atrocities just as I do [or don't]. You have not lived through the horror year by year, day by day, awake and asleep. In Claude Lanzmann's film Shoah a survivor of the Warsaw ghetto says, 'If you could lick my heart you would be poisoned'" (126). This retort implies that the author has enough poison left in her to kill anyone she wishes; but in contrast to Jews who were caught in the Warsaw ghetto, she should not have had the analogous experience that left her in this state.

The argument for a unitary German identity becomes even more explicit as she disclaims anything that might have qualified her for this kind of suffering. Still in her own voice, she adopts two standards for ascertaining whether someone is Jewish. First, one has to believe in the God "invented by the Jews," and, second, one needs to share an emotional bond with contemporary Israel. The reasoning is obviously flawed, since long before Weil formulates these criteria, it is evident that she does not meet either one of them. She goes on to show in the intertext a similar lapsing of belief in Michal, rewriting Michal's stance far beyond anything the Old Testament story offers or even implies. To correlate with her own rejection of Judaism, Weil has the quintessential Jewish daughter and wife express profound skepticism in God and has her challenge the rationale of Israel as David's created nation along with the methods used to establish it. The re-creation of Grete Weil into a German thus works largely because of the Jewish intertext and narrator, both reversing initial arguments into biographical and cultural critiques.

In the closing pages of the book, Weil attempts to revitalize the spirit of the earlier chapters by describing a brief visit she made to Israel. Through that description she produces a profound acknowledgment of her Jewishness, which might have counterbalanced, were it convincing, the hostility toward her heritage engendered in the narrative through the tropological effects of her stroke. In this section Weil identifies her instinctive love of Israel's landscape with the identification she has built up with Michal as she has imagined her in the biblical discourse. Simultaneously, she also acknowledges an affiliation with other elderly Jewish women visiting Israel as a sort of pilgrimage, just as she presents herself doing in the autobiographical text. In both cases, rather than reasserting a connection to her Jewish heritage, Weil only succeeds in confirming her distance from it. She is forced to concede that while she is enamored of Israel's topographical beauty, the country is "too foreign" for her to maintain a lasting relationship with it. More emphatically, in the process of acknowledging resemblance between herself and the other aging, middle-class visitors, she again sees herself suffering because she is Jewish. She narrates her response to these women in much the same way she describes her stroke and coma, as physical aversion overtaking her in the form of a "shock." The shock again renders itself tropologically in the text as direct persecution by the Nazis ("that any moment the SS will come marching in and take us all away"). As such, it triggers a dramatic reliving of the feelings of victimization in relation to her Jewishness that she has always despised: "The shock lasts throughout the whole sleepless night, only the next morning does the beauty of the desert drive it away" (171). Weil's disproportionate response to a group of aging tourists is heavily ironic. The emotions necessary to a reidentification with her Jewishness are precisely the ones she does not want to have and believes she was never meant to have. Any relation to Israel must finally be fleeting, an effect of the power of the landscape rather than a bond with its inhabitants or even just a vague connection with other tourists. The effort to resituate herself within a Jewish framework is unlikely ever to succeed, and Weil admits to the difficulty, saying, "I belong there, I don't belong there" (171).[28]

Continuing to perform at least the rhetoric of a dual subjectivity, Weil writes both of her narrators at the end of *The Bride Price* returning to their previously held (then previously rejected) balanced stance toward David and what he represents. Weil's earlier adolescent view of David as equally heroic and vulnerable comes up now as the narrator refers back to Michelangelo's and Rembrandt's contrasting representations and comes down slightly in favor of Rembrandt's gentle version, though without completely rejecting the classical one. In corresponding fashion, the author has Michal, in the last biblical chapter, rearticulate her love for David rather than dwell on his willingness to murder. She goes so far as to recount a meeting soon before he died, when David played on his harp and carried her "to unimagined heights as once long ago. As beautifully as no other can" (179). With Michal's emotions for and against David momentarily stable in this closing part of the text, the implication is that a reconciliatory gesture and identic balancing act may again be possible. For most readers, though, the Old Testament has been used too powerfully as an argument against itself for either one of the narrating widows to recover an equilibrium of contrasting points of views and ideological commitments. The evidence of the text, despite a rhetoric of moderation and conciliation, is too removed from the portraits of these women developing ever since the recounting of Weil's medical catastrophe. At this point in *The Bride Price* the narrator's self-imaging is too extreme, too radical a maneuver, in view of all the preceding images, to be feasible.

To assess *The Bride Price* primarily in the context of late-twentieth-century Germany means that the terms "Jewish," "Christian," and "German" must be defined very carefully, and throughout the book the definitions undergo slippage. Appearing in West Germany during the years of the "Historians' Debate," when questions on the cultural status and representations of the Nazi period were being argued over in both the popular press and academic community, *The Bride Price* came under fire for its volatile assertions."[29] But since the book was translated into English and published in the United States in the aftermath of Germany's reunification (and a new set of public debates in Germany), we are able to see *The Bride Price* through our own cultural lens, which allows more fluid identity affiliations within a single nation-state. Our own national discussions on the shifting roles of religion, race, ethnicity, gender, and borderlines help us in examining Weil's colliding politics and subjectivity without simply calling them objectionable or out of hand. From a life writing perspective and in a comparative study such as this one, the book's generic shifts enact the author's intellectual and emotional vacillations and in many ways bring *The Bride Prince* into conjunction with other women's self-representations driven by crises and catastrophes. The modes of displacement and distantiation through which the text evolves allow the author to explore the tensions of a lifetime through other characters' lives, filling in the ostensible biographical details with autobiographical allusions. *The Bride Price* is much like other books that, in responding to excessive or unimaginable conditions, adopt extreme counterpositions.

Considering the elaborate political and narrational maneuvering that goes on, it is hardly surprising that in the final autobiographical chapter Weil, in her own voice, tacitly acknowledges the failure of integrating Judaism into a self-image that allows her sometimes to despise her religion. Her closing self-portrait is of a very old woman still writing but with nothing left to say, and with no one desiring to hear it. With the process of recounting her ideological ambivalences exhausted, she admits "it is getting to be time for me, Grete, to depart from this story" (182). Declaring her life nearly over and her endurance exhausted, she no longer has any conflict, guilt, or anger to express, only an obsession with the manner of her dying: "Like Michal's life, my life is also over. Not much more will happen beyond the one thing about which I, who have liked reporting about everything, will no longer be able to report: my own death" (183). In effect, the narrator is deleting herself from the text through an image that, given all the images and counterimages, is perhaps the most radical self-image of all. It is a portrait possessing an outer frame but with almost nothing remaining of its central female subject. Moving herself out from the story, Weil becomes the vanishing point of her own autobiographically figured fiction. Other women who write in dire circumstances make efforts to resist being victimized and work to become active agents of resistance and sometimes of social change. In addition, they generally locate themselves empathetically within a supportive community of other survivors and produce manuscripts that anticipate some vision of a future. The last image of Weil's self-representation, however, is confined to one woman's isolated body. The efforts toward community and toward a capacious self-understanding capable of absorbing competing beliefs have been reduced to rhetorical exercises. Concentrating on this single outline of herself—an aged body nearing extinction and about to slip out of the frame—the narrator reformats her life according to the very narrowest of terms, a death watch. Because loss of consciousness is always imminent, survival is experienced as a disaster about to happen; survival is the last ironic reversal, for it becomes the catastrophe, rather than a response to catastrophe.

As literal as an experience defined only by the body's materiality may be, it is also the trope of all *The Bride Price*'s tropes. A life based on *imagining* that death is about to strike creates a *real* existence, which nonetheless metaphorizes the real existence of living as a prisoner about to be tortured or killed. Whatever the distance between Weil, the woman who evaded the Nazis, and the autobiographical narrator that represents her, the flesh-and-blood woman lived much longer than the narrator anticipated. If she lived in any way similar to what her narrator describes, the time must have seemed endless. Over a decade later, on May 14, 1999, Grete Weil died at the age of ninety-four in Germany, "the land of [her] murderers, the land of [her] language."

Autobiographical Discourse as Biographical Tribute

Isabel Allende's *Paula*

I SABEL ALLENDE DID NOT START to write novels until she was almost forty years old. She composed a letter to her grandfather as he was dying in Chile in 1981, which she continued after his death and expanded into *The House of the Spirits*.[1] In less than a decade Allende established a reputation as a major writer of fiction, publishing four novels—*The House of the Spirits, Of Love and Shadows, Eva Luna,* and *The Infinite Plan,* and the collection *Stories of Eva Luna*—between 1982 and 1991.[2] These works were translated widely, sold millions of copies, and two of them, *The House of the Spirits* and *Of Love and Shadows,* were made into films in the 1990s. When asked by interviewers in May 1991 about forthcoming projects, Allende responded that she had many ideas for other volumes of fiction and anticipated few obstacles to her productivity.[3] She was eager to write, no longer occupied with the personal, career, and political activities of her earlier years. In Chile she had written primarily for magazines and television. Going into self-imposed exile after Pinochet's military coup in 1973, she had raised her children in Venezuela while working as a journalist and school administrator. Allende also told interviewers in May 1991 that because she did not publish her first novel until her middle years, her chief problem was time: "There are so many things that I want to write about, so many stories that I want to tell."[4]

The book that Allende began approximately eight months after this interview shows how mistaken she was in thinking that the pressure of time would be the most serious obstacle to her career as a fiction writer. She could never have anticipated the catastrophe that devastated her family and irreversibly changed the course of their lives. In December 1991 her twenty-seven-year-old daughter, Paula, became extremely ill and fell into a coma. She remained in this state for several months in a Madrid hospital and then was moved to her mother's home in California. Paula died in December 1992, one year after the onset of the coma. According to Allende, her daughter had learned earlier that she had the genetic disorder known as porphyria but believed that she was successful in managing it.[5] When Allende arrived in Madrid to launch the publication of *The Infinite Plan,* she found Paula suffering presumably with the flu. Her condition worsened, however, and she soon had to be rushed to the hospital. Allende recounts that just after the two of them exchanged words of love, "true horror was unleashed" (20). Her daughter's body convulsed in a series of violent spasms. Looking blank but directly at her mother, Paula sank into a coma and, as Allende recalls, "From that moment life stopped for you. And for me" (21). Written from January 1992 through December 1992, *Paula* is the literary product of this catastrophe.[6]

Unlike the other catastrophes that this study examines, Paula's illness is the only event that was entirely personal and not seen as part of a larger crisis. Allende states that even though she knew her daughter had inherited the disorder, she did not consider Paula to be living in a medical crisis situation. To the extent that her text describes Paula's young adulthood, it presents these years as uneventful and unburdened by medical concerns and certainly without the oppressive political conditions that Allende experienced when she was the same age. Paula simply finished her schooling and then fell in love. After marrying, she and her husband settled down and worked in Madrid. Nor are there passages to suggest that either she or her mother harbored fears that the genetic condition would lead to an impending catastrophe. In 1991 when Paula was beginning to sense that something was wrong, Allende associated the symptoms with depression or fatigue, never with porphyria. From her perspective, the sudden attack seemed to emerge without any cause and in the absence of a defining context. For a parent such as Allende, who describes herself as challenging boundaries and always seeking larger contexts of experience, Paula's medical disaster—occurring in isolation and not given quick, appropriate treatment—was inexplicable. [7]

Paula is comprised of two extensive narrative segments, each one following Allende's perceptions of the illness as it progresses, and an epilogue, written after Paula's death. Parts 1 and 2, which are contemporaneous with the events they describe, rely on different modes of narration to respond to Paula's illness. Part 1, dated and entitled "December 1991 to May 1992," begins soon after Paula loses consciousness and continues over the next few months. Composed as a letter directly *to* Paula, which Allende expects to present her with after the illness is over, Part 1 develops as a catastrophe narrative. Its immediate drama is intense and heartbreaking, and the possibility that Paula might, at any time, regain consciousness remains an active expectation. Allende also contends throughout this segment that Paula is aware of her mother's commentaries. In her role as author, Allende therefore writes as if her work might literally revive Paula: "On this January 8, 1992, I am writing you, Paula, to bring you back to life" (10). Part 2, dated "May to December 1992," narrates what takes place after Paula is moved to her mother's home in California. Although this segment is also contemporaneous with the illness, its text is not addressed to Paula but to a public readership. Describing Paula's unchanging comatose state, Part 2 implicitly concedes that the patient is not going to recover and will never be able to read the text. The writing thus evolves into a crisis narrative. The emotions remain powerful, but the guiding belief that Paula will awaken turns largely into resignation. The narrative patterns become more conventional and their tone elegiac. Only in the epilogue, entitled "Christmas 1992," does Allende know for certain that Paula does not survive the ordeal, for she dies in early December.[8] The epilogue contains a final narrative shift in order to portray Paula's death. Allende's voice severs the present-tense relationship between mother and daughter that characterizes parts 1 and 2 and describes Paula in her last hours from a strictly retrospective stance.

   Paula is a biographical text with a minimum of biographical content. It purposely avoids becoming a biography, at least in the conventional sense, because its author insists on not providing the full retrospective life story of her subject. Allende instead wants to safeguard most of Paula's history for Paula herself someday, perhaps, to use as her own *autobiographical* material.[9] To claim her daughter's story, even in the role of a biographer, would mean giving up and conceding that Paula will never take possession of the history of her own life. Allende is thereby left with a gap between intentionality and genre that she tries to close, partly by staying fixed on Paula in her present condition. Focused on a single illness, she produces writing as biopathography, to reflect Allende's perspective and offer a version of Paula from the outside.[10] The assumption is that when Paula revives, she will have access to this version of herself and find it useful, for she will not have any memory of it. Until then, Allende respects the boundaries of her subject's precatastrophe life. Allende's purpose calls for giving Paula the letter composed in the interval of time during which she had crossed the threshold between life and death.

Because Allende wants to protect the details of Paula's life story while she also feels compelled to write, her text moves beyond its limited biographical content to explore other subjects and discourses. It adopts an autobiographical mode, and this brings ethical consequences along with it. The writer is left to give her ostensible subject a truncated historical treatment, creating tension between Allende's biographical intentions and her nonbiographical content. So by acting on her feelings of responsibility to her daughter, the author neglects her subject and centers on herself. Paul John Eakin examines the difficulties in judging what is, or is not, responsible subject matter in life writing texts, especially as we have come to reject the philosophical notion of the self as "free-standing" for one that is relational and interdependent. In *How Our Lives Become Stories* he observes there is no escaping the ethical and privacy issues raised when an author asks, "What is right and fair for me to write about someone else?"[11] Responding to this question, Allende protects her daughter's privacy but creates a different problem, as if she does not adequately consider the complementary question, "What is right and fair for me to write about myself?" By focusing on her own history, she leaves herself open to accusations of both egotism and exploitation, and these show up in the early reviews of *Paula*. Doris Grumbach suggests that if the book is principally an autobiography, there is too much of Paula. There is too much, Grumbach writes, because the daughter is a literary device, not a subject in her own right, and merely a springboard for the mother's autobiography.[12] Yet Suzanne Ruta sees *Paula* philosophically and conceptually as a biographical text and argues in this case that there is too little material on Paula.[13] Ruta says that she "strains to know Paula better." She implies that the protective silence around Paula gives Allende license to stress "the distance between herself and Paula—the confident survivor [from] the stricken young woman." The question, then, of how to make literary use of others' biographical material is unsettling in this instance. It involves our cultural expectations of mother-daughter relationality, which are especially acute here because the daughter is so vulnerable.[14] In other words, must we view the mother's abounding recollections and rich autobiographical narrative against the daughter's physical incapacitation and

Isabel Allende. © *Miriam Berkley*

silence? How do we judge a lavish display of maternal self-representation under the rubric of biographical writing?[15]

My approach to the question of autobiographical ethics is to view the autobiographical sections as a substitutive discourse. This means that I do not examine the biographical and autobiographical sections in competition or in ethical conflict with each other. Instead, I consider the autobiographical material as an embedded discourse, passages set inside of, and fully determined by, the biographical situation and the project's biographical goals. The autobiographical sections, which occupy the empty spaces of the biographical text, exist because of the restrictions Allende imposes on her content and the way she breaks the impasse of composing a biographical text without appropriating biographical material. This means that the more the embedded autobiography develops, the less it is likely that Paula will ever articulate her own life story. Allende's history is thus infected, and always diminished, by the irony that allows it to progress. As the author chronologically develops her own story, we realize that she will fail to accomplish what is far more important to her. She will not have the choice between two alternatives. The first would be to change the narrative into a biographical text, whose climax is her subject's awakening and whose denouement is her gradual recovery. The second would be simply to abort the text once its raison d'être disappears.

Throughout this chapter I examine the tropological tensions of Paula's life writing discourses in the context of the book as a biographical tribute. I consider the ethics of narrative appropriation and self-assertion while following the evolution of its segments responding to Paula through different stages of her condition. From my own perspective, Allende makes certain that Paula infuses Paula because her unique drama prevents any other story from becoming a freestanding segment or even achieving a central position. Most important in recognizing Allende's narrative relationship to Paula is the way that the text becomes subject to Paula's authority. On the one hand, as Paula falls more deeply into a coma, her position as a passive biographical subject is confirmed. On the other hand, Allende's narrator reveals her to be an active agent of the text, governing its momentum and affecting its composition. Despite the annihilating effects of porphyria, Paula is given—because of a letter she wrote to her mother, which her mother finally reads—total control over Allende's book and, crucially, over her own life and death. It is, very dramatically, the biographical subject who decides how and when Paula will conclude.

CATASTROPHE NARRATION AS BIOGRAPHICAL STORYTELLING

According to Linda Wagner-Martin, a biographer's most difficult task lies in conceptualizing the project. This is especially the case with biographies that chronicle women whose lives do not conform to the white male success story. Wagner-Martin demonstrates in *Telling Women's Lives* how feminist biographers have used innovative concepts in presenting their subjects as well as experienced critical and public resistance after their books were published.[16] Some of these biographers have written on the critical reception and legal resistance that they encountered. The best known examples are Diane Wood Middlebrook on the right-to-privacy issues pertaining to her biography of Anne Sexton and Wagner-Martin and Janet Malcolm, each recounting the legal convolutions in dealing with the Sylvia Plath Estate.[17] Sparked by Malcolm's description in her 1993 *New Yorker* essay, "The Silent Woman," of the biographer as a professional burglar, Phyllis Rose admits to having misgivings after spending decades on her biographies of Virginia Woolf, Josephine Baker, and the Victorian wives whom she covers in *Parallel Lives*. She calls herself a "burned-out biographer" who knows full well "that at the heart of the biographer's motivation is some act of personal appropriation, some sort of psychic exploitation." Every biographer "in a different way exploits his or her own subject," and "some of us, perhaps too aware of the morally tenuous nature of our enterprise, will pay the price of our art in guilt."[18]

The author's relationship to her subject, questions of appropriation and interpretation, the concept underlying the biography, and what Middlebrook calls the "excruciating particulars of real choices" in balancing the interests of all the different parties influence the project conceptually and pragmatically.[19] But Allende's challenge, even without legal dimensions, was extreme. Few writers have the uncommon task of generating a biography without featuring the biographical subject, especially when the subject is one's daughter and especially when the daughter is suspended between life and death. Paula's catastrophe does not lend itself to a particular narrative form and makes conceptualizing a manageable framework extremely difficult. A retrospective structure would appear to be eulogistic before the fact, and an ongoing dialogue would need active collaboration, such as Sandra Butler's and Barbara Rosenblum's shared discourse in *Cancer in Two Voices*. A sustained biopathography would be unsuitable in the context of the subject's recovery and the writer's expectations for her recovery. Generated for the most part before the catastrophe is resolved, the material has to reflect the highly contingent, tenuous nature of all the contributing factors. In particular, it reflects the fact that while most biographers at least have the certainty of a narrative to be told, Allende has no legitimate story to tell; what eventually takes place could very well render the text incomplete, ethically problematic, or irrelevant if the subject suddenly revives.

Allende's spiritual beliefs, which fuel *The House of the Spirits* and all of her subsequent fiction, create difficulties for a life writing project. The most problematic of these is Allende's reluctance to express pessimism and her refusal to dwell on the fatalistic views of other people who come in contact with Paula. Characterizing her spirituality as a form of sentience of the universality among all things, living or dead, Allende explained to an interviewer: "I believe that there is a spirit, a spirit of life in everything that surrounds me—in plants, animals, people, towns, in the air, in the water, everything. And, in a way, like the ancient Indians, I try to be in touch with that. I have the feeling that if I damage anything that surrounds me, it will come back to me. So I am very careful about the world that surrounds me and the people that are around me."[20] Guided by these correspondences, Allende's vision for her book is thereby limited. Saying too much and venting the worst of her fears could have ill-fated effects. Midway through *Paula* she avers, "Now I am more careful about what I write, because I have found out that although something is not true today, it may be true tomorrow" (174). There is too much she does not know about Paula's illness and too little that daughter and mother can share for her writing to be incautious and somehow be connected to the outcome she most dreads.

More than most biographies, including the ones that Wagner-Martin covers in *Telling Women's Lives*, Allende's work brings into play Elaine Scarry's ideas on experiences that are unshareable and inexpressible.[21] To be sure, in *The Body in Pain* Scarry focuses on conscious physical pain, which is a state of heightened sensitivity, while coma is the absence of consciousness and therefore the absence of pain. But from the standpoint of witnesses, the two afflictions have a number of similar effects and symptoms, and this is where Scarry's analysis of the relation between language and pain is especially relevant. What takes place inside of the sufferer's body cannot be shared, for it "has no referential content. It is not *of* or *for* anything. It is precisely because it takes no object that it . . . resists objectification in language." The verbal inexpressibility of both conditions is particularly striking as a symptom that "comes unsharably into our midst as at once that which cannot be denied and that which cannot be confirmed."[22] Indicating this is a problem common to all languages, Scarry looks at the political and perceptual complications of pain. It is, however, the latter complication that connects her discussion to Allende's work. *Paula* exposes the unbridgeable distance between the biographer and her subject and shows its narrator trying to anchor her portrayal onto something capable of embodying and conveying a sense of Paula's "aliveness." As a biographical evocation and tribute and especially as a work-in-progress vulnerable to external changes, the book is intended to mediate between the two women and to close the hiatus in a performative and symbolic sense, if not in actuality. Paula may not be in pain, but neither the doctors' opinions nor the machines tracing the rhythms of her body translate the essence of coma into a shareable, comprehensible terminology. Even victims who survive the experience cannot do this, since a comatose state precludes consciousness. Scarry examines acts of representation linked to inexpressible conditions, making two observations especially important for *Paula*. Art that is made because of these conditions is weighted with ethical consequences and, by necessity, also bears an "analogical" relation to the event it represents. The event *must* be shown as something else, because its deepest elements are unfathomable to others. In terms of the thesis of this study, catastrophes trigger forms of representation that incorporate tropological and substitutive discourses. However, the distance between subject and referents signals the dire qualities of the event rather than a diminishing of life writing intentionality.

The early part of the book carries out its biographical function by including present-time events of which the subject has no knowledge. These passages directly address Paula as "you" and narratively perform Allende's hope that there is a spiritual or sentient connection that enables Paula to receive the story. Contrary to the doctors, Allende believes Paula can perceive certain sounds and wants her, also, to realize this: "I know you hear because you flinch at the sound of metal on metal." Yet she does not know whether Paula's damaged brain, to any small extent, can translate sound into signifying content (34). The private nature of these second-person passages is confirmed by the details Allende chooses in order to keep Paula informed on the condition of the porphyria: "You have no control over your body; you cannot move yourself and you suffer violent spasms like electric shocks. In one way I am grateful for your state of complete innocence; it would be much worse if you understood how ill you are" (127). Whatever other directions the narrative takes, it returns to this basic, unchanging state of Paula in a coma. The return is always dramatic, accomplished through what Gérard Genette identifies as simultaneous narration.[23] This technique eliminates the temporal space between the activity of narrating and the events or conditions being described. The material conveyed in this manner bears the anxieties of present time but not the ethical weight of possible appropriation; if not committed to narrative form, it will be lost.

In the process of conveying her observations to Paula, Allende concentrates on details that will establish a close relationality between mother and daughter. The present-time stories that she wants Paula to sense or in some way hear could temper the absolute solitude of her daughter's state, for they assume as well as perform the capacity to move beyond the limits of their individual physical and psychic states. Indeed, the opening words of the book, "Listen, Paula. I am going to tell you a story, so that when you wake up you will not feel so lost," demand not only that she hear but that she store away—in the memory by all rational accounts she does not have—the family accounts that follow. Even the descriptions addressed to Paula of the terrible state of her health are phrased so as to counteract the isolating effects of the coma and make the text rhetorically perform as if those effects do not entirely exist. The descriptions also tend to show both women simultaneously, with Allende watching over her daughter and the two of them symbolically joined, rather than showing just Paula: "I bend down to you, and sometimes I dislodge some cable and an alarm sounds. I examine you inch by inch, observe the numbers and lines on the screens, the entries in the open book on a table at the foot of your bed.... I place my hands on your head and your breast and try to transmit health and energy" (79–80). As remote as Paula may be, Allende draws her into intimate contact, explaining, "By trial and error I am learning to care for you; at first the opening in your throat, the tubes and probes, horrified me, but I'm used to them now; I can bathe you and change your bedding without help" (127). Comments such as this throughout part 1 confirm the empathetic bond while continuing to provide details of the biographical portrait.

Many parts of the simultaneous narration are intended to engage Paula, to prod her into consciousness and involve her in the biographical process that is taking place without her consent. Though biography is often viewed as a single-voiced narrative, Allende is fighting to make it double-voiced. Langness and Frank, who describe biography from an ethnographic perspective, invoke the phrase "voices in harmony." This is exactly what Allende wants. Instead of describing just her own ruminations, she embraces the chance to incorporate another voice into her prose and, as Langness and Frank explain, to rely "as much as possible on the subject's own expressive statements and deeds as the point of departure for interpretation."[24] She tries to activate the missing voice by posing questions to Paula. Some of them plead for subjective information: "What do you want to teach us, Paula?" (73). "Will you get well, Paula?" "What goes through your thoughts?" "Do you want to live, Paula?" "Do you want to die?" (34). Other questions are so open ended they are meant to provoke Paula into reacting: "Where are you wandering, Paula?" "How will you be when you wake up? Will you be the same woman, or will we be like strangers and have to learn to know one another all over again? Will you have your memory, or will I need to sit patiently and relate the entire story of your twenty-eight years and my forty-nine?" (7). "Will you know I am your mother when you wake, Paula?" (75). Still other questions, and their answers, are reported *to* her so that she can know what other persons are claiming about her prognosis. A close friend of her mother, a physician, arrives from Caracas and examines the patient. Allende questions him:

> "Tell me the truth, then. Do you think she might die?"
> "I do," he replied after a long pause.
> "Might she stay in the coma for a long time?"
> "I hope not, but it is a possibility."
> "And if she never wakes again . . . ?" We stood silently beneath
>   the rain. (79)

Allende records this foreboding dialogue but not from a biographer's urge to report all accessible information. She hopes that Paula, like her own grandmother and some of the women she portrays in her novels, has extrasensory abilities. If these abilities enable her to sense what her mother is writing, then this recorded conversation could galvanize Paula to challenge its pessimistic conclusion.

Other storytelling strategies in the simultaneous narration are meant to lure Paula back, reminding her that a supportive network of husband, family, and friends awaits her return. Paula's husband of one year, Ernesto, is her closest spiritual lifeline. "He tells us he is in contact with your soul, that you can hear him, that you have feelings and emotions, that you are not a vegetable as the machines you are connected to attest. . . . When he takes your hand the readings on the screens change" (82). When Allende begins to recount the story of Paula's great grandparents, she works to centralize Paula within the family circle. The goal is to demonstrate that she is more here, with family, than in a place where they cannot reach her. She must see herself in the photograph of her great-grandfather, her grandmother, and mother, pregnant with Paula's younger brother. "Look, Paula, this is Tata's picture. That's you," her mother says, pointing to the three-year-old child in the middle of the family unit. As the days pass, she assures Paula of her family's attention and love. Allende and her own mother live nearby, rise before the sun does, and arrive early at the hospital. They spend most of each day in "the corridor of lost steps," their name for the hallway just outside the hospital room. Allowed just two visits a day for the first few weeks, they remain as close to Paula as they can for as long as they can: "At least we are not alone, we are three" (94).

In addition to the stories that comprise the simultaneous narrative, Allende, in the role of biographer, also has some past-tense stories that carry no risk of appropriating Paula's life history. There is no risk because the time span for this retrospective material extends back only to the start of the coma. Any episode between that point and her current narrating time is information that Paula lacks and upon awakening will remember little or nothing about. The analogy between the biographer and the burglar is not applicable in any way; there is no possibility of what Malcolm refers to as "voyeurism" or what Rose calls "psychic exploitation."[25] In fact, if Paula is ever to understand this catastrophic period, she will want first-hand access to it, requiring her mother to function as her primary source. The biographer's ethical responsibility in this case is clearly to share what she knows and has witnessed, as long as she limits it to the very recent past tense. As a result, events of this limited, retrospective narration tend to be dramas of Paula's medical emergencies. Each of these, a catastrophe unto itself, takes place within the larger catastrophe of the coma. The narrator is unable to give complete treatment to the larger problem but can be extremely detailed with the retrospective events. From her enunciating position, she knows that Paula has survived each of them.

When Paula withstands an immediate new threat to her life, Allende can use the event as an exemplary tale of courage and victory. She then directs her account right back at Paula as a means of encouraging her to keep trying to cross the threshold into consciousness. Since each new catastrophe is capable of sending Paula deeper into the coma, Allende's presentation is fraught with emotion: "Death laid its hands on you Monday, Paula. It came and pointed to you, but found itself face to face with your mother and grandmother and, for now, has backed off. It is not defeated, and is still circling around, grumbling, in its swirl of dark rags and clicking bones." She describes the attack for Paula's benefit:

> We could hear a terrifying rumble from your chest and see the whites of your eyes through a slit between your eyelids. Suddenly your blood pressure plummeted almost to zero and the alarms on the monitors sounded and the room filled with people, all working so hard around you that they forgot about us, and that was how we came to be present when your soul escaped your body, as they injected drugs and administered more oxygen and tried to make your exhausted heart start beating again. . . . The bodies of the people attending you blocked our view, but your anguish and the triumphant breath of Death were all too clear. (92)

Because the passage personifies death into the form a predator, mother and grandmother have a visible, material enemy to conquer, and this implies that the struggle to defy death will continue on a more level battlefield. Regardless of what the physicians think happened during the episode, the narrated version develops into a parable of female strength allied with preternatural forces. The mother and grandmother need only to hear one physician say that nothing further can be done and another one actually proclaim, "She's gone," for the two women to be presented in the act of marshaling their own aggressive, offensive strategy:

> Then I felt my mother's hand in mine, pulling me forward, and we walked to your bedside and without a single tear we offered you the entire reservoir of our energy, all the health and strength of our most recondite genes from Basque sailors and indomitable American Indians and in silence we invoked all the gods known and yet to be known, and the beneficent spirits of our ancestors, and the most formidable forces of life to race to your rescue. Our unvoiced wail was so intense that from fifty kilometers away Ernesto heard it, clear as a bell; he knew that you were on the edge of the abyss and started immediately for the hospital. In the meantime, the air around your bed was frozen and time was suspended, but when the clock again began to mark the seconds, Death had lost. (93)

As Allende presents this event, it is a triumph in which the previous storytelling elements culminate. It incorporates the power of supportive family members, a spiritual telepathy, the salutary effects of voices in harmony, a profound, unexplainable relationality, and a felt sentience among persons who are physically distant from one another. On the level of text, these elements are all reinforced by the tension between the time period this catastrophe took place and the time that Allende is record- ing it. The experience is still recent, and she continues to feel its disori- enting effects as she writes, without having a reliable assessment of Paula's condition. The doctors do not know what drove Paula into the coma (porphyria or the drugs treating it), nor do they agree on whether she is aware of movement, touch, or sound. This uncertainty is reflected in much of part 1, especially in the passages that recreate very recent, tenu- ous developments.

Although readers cannot verify what "really" happened when Paula almost died, the episode of the mother and grandmother collaboratively saving her is a pivotal moment in the narration. It clarifies how the author, throughout part 1, uses the book performatively to exhibit a kind of control that she does not actually have. She offers evidence, or textu- ally creates evidence, that feminine resolve and maternal solidarity are powerful enough to vanquish "Death." The event is a starting point for additional narration in a similar mode. Other smaller triumphs follow, and these participate in Allende's ongoing argument for recovery, which is set against the physicians' judgment that Paula will never rally. Within the limits of the retrospective narration of recent events, Allende strategi- cally describes a series of challenges, most of which Paula meets. Ruta addresses this staged aspect of *Paula*, noting that Allende eliminates "the negative" aspects of the family's responses to the illness and that her "high-flown rhetoric" draws attention away from the more introspective and presumably skeptical passages.[26] Ruta's comments are accurate, but they fail to recognize the reason behind Allende's narrative decisions. Because part 1 is addressed to Paula and is intended spiritually to reach her, its rhetoric performatively argues with Paula that she must fight her way back to consciousness. More pragmatically, of course, the rhetoric helps Allende stay faithful to her own point of view. It also provides her with additional instances where she and Paula both appear to have some agency. We see, for example, that Allende convinces the doubting neurol- ogist to test whether his patient can take a few breaths on her own. Paula fails the challenge at first, and the doctor quickly turns the respirator back on. Yet when Allende describes the second attempt, a few days of writing time have passed and Paula has already managed to breathe by herself for short intervals. Allende joyfully tells Paula—which is to say that she "informs" her in writing—that she achieved freedom from the machine. And there is more: "I took you in my arms, then held your face in my hands and kissed your forehead, your cheeks, your eyelids; I shook your shoulders, calling Paula, Paula.... And then, oh, Paula ...! and then you opened your eyes and looked at me!" (126; ellipses in original). Successes such as this, however, are narratively established and enacted in patent opposition to the overall medical prognosis. Even at the climax of this victory, Paula remains in limbo and is still in the midst of her larger catastrophe. Though we may wish to be convinced by the intermittent episodes that suggest possibilities of health, we also realize that the distance between the text and some of the ongoing events that it reflects is increasing.

The simultaneous and limited retrospective narrations do not entirely eliminate more conventional past-tense biographical storytelling. References to earlier times in Paula's life suggest the kind of child and young woman she was, but more significantly they indicate how much there is to know and how little the text reveals. Rather than convey much information, these references evince Allende's decision to move far away from a conventional biography. They are clues to Wilson Snipes's point that biographers are always at the center of their biographies because, visibly or invisibly, they are "the psychological center of reference." The answer to "how does the biographer perceive himself: as artist, historian, scholar, dramatist, lyricist, moralist" will determine the kind of biography that is written.[27] Allende realizes that she has to be her book's psychological center, for Paula's does not exist as long as the catastrophe goes on. This unique condition ethically compels her to protect her subject far more than most other biographers and to write about Paula without directly taking up her biographical story. When she informs her daughter that she stood out from all the great-grandchildren in the family, this statement emerges from the larger portrait of Allende's grandfather. Likewise, when she reminds Paula that she was partly raised by her paternal grandmother, Allende is primarily recounting her own busy career in television in the early 1960s. In a portrait of her stepfather, Allende adds tangential details about Paula. Her characterization of the daughter who wanted to educate everyone around her occurs in the middle of a passage about the persons who helped Allende to raise her son and daughter. Biographical descriptions such as these are incomplete, implicitly signaling that Paula's life is her own and not a subject for extensive display.

Because the catastrophe limits what the biographical modes can portray in either the past or the present, Allende's text is pressured into narration that looks to events in the future. This is a logical response to the drama of catastrophe and to the fear that the outcome will be unpredictable and uncontrollable. In Paula's case the doctors' conflicting opinions and the impenetrable nature of the medical catastrophe exacerbate the lack of power of everyone concerned. Resorting to passages that anticipate events that will come *after* the narrating time (what Genette calls prior or predictive narration) allows Allende to insist, in a medium she does control, that Paula will have a future.[28] The passages that project future events are far from imaginative flights of optimism or magical realism, and their tone goes from optimism to despair. Still, insistent hopefulness predominates in most of them. When, for instance, someone asks "why I put so much effort into this endless letter you cannot read," Allende informs Paula that "you will read it some day, I'm sure, and you will make fun of me in that teasing way you use to demolish my sentimentalism" (162). While the text concedes to the limited expectations for Paula's future, it nonetheless performs the mother's desires that catastrophe will be replaced by convalescence. Only then will Allende seriously consider picking up longer threads of Paula's biography, and only if it becomes necessary. If Paula has amnesia or brain damage, Allende can recount a full biographical narrative of her life without appropriating it, in effect giving to her daughter the narration that she has been withholding. That discourse will also be a series of shared episodes centering Paula in the midst of her family network.

The simultaneous, retrospective, and predictive narrating techniques create *Paula's* rich texture, but even working together they are only partially successful in their biographical purpose. They are limited in scope and their time frame, bounded by the subject's unchanging pathology and by the author's caution not to exceed ethical boundaries. With many restrictions, all of the biographical attempts converge at a single point of impasse—Paula as an impervious and inaccessible biographical subject. The problem is compounded by the fact that her immobile state could (and, from the narrator's perspective, will) change at any time. The biographical storytelling cannot proceed beyond these limited modes of presentation until Paula awakens and exerts her active presence over the text. Allende urges Paula to embrace the role of heroine and present her own version of the catastrophe. She wants her to be strong enough to share the task of narrating and transform the project into a collaborative work: "You are the star of this illness, you must give birth to your own health, fearlessly and with great fortitude" (189). When this does not happen,

Allende must turn her writing back to what Snipes designates as the center of reference in all biographies, the biographer. Allende turns to herself and to her own life narrative as a substitutive and interim discourse.

CATASTROPHE NARRATION AS AUTOBIOGRAPHICAL STORYTELLING

With options for biographical development limited from the start, Allende finds it necessary to make extensive use of autobiographical materials. Perhaps the most important aspect of this autobiographical storytelling is that Allende does not consider it to be autobiography. She describes the book as a memoir and entitles it *Paula*, indicating that her interest is not in having herself be the central figure. As Eakin observes, the lives of other family members, in a memoir, are rendered equally or more important "than the life of the reporting self."[29] In fact, in mid-1995 after publishing *Paula*, Allende told an interviewer that she had no interest in autobiography:

> I would never write an autobiography because I am not interested. An autobiography would be about name dropping, dates, awards that I have received. Of course, it would also be about moments of defeat and failure, about moments of success and the great things that have happened to me. In other words, I would be letting the world know how important my life has been. I'm not interested. I think that is boring.... The problem with autobiography is that I don't remember anything. I suppose if I look through my files my memory will be sparked, but I really don't remember much. I remember emotions. I remember those moments in my life that I have already related in *Paula;* the moments that have carved me into the person that I am today. The goals, achievements, those things are not what have made me what I am.[30]

The way in which she defines autobiography is surprisingly restrictive for a woman who writes as much and as freely as she does. The emphasis on external data, the movement from failure to success, and informing "the world" of the author's importance are criteria, which, hearkening back to Georges Gusdorf and Georg Misch, have been deconstructed by life writing critics and authors over the past few decades.[31]

However, even by the standards that Allende explains, much of the information in *Paula* has to be considered autobiographical. The first-person narrator is clearly the author, who goes back in time to her childhood, her parents, and grandparents. She may not be preoccupied with "name dropping, dates, and awards," but neither does she completely ignore these elements. Following Lejeune's early definition of autobiographical writing, *Paula* is certainly a "retrospective prose narrative written by a real person concerning his [her] own existence, where the focus is his [her] individual life, in particular the story of his personality."[32] A significant portion of the letter to Paula recounts Allende's first marriage, her raising of two children, and her career as a journalist against the backdrop of politics in Chile. She traces the evolution of her political awareness to her support of the socialist government of her uncle, Salvador Allende, from 1970 to 1973, and the repression and violence of the Pinochet government after the military coup and her uncle's death.[33] The stories of her failing marriage and the beginnings of her writing career unfold during her seventeen years of exile in Venezuela. They take up most of part 1 and lead Ruta, in reviewing *Paula,* to call it a "brilliant flood of autobiographical reminiscence spanning three generations on four continents."[34] This "flood" of material follows the path of the autobiographical protagonist experiencing defeats and successes and shows that the author's life and work have had an impact on the public. If, according to even her own standards, so much of *Paula* is autobiographical, why does Allende not identify the book as her life story?

She avoids classifying it as autobiography and adheres to her generic label of "memoir" because her goals are not autobiographical despite the fact that her methodology often is. The segments of text that go beyond the biographical scheme, regardless of their length and development, always remain secondary. They are part of a default narration, activated when the biographical approaches are unable to progress and when Allende is forced to admit: "Nothing exists but you, Paula, and this space without time in which we both are trapped" (23). To break out of this space, at least in a narrational sense, Allende shifts into memories where time is retrospectively fixed in place. Functioning in a surrogate capacity, her self-representation lacks the import it would have in a book whose overriding purpose, in addition to its content, was intended to be autobiographical. Rather than cherish her life experiences, she insists that her past has "little meaning" and now seems "only a blind journey guided by instinct and detours caused by events beyond my control" (23). In his seminal essay "Conditions and Limits of Autobiography," Gusdorf establishes a prerequisite for traditional autobiographies. The autobiographer should believe it "a useful and valuable thing to fix his own image so that he can be certain it will not disappear like all things in this world."[35]

This is diametrically opposed to Allende's belief concerning her life as it appears to her in 1992. In writing *Paula* she is trying to make certain that her daughter is the person who "will not disappear," and though Allende recounts many scenes from her own memories, she does not attach enormous significance to them.

Allende's refusal to characterize her life as either singular or exemplary enables the autobiographical segments to serve biographical purposes in a literal as well as a figurative way. Turned into text, her memories are nothing more than a narrated story, which can be used by persons who need it.[36] In a literal sense, if Paula awakens and suffers from amnesia, she can listen to, or read, the manuscript and make use of the contents in any way that is helpful to her. The stories might have a "real" impact by stimulating her memory. If this does not happen, Allende insists that Paula should simply make a claim over any recounted episode she wants: "Take it [my past], Paula, perhaps it will be of some use to you, because I fear that yours no longer exists, lost somewhere during your long sleep" (23). The assumption is that every human being must have a past, and if one person's memories substitute for another's, the distinctions between fact and fabrication hardly matter. Allende thus tells Paula that "happenings fade from memory; people forget one another," but "in the end, all that remains is the journey of the soul, those rare moments of spiritual revelation." Oliver Sacks observes in his published accounts of treating patients with neurological and memory disorders that our stories are what make us recognizable to ourselves. "To be ourselves we must *have* ourselves—possess, if need be re-possess, our life-stories. We must 'recollect' ourselves, recollect the inner drama, the narrative, of ourselves." According to Sacks, when memory and narrative are lost "there is always a reaction, on the part of the affected organism or individual, to restore, to replace, to compensate for and to preserve its identity, however strange the means may be." [37] Allende's plan is less strange than it is an improvised means of figuratively and, if required, of actually transferring memories-as-stories over to her daughter, who may need them more than her mother does.

When self-representation is a compensatory reaction such as Sacks envisions, the triggering action or event may also control how the writing develops. If the triggering agent continues, and the writer continues to react to it, the autobiographical material may never achieve independent status. This explains, in large measure, Allende's personal narrative, which, regardless of how well developed it is, remains tethered to the biographical tragedy and impasse. Her history comes out as segments of interpolated material between moments of more important primary actions.[38] In the context of Allende's letter, primary actions are narrating instances that construct the biographical portrait. When there is virtually nothing further to narrate, Allende switches over into autobiographical text. This has its own dramas and cast of characters, but the content in no way changes its secondary position. The narrator is clear about this, attaching the autobiographical segments to some aspect of the biographical process or situation. She deliberately grounds her initial genre switch to her failure in making contact with her biographical subject. She marks the day, January 8, 1992, one month after the coma began, and explains that she will "give form to this devastation."[39] What follows is a segment on her mother's early marriage, which lasted four years and left her with three babies. The narrator likewise marks the one-hundredth day of the coma, which then serves as a pivot for describing Chile in the 1960s when the politics of the Christian Democrats paved the way for Salvador Allende's presidency in 1970. Sometimes the narrator shifts into self-representation because the waiting in present time becomes too difficult. "The empty moments of this nightmare" lead her to counter with moments of fulfillment, including those in her own recent remarriage. Other times, the narrator interpolates autobiographical segments between consequential events occurring in the present. Passages on her courtship with her first husband and her early career as a translator and journalist are certainly interpolated material. They come between two of the most dramatic sections of biographical narration: the success of mother, grandmother, and daughter in fighting off death ("You were on the other side for a few minutes, and in fact, no one can explain how or why you are back") and the initial failure to get Paula to breathe without the respirator ("Watch in hand, I counted the seconds, begging, commanding you to breathe"). Though expansive, the autobiographical interruptions do not match the emotion and pathos of the biographical forms of narration in *Paula*, and they remain secondary material.

The autobiographical segments are intended to have less, or at least a different kind of, emotional concentration than the biographical passages. As interpolated material, their function is to take the emotion of the present and displace it onto a more distant memory or even onto anticipated events that are still to take place. When Allende explains that the neurologist will make a final prognosis on Paula's nervous system, she does this, for example, by troping the all-important battery of tests into memories of the political coup in Chile. With the first day of testing taking an emotional toll, Allende transitions over to material that becomes a replacement narrative. She links the electric charges that were sent through Paula's body to the electric tortures that men, women, and children were subjected to by the political police during Chile's coup. She also extends the torture to her own body so that she suffers each charge administered to Paula, which is "exacerbated by terror" (187). The remaining fifteen pages of part 1 are primarily substitutive discourse. They avoid saying anything more about the testing, even though it is ongoing with the activity of writing, and move off in two other directions. The first is clearly predictive with content as different as possible from what is happening in present time. It concerns the forthcoming birth of Allende's grandchild and Paula's niece in May. Allende pleads with Paula to get healthy so they both can return to California for the event. The second and more developed direction is just as clearly retrospective. Rather than replace the situation with one that evokes an opposite emotion, this section disperses the immediate, personal pain by shifting it onto and through the broader political and social tragedy of September 11, 1973, the day Salvador Allende's government was overthrown. It describes the violence of succeeding days as well, stressing the news blackouts, mass arrests, and executions ordered by the military junta. Allende rejects the official version, that her uncle's death was suicide, and lingers over his radio address, showing that he knew he would be executed: "*The tranquil tone of my voice will no longer reach your ears. It does not matter. You will hear it still. I shall be with you always*" (194). The speech is important in its own right, but with Allende's link to Paula always subtly present, her uncle's final message resonates with words of farewell that Paula, in her own letter, communicates in a few months' time to her mother. The substitutive discourse serves as a repository of knowledge and emotion that the narrator is experiencing but that she needs to suppress for a certain period of time.

The text works to keep readers mindful of Paula as the primary subject even though she slips out of sight for intervals in which the interpolated material takes over. To do this, readers must view Allende's self-representation as a substitutive discourse operating on two levels. First, it provides content for the book by taking the place of biographical modalities, for otherwise Allende can prolong her descriptions only by making the same observations and articulating the same fears. Second, Allende's narration works as a tropological projection signifying Paula's impenetrability and the inability to find direct language for it. However, Allende uses her own history not just to talk about herself but to reflect the potential of Paula's story. In this sense, the tropological relationship is not based on resemblances or commonalities but on the painful contrast between absence and presence, between what the daughter lacks and what the mother possesses. As a result, the distance between the literal situation and the tropological representation is considerable. Scarry's discussion of how objects and artifacts can represent "unshareable" experiences applies to some extent to Allende's tropological narrations. Scarry gives the example of a bandage of gauze placed over a wound as an object that takes the place of the missing skin; Allende's autobiographical sections similarly take the place of the missing biography. On a second and metaphoric level, the weave of the fibers does more than replace the skin; it "mimes" the skin's texture and creates something that extends and reflects what it replaces. In Scarry's example we recognize the wound because we see the bandage and infer that the wound is immediately under it. Being able to recognize this correspondence between the injury and its external referent is essential, for the link conveys the "sentient fact of the person's suffering" and enables other people to sense it.[40] Allende's tropological discourse is somewhat different. Built on contrasts instead of the similarity or proximity of mother and daughter, the link between them can be unclear. When this happens the distance between Paula's life and the contrasting narrative that represents her is so large that we come close to forgetting the daughter.

Although the effort to establish an empathetic and tropological bridge between the author and her biographical subject addresses certain problems, it also creates new ones. On the one hand, it circumvents the questionable ethics of taking over the biographical story without Paula's consent. On the other hand, it introduces the equally questionable ethics of indulging in self-display, especially under the guise of a biographical tribute. It also brings into play the added difficulty of making use of political narrative, even partially, as a substitutive discourse for individual autobiographical material. Allende realizes that she is burdened by her own narrative design, which she has improvised in order to confront the ordeal of the medical tragedy. As an author she comes to doubt what she is doing but lacks a more satisfactory course of action. So she perseveres with her writing and incorporates her reservations within the text, "asking" her daughter, "What good are all these words if you can't hear me? Or these pages you may never read? *My* life is created as I narrate, and *my* memory grows stronger with writing" (8; emphasis added).

The most conspicuous problem, or contradiction, is the letter format of part 1, because it is both a sincere effort as well as a dramatic strategy.

By articulating the text to Paula, Allende assumes the presence of a second person along with an eventual answer, which signifies narrative engagement and collaboration. The expectation is that Paula will be able to read the material, reply to the questions, and offer information that no one else can possibly know. She will be in a position to supplement her mother's accounts and provide a daughter's perspective on the self-representative discourse. The manuscript resulting from both women's participation will be broader in scope and more dialogic than Allende's initial pages. Another possibility involves the stories' potential as oral narrative. If Allende is reading aloud while they are together, Paula may in some fashion absorb the contents and be provoked into responding orally. In either case the choice of narrative form introduces the idea of dialogue and collaboration. Egan emphasizes that techniques that involve dialogue, double voicing, and double perspectives help authors writing on crisis to avoid giving isolated accounts of themselves. They can transform "the narcissistic by means of the corrective lens of the other, developing linguistic strategies that enable plural voices and that contain the oral and the written within each other."[41] The letter in *Paula* derives from Allende's belief that the catastrophe pressuring her to write nonfiction will come to an end and that the addressee will respond to the oral or written and participatory aspects of the work-in-progress.

The letter may be definitively grounded in the circumstances of the illness, but at the same time it is also a dramatic enactment. Allende longs for Paula's breakthrough, but when it does not take place, the reality of a dialogue or collaboration becomes unlikely. The author continues on in the second-person mode of address, but her intended reader devolves from the flesh-and-blood Paula into a literary construction, a persona having less in common with the actual human being as time goes by. Consequently, the questions that are intended for Paula only seem intended for her. Remarks that are directed right at her at some point become largely rhetorical, and the letter that is exclusively meant for Paula to read only appears to be exclusive. Given this aspect of the text, that the letter is just as figurative as it is real, it is hardly surprising that despite persistent references to "you," there is no salutation at the start or any formal closing. The letter and its framework actually break down even though they seem to blend gradually into the account of the Chilean coup, which ends part 1. The fundamental contradiction, then, which runs throughout the book's first half, is that the letter is as performative as it is genuine. It is an act of faith that a positive development will occur while at the same time it textually dramatizes a set of circumstances that does not exist—Paula aware of ongoing activity and wanting to take part in it. Until this happens and then when it fails to happen, all the questions, prodding, and reassurances create a fiction, but not the actual practice, of collaboration and reciprocity. As a result, the ultimate performance may well be Allende's choice of narrative form, which requires circumstances that do not exist and are unlikely ever to exist. The ultimate performance is Allende's professing, "I am writing you, Paula, to bring you back to life" (10).

STORYTELLING AND CRISIS

Critics tend to show how crisis texts are linked to patterns of failed narrative. When familiar assumptions and hopes break down during extended crisis experiences, writers have difficulty with chronology, familiar modes of characterization, and customary narrating forms. Egan's ideas on how "failed narrative or disrupted processes of narrative posit the impossibility of traditional story" generally hold true for autobiographical and collaborative texts from crisis conditions, especially in the "ultimate crisis," death.[42] Nevertheless, the second part of *Paula* is the very opposite of failed or disrupted narration. The writing is predominantly autobiographical, and the evolution of its storyline is chronological, detailed, and fairly continuous. Certainly, death is the one experience common to all people, yet it remains unique in its particulars, and the response to it can be highly individualized. Regardless of when and how death takes place, nothing prepares us, and nothing in our experience is similar enough to make dying—our witnessing it as well as our own—anything but extraordinary. The circumstances of Paula's illness are so unusual that they intensify what is in any case a crisis. Porphyria is rare, its effects poorly understood, and without reasons for the coma conclusively traced to either the illness or to mistreatment, even the most basic questions surrounding the death go unanswered. Given the unlikelihood of this catastrophe and the high degree of drama, it is not surprising that the text breaks away from the patterns of crisis and illness literature that critics have often outlined.[43] Major segments of *Paula* appear remote from the destabilizing events that Allende experiences and that keep her focused on her project. Yet her clinging to certain autobiographical conventions—just when doing this would seem "impossible"—does not suggest she is neglecting her daughter. It accentuates the difficulties in attempting to confront and understand death. Beyond that it dramatizes the unimaginable punishment of witnessing, seemingly without end, the dying of one's own child.

The reason for the shift back to traditional storytelling can be further understood by distinguishing between catastrophe and crisis. If we reject crisis as an all-inclusive category and regard these two states as distinguishable from each other, we can appreciate how the writing drastically changes when the external and medical conditions change. There comes a point when Paula's condition is no longer a catastrophe because it enters a crisis stage. A crucial aspect of catastrophe is sudden or unpredictable change, and the letter that constitutes all of part 1 is predicated on Paula's breaking through to consciousness and her body rallying to sustain itself without the help of machines. In contrast, part 2 responds to the probability of a long-term condition, with no end in sight. Part 2 is generated by a crisis. Occurring over time, a crisis acquires stability or momentum of its own as its constitutive elements lock into place. People who are most affected by the crisis slowly lose their initial sense that conditions are "unreal" or capable of reverting to what they previously were. People find ways to adjust, and Allende, finding her own ways, turns to different writing strategies.

The most important of the changes is that the narrator stops addressing her daughter, shedding both the epistolary performance and her belief in a recovery. Abandoning the letter format, part 2 is more conventional than part 1. It lacks the expectation of reciprocity and thus has no reason to direct its material to the "you" who signifies Paula. The narrator refers to Paula now as "she" and "my daughter" in the third-person voice. We know, of course, that Allende talks to her daughter during this period. Occasionally she records what she says, but the text itself is not directed to Paula. This shift indicates that the text is no longer intended to be private or, alternatively, that it is being written to appear to be private. In fact, it is very likely that Allende, marking this section as May to December 1992, which was six months to one year after the coma began, realized that one day she might want to make this manuscript public. There are three major autobiographical segments, and none of them is dotted by the kind of commentary to Paula that runs through part 1. This new pattern, far from disrupted or dialogic, is monological, retrospective, and traditional. It is so substantively different from the material that precedes it that it revises the way we interpret the earlier letter. From the perspective of a situation with no improvement for nearly a year, the hopefulness seems misplaced. The narrator's precautions regarding what she commits to writing seem all the time unnecessary, and her efforts to engage Paula valiant but unrealistic. The performative aspect of the letter—hence, its fictionality—is made dramatically apparent by part 2. As a result, the very effort at engagement seems diminished and ironically more affecting and poignant than if there were no narrative change in part 2.

With her writing now aimed at readers, Allende backs off from the single most important restriction she has kept until this point—not using biographical content. The narration indicates that Allende is less concerned with gauging its impact on Paula, and she reveals the essential information omitted from the letter, that the medical tests indicate no brain activity and no chance of recovery. Allende does not detail the family's grieving over the terrible prognosis, but the way that the narrative responds is sufficiently telling. Responding to the certainty that Paula won't ever use them herself, the narrator suddenly releases biographical details and they come out like an extended epigraph in one long paragraph. Each sentence formally designates a landmark in her daughter's life. She describes images of Paula in successive stages, first as an infant staring wide-eyed at her, then as a toddler taking her first steps. She recalls her daughter graduating from high school, then on her wedding day, and finally on the day "when she began to die in my arms" (206). This memorializing paragraph is not something Allende shares with the doctor or addresses to Paula. It is her connection to Paula, which she extends to readers now that her text is openly declared to be public. Since most earlier references to Paula come in the recollections about other family members or as part of Allende's autobiographical segments, the passage is also the most compact and comprehensive section on Paula's life in the book. Even though she gestures toward biography, the narrator does not develop the epigraphic modality further. It evokes death and memorializing activity too strongly regardless of the reality of the tragedy.

Another narrative change caused by the turn from catastrophe into crisis concerns the narrator's perception of time. During catastrophes such as the one that Allende experiences, temporal patterns break down as daily activities are interrupted. Allende, then, composing with the limitations of a catastrophe scheme, marks time in only very general ways. She comments, for example, that a day or a week has passed, but which one in particular scarcely matters. The calendar has significance only for what it suggests about Paula, namely that with the passing of time, hope fades. Remarks about time are contextual, part of a larger description of what the family can anticipate or their apprehensions over the ostensible lack of progress. Indeed, the narrator is more specific about days and dates from twenty years earlier in her autobiographical narration than she is about the present. Against these factors, any specific reference to time is striking, especially the one remarking that it is exactly one hundred days since the onset of coma. This comment suggests that the catastrophe is beginning to move toward a protracted crisis, where, in part 2, time is more methodically noted. To be sure, Allende perceives these later months, May through December 1992, as immobilized, but her accounting of them is progressive and chronological. As often happens in crises and crisis narratives, time moves ahead, lacking the expectant tensions of imminent, sudden change found in catastrophic situations. Now in the context of crisis, Allende describes her decision to bring Paula to California, where she lives with her second husband. The progression of time becomes very clear and very specific. The trip from Madrid to San Francisco takes twenty hours. She recounts that less than one week has gone by since the arduous trip. Paula's husband is in California just four days because his job requires him to return to Spain. Paula is in a rehabilitation clinic for one week. A granddaughter is born in May in Allende's house. The doctor and Allende agree to give themselves three months before reviewing the effects of nontraditional treatment, and she marks off time within this perimeter. Allende takes note of her fiftieth birthday in August. Autumn arrives, and she thinks about the years ahead and whether she will ever return to writing fiction. In other words, as the possibility of change diminishes, time in the crisis narrative acquires a superficial but quite noticeable progressive structure.

The author's life becomes the dominant narrative of part 2, but it never completely loses its interpolated or secondary status. If it appears unhinged from the crisis of the present, this is because the narrating moments, which it links, are less dramatic than those it links in the previous catastrophe section. Because there is no longer a tense expectation that Paula will regain consciousness, the narrating moments quickly recede into the background as the autobiographical passages expand. This happens despite the fact that the present-time narrating moments are actually more distressing here than in part 1. Previously they were based on hope, but now they reflect resignation. The pages in part 1 on Allende's childhood are interpolated between very dramatic narrating moments. They begin by insisting that Paula take possession of her mother's past; no one can survive without memories, and Allende is more than capable of generating additional ones for herself. The pages end as the narrator is almost belligerent toward Paula's silence. She casts out questions that she defies Paula to answer ("Do you want to die?") and practically accuses her of listening but not answering. In part 2 the narrating moments are calmer and elegiac in tone. The first autobiographical segment starts with just a reminder that the Allendes have gone through other ordeals, leaving them all stronger than before. Allende admits, however, this is the only time she has been so oppressed by the lack of hope that there are no dramatic events to fuel her memories and her writing. Because she is consumed with despair over her daughter's condition, the sense of possibilities, which has been taken from Paula, is gone for her too. She sees herself with nothing to offer: "I close my eyes and before me rises the painful image of my daughter in her wheelchair, her eyes staring toward the sea, her gaze focused beyond the horizon where death begins" (260). While writing the catastrophe narrative a few months earlier, there was something to tell, or to anticipate telling: her daughter's recovery. In the crisis narrative, there is little to reveal because there is so little to anticipate.

The unfinished autobiographical narration, which becomes dialogical, reaches beyond self-representation to work substitutively and tropologically. It simply takes the place of the illness narrative. Then it also serves as a displaced argument against the inevitable death of the biographical subject, Paula. Becoming dialogic, the autobiographical segments counteract and suggestively protest the very fact that Allende feels impelled to write these pages. Egan refers to dialogic narrative written in response to terminal illness as a way to "reconstitute the self that is threatened with isolation *in extremis*," which is precisely what happens in *Paula*. Egan also distinguishes narrators in such cases from conventional biographers because the former are so deeply implicated in the process.[44] Trying to reconstitute her isolated subject, Allende qualifies as an unconventional biographer, yet reconstituting the biographical self through the autobiographical self is, by all measures, an extremely tenuous process. The substitution may be obvious, but the technique of troping the dying self with the self who survives is harder to recognize. Consequently, the tropological correspondences again raise the ethical issue of the mother writing about herself while facing her terminally ill daughter. Lejeune says that classifying something as autobiographical is a question of "proportion," a decision on what the author "mainly" or "primarily" intends.[45] If so, much of the second half of *Paula* is mainly or primarily autobiography, yet to categorize it this way misrepresents its intentions. The book is autobiographical in the literal sense that it recounts the author's life. Given the context in which it is written, however, self-representation is meaningful "primarily" as a tropological reflection, one that displaces the biographical subject and the problems that follow from the particular illness.

As a matter of fact, while the autobiographical sections in part 2 substitute for and tropologically counteract the biographical tragedy, they take on attributes of a quest story, describing situations that can be ameliorated or redeemed by a forceful protagonist. Arthur W. Frank's discussion of how physically ill autobiographers sometimes adapt the quest story to their own purposes is relevant to Allende. As a surrogate for her daughter, Allende writes against the illness, offering a contrasting narrative of feminist choices and political resistance. Frank explains that quest stories "meet suffering head on; they accept illness and seek to use it. Illness is the occasion of a journey that becomes a quest."[46] Allende meets Paula's suffering by reconstructing her own life journey and symbolically sharing it with her daughter. This means that the autobiographical segments in part 2 have a conscious relationship with the missing biographical segments. They are set against them, with the expectation that readers will avoid unhinging the two genres and continue relationally to link the two women. Allende's life is presented as a series of challenges and successes. The first part, for instance, after the overthrow of the socialist government, portrays Allende caught up in a national crisis. She participates in underground networks to get political dissidents safely out of Chile, and eventually she and her family go into exile for thirteen years. Other parts depict her in Venezuela, learning the social codes of a new culture, ending her marriage, and raising her children to adulthood. Closer to the narrating time of 1992, other episodes trace her late career as a fiction writer and then her second marriage. Each piece of this quest story uses one person's life as a figurative expression of another's. The fact that it is just marginally Paula's history confirms Scarry's basic point that objects and art that represent an unshareable and unfathomable subject are "analogical" and should be seen in correspondence with one another. "In the attempt to understand [the act of] making, attention cannot stop at the object," Scarry writes, "*for the object is only a fulcrum or lever across which the force of creation moves back onto the human site and remakes the makers*."[47] The quest story in *Paula* is the lever, the narrative mechanism that connects to, and suggestively reflects, the biographical subject, while attempting to remake absence into a vital past, present, and future.

COLLABORATIVE STORYTELLING AND CLOSURE

When Allende is no longer shaping her text in anticipation of Paula's recovery, collaboration occurs in a manner that is different from all her previous expectations of dual participation. The form of the collaboration ruptures the project in ways that Allende must be convinced into accepting and introduces elements of dialogism and argument. Paula exercises her authority by creating her own text, which insists that certain events take place in her own life. Her authority extends to her mother's writing as well, for Paula implicitly gives Allende approval to describe these events at the end of the manuscript. The final result will convert the project back into nonautobiographical writing and return *Paula* to Paula as its primary focus. Throughout part 1 Allende may look forward to Paula's awakening, but in no way does she expand the hoped-for event into a detailed scenario. The end of part 2, however, depicts Paula as not merely conscious, but sufficiently "real" for Allende to recount an episode in which she "visits" with her mother and gives directions for the biographical closure the manuscript will have to incorporate into its final pages.

The meeting of mother and daughter, occurring in a dream that Allende has, allows Paula to present dialogically her own choice of denouement, and, from a broader perspective, it literalizes the metaphorical representation. Regardless of how the dream struck Allende at the time, once she renders it into narrative, it reveals Paula as simultaneously "real" and "fictional." There is no way to reconcile these two versions, and indeed it is the combination that gives Paula a remarkable agency and authority. As the comatose subject of the story, who has been narrated over and to, she is unexpectedly perceived as conscious, alert, and decisively expressing her own views. Paula emerges through the medium of the dream, insisting on a new course of action in her life and consequently a new direction for her mother's project. By having Paula enforce her active presence into her mother's unconscious dream, Allende succeeds in the paradoxical task of fictionalizing her daughter into reality. This takes place because the text that Paula utters enables her to break through the restrictive framework of the dream. The narrative locates Paula *in* the dream, coming *out* of the dream and miraculously positioned physically beside her mother. On one level the dream signifies Paula's communication as imaginative and tropological. On another level the dream is real, with the narrator providing evidence in passages that describe the incident, intentionally keeping the details ambiguous and contradictory. What happens is that Paula finds her voice and briefly becomes a storyteller herself when she enters Allende's room one evening and sits at the foot of the bed. As Allende tells it, Paula urges her to wake up for the express purpose of making certain that her mother understands their time together is real. The final evidence of the literalness of their encounter is a pair of Paula's slippers, mysteriously left by the bed. Addressing her mother as "you" and speaking in her own voice, Paula invokes Allende's aborted letter of part 1 and answers all the important questions in it. She goes on from there, seizing the event for her own necessary purposes. She regards her own life as reaching a new stage of a quest, with a "radiant path" before her, but she needs help to embark on it. She assures her mother she is aware of everyone around her, yet while they believe that she hears nothing, she believes none of them has been able to hear *her*. In effect, the text shows Paula forcing it to be collaborative not only by dictating its denouement but also in rejecting the biographical script that keeps her attached to machines forever and simply breathing. She similarly rejects one of the doctor's scripts, which predicts seven years of existing in this condition. In a larger sense, of course, the narration shows Paula arguing for control over her own life, which is to say that she wants to be allowed to die.

This incident, hovering between the tropological and the literal, is in keeping with Brian McHale's observations that the only way to process the contradiction is to register "the two possibilities and the tug-of-war between them."[48] However, because Paula also corroborates her "spoken" text with a written text, the balance begins to tilt in the direction of a literal trope. This time, with no dream mediating and problematizing Paula's text, her written prose emerges as a compelling, incontestable document. A letter that she wrote on her honeymoon, to be opened at her death as her last will and testament, becomes, in the context of her mother's life writing project, Paula's own predictive narration. Reading it, Allende has no choice but to see the current stage of the illness as penultimate to death, and, as a result, she must use it as the turning point toward narrative closure. The letter sets itself against the trajectory of the mother's narratives, all of which are capable of continuing on without end, if that is what Paula's condition requires. But Paula's text is unambiguous in its dialogic opposition to her mother's writing. It disputes the very passage in which it is embedded, where the narrator is discussing the endlessness of the crisis. Paula predicts that her body will imprison her. She explains that if this comes to pass, "*I do not want to remain trapped in my body. Freed from it, I will be closer to those I love, no matter if they are at the four corners of the planet*" (321–22). She further explains that she is already a spirit and wants to be cremated, her ashes scattered and have no tombstone erected for her anywhere. Paula thereby directs the course of her own life and, presuming that her family will accede to her decision, she narrates her end and writes her farewell. Scarry emphasizes that art and artifacts that come to represent this kind of incommunicable suffering are imbued with a special moral pressure. They allow "events happening within the interior of [another] person's body" to be understood and encourage the receiver or observer to respond. Scarry describes this reciprocal correspondence with two stages, "projection" and "reciprocation," both of which operate at the end of *Paula*. Allende experiences the pressure to reciprocate and fulfill the moral responsibility that her daughter expects from her. Although Paula frees her mother from having to generate additional autobiography, she requires Allende to serve as the catalyst of her dying.

Allende's reciprocation, understandably slow to conform to Paula's text, illustrates in an extreme fashion the difficulties of collaboration. The narrator is depicted as wrestling with Paula's point of view and continuing the dialogue that Paula initiated in verbal testimony and reiterated in her farewell letter. Her intermediate response is to imagine her own theoretical possibility for a subjectivity that could offer Paula more years of life. Harkening back to what Kristeva calls "incorporation," she pleads for identic fusion, somehow to absorb Paula inside of her own body. Using the second-person address that her daughter has forced back into *Paula*, she asks, "Can I live in your stead? Carry you in my body so you can recover the fifty or sixty years stolen from you? I don't mean remember you, but live your life, be you, let you love and feel and breathe in me, let my gestures be yours, my voice your voice. Let me be erased, dissolved, so that you take possession of my body" (323). Kristeva wonders "on what ground, within what material does *having* switch over to *being*" as she questions the dividing line between very close identification with another person and psychological unification.[49] Applied here, the questions are: At what point does *having* a terminally ill daughter switch over into *being* the daughter? And at what point does the tug-of-war between the literal and the figurative come to an end?

These crucial questions are addressed in the epilogue dated Christmas 1992, which narrates Paula's death just before sunrise on Sunday, December 6.[50] While focusing on the ceremony that carries out Paula's instructions, the author merges the spiritual, literal, and tropological elements

in a few dramatic pages. The sense of oneness does not extend to a relationality that erases the mother but incorporates metaphysical faith and
poetic expression. In addition, the tension between what is tropological
and what is literal diminishes as the prose concentrates on giving a moving and eloquent account of the denouement. These pages describe Paula's
death, yet they also narratively seal the event off from outsiders. They
effectively distance us from that morning by avoiding descriptions in the
present tense. With the epilogue, Allende's voice shifts back into the past
tense and uses retrospective narration, effectively barring readers from
the illusion that they are "present" at Paula's death. This means that the
most significant development in the text is not immediately and simultaneously narrated but rendered in more private terms than the other biographical events.

   As a biographical tribute, Allende's book might seem to contradict
Paula's instructions that there not be "a tombstone with my name anywhere" (322). Her name, after all, is everywhere from the title to the
closing sentences, and Paula motivates all the pages where she does not
actually appear. More importantly, *Paula* is a "living" text, which is totally
unlike an epitaph or tombstone. It follows Paula as if she will regain consciousness, and even when this seems impossible, it still refuses to come
to an end. Recovery may be impossible from the start, but the text that
bears Paula's name continues to be tense with expectations and anxieties.
In the most developed autobiographical sections of part 2, Allende's narrator insists that she has lost all hope. Despite this rhetoric, the text itself
is evidence that she is not completely devoid of hope, for *Paula* is meant
to go on, in one way or another, for as long as Paula goes on. The book
aligns itself to the rhythms of Paula's catastrophe and eventually to her
crisis, modifying its life writing genres and trajectories in response. Written in the midst of catastrophe and anticipating a renewed Paula, the book
is fairly focused on present time. Shifting into autobiography, it stays
attentive to its addressee and listener, presuming and imagining that she
is sentient to things around her. When catastrophe reverts to crisis and
recovery is no longer foregrounded, the autobiographical passages occupy
more space and are directed to readers rather than Paula. If in these long
interludes Allende looks away from Paula to her own exilic history, it is
because she reaches an impasse in the biographical situation and is compelled to look elsewhere in order to continue writing. This leads her to
find analogical and substitutive modes of representation to compensate
for gaps in the biographical discourse. As Scarry reminds us, the effort to

make pain (or inexpressible suffering) visible and shareable is a deeply ethical and moral project fraught with its own contradictions. The attention that Allende pays to her own life is unsettling, but it illustrates Rosenwald and Ochberg's point that "the movement of a life cannot be stopped by a story" just as the movement toward a death cannot be stopped. The movement can only be shared as it bares the "wounds" and predicament of the writer who struggles to make the effort.[51]

It is generally the case that narrative accounts of catastrophe and crisis are triumphs over adversity for their authors. This is particularly true for women, who historically have had limited access to channels for putting their resistance into action. Lili'uokalani found a way by publishing her autobiography and using it as a pretext for triggering public debate on U.S. policy in the Pacific. She achieved this purpose even though she was unable to reach her ultimate goal of preventing the American annexation of Hawai'i. Banti published *Artemisia* in a postwar environment when her readers would recognize her destroyed manuscript as a trope for larger losses and her revised, published manuscript as a trope for cultural reconstruction, along with its being an argument for appreciating the life and work of Artemisia Gentileschi. H.D.'s manuscript of *The Gift* is clearly one civilian's triumph of will over constant threats to life in wartime. Even Weil, whose book becomes increasingly self-involved and defeatist, has the accomplishment of finishing *The Bride Price* and living long enough to witness its publication—and years beyond. *Paula*, though, is unique among these life writing works. It is the only manuscript whose completion and publication represent the failure of the original project.[52] Its completion corresponds to the death of its primary subject, and its publication signifies its function as a biographical tribute rather than a memoir of renewal.

Conclusion

THIS STUDY USES CATASTROPHE as a narrow and significant point of entry into current discussions of autobiography. Despite a great deal of scholarly interest in autobiographical representations of life-changing events, the generic terminology has been confined in specialized cases to trauma with belated psychological effects and, in more general cases, to crisis with ongoing, continuous characteristics. In proposing that catastrophe be adopted as a related, yet discrete category, I have argued that catastrophe narratives exhibit important features of their own. These differences are created when particularly extreme circumstances drive individuals to life write and then constitute the primary subject of their texts. While the broader categories tend to minimize differences, the more restrictive category that I propose foregrounds the impact of catastrophe on all levels of text in ways that trauma and crisis do not. A more restrictive category also brings into focus what my chapters attempt to theorize and illustrate as the distinguishing element of catastrophe narratives: an unleashing of the past as a dynamic response to exigencies of the present, making self-representation predominantly or entirely tropological. Not only is the past seen *through* the present time frame, as is always the case; it *is* the present, in displaced and substitutive forms. However much the past may be shaped into a discernible storyline, it is the uncertain present that preoccupies the writer, for whom process and product come together. Two narratives are being told, and two levels of representation, literal and tropological, are present.

The texts presented here illustrate that by distinguishing catastrophe from crisis, we can see more clearly how autobiographical writings related to catastrophe serve as channels for making public little-known, censored, or especially private information and, more expansively, as vehicles of criticism or social action against events that exceed the writers' control. Even when catastrophe texts seem isolated in their concerns or highly focused in their biographical details between, say, mother and daughter or with one woman's story, sociopolitical events of a widespread and calamitous nature come into play as important elements of their discourses. Considerations of gender run through these recounted events as women, limited and defined by their vulnerable positions, publicly self-identify with their respective catastrophes. To be sure, other catastrophe narratives that represent events occurring to a single geographical region or to a violently oppressed population will likely generate somewhat different conclusions. Texts, artifacts, photographs, testimonies and, increasingly, videographic accounts of a single catastrophe are also likely to yield related yet different patterns from those I have traced. Despite what will be significant variations in each localized situation, the most important point is that catastrophe life writing exists and needs to be recognized and theorized on its own terms.

My intention throughout this study has been to expand and refine ideas of genre by discussing catastrophe narratives as more unstable and variable than crisis narratives, mainly because they are the products of more volatile conditions, whether they appear to be intimate elements of a catastrophe or are depicted as immediately relevant to a broader population. The etymologies of the terms provide a clear rationale for doing so. "Catastrophe," most often used in critical analyses as a synonym for trauma or crisis, is rarely invoked as a term with its own set of conditions and effects. However, from the Greek *kata*, meaning away from, and *strophe*, as a turn, catastrophe can rightly be viewed as a change that is extreme enough to constitute an overturning, a revolution or subversion of the established order or system of things. In particular, catastrophe points to changes that may be as irreversible and widespread as they also are sudden and violent. "Crisis," from the Greek word *krisis* and the verb root "to decide," indicates merely a separation or division. Crisis narratives therefore seek out, depict, and follow the long consequences that come out of decisive changes and turning points. The ongoing, continuous nature of crisis practically demands it, and critics have generally emphasized the importance of adjusting or accepting crisis since it is resistant to change. But catastrophe is a more extreme condition. Catastrophe narratives are linked to radical upsets that defy accommodation as well as literary attempts to enfold them smoothly into representational narratives. I should add, however, that this study does not view radical change exclusively as one specific kind of experience rather than another, but on the basis of *how* an event or phenomenon is responded to and perceived, with the factors of surprise, intensity, severity, and rapidity of change all coming into play. In closely examining five representative works by women who suffered catastrophe as well as long periods of crisis, I demonstrate how catastrophe, to a greater extent than crisis, remains outside the narrative while it is also made, in direct or deflected ways, to be its primary internal focus. This duality generates text while simultaneously thwarting it, and, as a result, catastrophe narratives are highly dynamic, with the urgencies of their conception dispersed throughout their progressive, yet irregular structures.

Although some of the selections I examine are initially set off by a catastrophe occurring in present time, catastrophe narratives are not limited to this basic cause-and-effect relationship. Crisis narratives can mutate into catastrophe narratives when their authors are subjected to an unexpected shock and respond through a textual project that is already underway. Lili'uokalani's *Hawaii's Story by Hawaii's Queen* is exemplary of this particular pattern; it witnesses the sudden threat of political extinction by abandoning a woman's bildungsroman design and the tempered criticism embedded therein to enact catastrophe while confronting it through much more aggressive argumentation and persuasion. Other catastrophe narratives, here represented by H.D.'s *The Gift* and Banti's *Artemisia*, owe their existence to catastrophe. Their women's stories would not have been composed in less dire circumstances, at least not in formats similar to those they actually assumed. Because catastrophe is also determined by how a phenomenon may be perceived, I use Weil's *The Bride Price* to demonstrate that the interpretation of a private event as a public catastrophe can trigger this kind of life writing; in a sense, catastrophe is always in the eye of the beholder, outlined by culture, gender, and history and other factors. Experiencing and troping one event into another—as Weil describes doing in responding to personal illness as if it were a wartime torture—carries enough force to actuate an experience of catastrophe and to pressure the writing into a catastrophe modality. Finally, because catastrophe is defined as a change of explosive proportions, the experience rarely goes on indefinitely, and Allende's *Paula* is a case study of how catastrophe narratives may break off into sections reflecting crisis or periods of resigned calm. *Paula*, initiated by a terrible illness, adheres to this pattern and progresses largely as catastrophe life writing, becoming a crisis narrative only when hopes for a second medical upheaval to reverse the effects of the first one prove to be futile. In addition, this selection illustrates ways in which a fairly insulated text may expand outward to serve as a highly public testimony. It operates figuratively as a displaced disaster story and literally as a political narrative, thus conjoining a discourse on national trauma—Chile's disastrous and violent political history—to a young woman's private medical disaster that the author, as mother, is compelled to witness.

By calling attention to these diverse examples of women's writing in catastrophe, I hope to make a case for the multiple possibilities they offer in how we think about additional categories and approaches to literary texts that are founded on catastrophe and crisis and how these two states may appear similar but conspicuously diverge. Indeed, one reason that these representative works have been neglected by life writing critics may be the difficulty of charting their unstable and reactive discourses according to the categories to which we are accustomed. At the same time, I recognize that crisis tends to involve more general and long-lasting conditions, a fact that will probably keep the category of catastrophe texts relatively small. Nonetheless, by reading back through the lens of catastrophe, we can refocus the way we look at the relationship of the narrating "I" to the autobiographical protagonist. We can also refocus our considerations of self-reflection and self-portraiture, as well as the strategic use of genres such as biography and fiction and sources such as letters, transcripts, and documents. The narrators' comments on their present time as well as the actual writing period, to the extent that we can accept them as referential and not entirely fiction, are crucial elements in the process of genre consideration. Reading back will be especially pertinent for autobiographical writings concerned with extreme circumstances that were produced in threatening environments—prison memoirs; resistance and revolution texts; political ephemera; testimonies of wars and regional, religious, and postcolonial conflicts; accounts of disease, disabilities, and epidemics. The tasks of foregrounding catastrophe, adjusting our debates, and recontextualizing our categories are therefore all important tasks for the future.

I began to work on these concluding pages during the week of December 7, 2001. Looking out over my computer screen, I could see the same mountains that bomber planes flew across on the same date exactly sixty years earlier to reach Pearl Harbor. To acknowledge the catastrophe that generated years of global crisis and, within that crisis, catastrophes taking place from tiny atolls in the Pacific Ocean to Central and Eastern Europe seemed an appropriate and symbolic end for a study on self-representation and catastrophe. I was also writing three months after catastrophe struck America, ushering in an extended period of crisis. Whatever events occur between my own writing time and when people read these pages, to live in conditions of crisis—whether characterized by a "high alert" or a state of "vigilance"—is to live on the edge between crisis and catastrophe, at least conceptually if not in actuality—for the latter remains uncertain until catastrophe again takes place. Although it could be argued that the blurring of these boundaries diminishes the value of making distinctions in the literature, I contend that it makes such distinctions more relevant than ever. If in America we now perceive ourselves, or actually are, or cause ourselves and others to be living in crisis, moving toward and then away from the edge of catastrophe, we have become closer to inhabitants across the globe who have long withstood similar conditions—in Northern Ireland, East Timor, Kenya, Malaysia, Indonesia, Afghanistan, Pakistan, and India, to name just a few. With so much incontestable catastrophe, the gap between actual and imagined catastrophe and between catastrophe and crisis may be narrow, but the space remains profoundly important. The differences, after all, are between an intact or wounded, disabled body, health and disease, or the life and death of large populations. It is a chilling thought that in a new century and a new millennium, the uncertainties between crisis and catastrophe are likely to reflect the way that we endure and, as a consequence, the ways that we will construct the narratives of our lives.

Notes

INTRODUCTION

1. The project for which I was reading H.D.'s prose canon was *Breaking the Sequence: Women's Experimental Fiction,* coedited with Ellen G. Friedman (Princeton: Princeton Univ. Press, 1989). See references to *The Gift* and *Palimpsest* as well as H.D.'s position as a second-generation experimentalist of the twentieth century in "Contexts and Continuities: An Introduction to Women's Experimental Fiction in English" in the same volume (7, 17, 24–26).

2. I explored this aspect of H.D.'s prose fiction in "H.D.'s *The Gift:* 'Hide-and-Seek' with the 'Skeletal Hand of Death,'" *Redefining Autobiography in Twentieth-Century Fiction by Women,* ed. Colette T. Hall and Janice Morgan (New York: Garland, 1991), 85–102, and in "H.D.'s Self-Inscription: Between Time and 'Out-of-Time' in *The Gift,*" *Southern Review* 26 (July 1990): 542–54.

3. In line with preferred current usage, Hawaiian words throughout this study are written with diacritical marks. However, the diacritical marks have not been added to the texts of any writers quoted in this chapter or chapter 1. Because diacritical marks were first used in the twentieth century, they do not appear in the passages that are quotations from Lili'uokalani's writings.

4. Lili'uokalani, *Hawaii's Story by Hawaii's Queen* (Boston: Lee and Shepard, 1898; reprint, Honolulu: Mutual, 1990); H.D., *The Gift,* abr. ed. (New York: New Directions, 1982); also *The Gift by H.D.: The Complete Text,* ed. Jane Augustine (Gainesville: Univ. Press of Florida, 1998); Anna Banti, *Artemisia* (Florence: Sansoni, 1947), trans. Shirley D'Ardia Caracciolo (Lincoln: Univ. of Nebraska Press, 1988); Grete Weil, *Der Brautpreis: Roman* (Zurich/Frauenfeld: Verlag Nagel and Kimche, 1988); *The Bride Price: A Novel,* trans. John Barrett (Boston: Godine, 1991); Isabel Allende, *Paula,* trans. Margaret Sayers Peden (New York: Harper-Collins, 1995).

5. Philippe Lejeune, "The Autobiographical Pact (bis)," *On Autobiography,* ed. Paul John Eakin, trans. Katherine Leary (Minneapolis: Univ. of Minnesota Press, 1989), 131–32.

6. Sander L. Gilman and Steven T. Katz, eds., *Anti-Semitism in Times of Crisis* (New York: New York Univ. Press, 1991), 14.

7. Suzette A. Henke, *Shattered Subjects: Trauma and Testimony in Women's Life-Writing* (New York: St. Martin's, 1998), xv. Other studies of life writing and therapeutic processes include Anne Hunsaker Hawkins, *Reconstructing Illness: Studies in Pathography* (West Lafayette, Ind.: Purdue Univ. Press, 1993); Judith Lewis Herman, *Trauma and Recovery* (New York: Basic, 1992); and the clinically oriented *Traumatic Stress: The Effects of Overwhelming Experience on Mind, Body, and Society*, ed. Bessell van der Kolk, Alexander C. McFarlane, and Lars Weisaeth (New York: Guilford, 1996). Also of interest are Roberta Culbertson, "Embodied Memory, Transcendence, and Telling: Recounting Trauma, Re-establishing the Self," *New Literary History* 26 (1995): 169–95; "Courtrooms and Therapy Rooms" in Susan Engel, *Context Is Everything: The Nature of Memory* (New York: Freeman, 1999); and Mary Elene Wood, *The Writing on the Wall: Women's Autobiography and the Asylum* (Urbana: Univ. of Illinois Press, 1994).

8. Cathy Caruth, ed., *Trauma: Explorations in Memory* (Baltimore: Johns Hopkins Univ. Press, 1995), and *Unclaimed Experience: Trauma, Narrative, and History* (Baltimore: Johns Hopkins Univ. Press, 1996).

9. Leigh Gilmore, "Limit-Cases: Trauma, Self-Representation, and the Jurisdictions of Identity," Special Issue on "Autobiography and Changing Identities," ed. Susanna Egan and Gabriele Helms, *Biography: An Interdisciplinary Quarterly* 24 (Winter 2001): 128. See also Gilmore's *The Limits of Autobiography: Trauma and Testimony* (Ithaca: Cornell Univ. Press, 2001).

10. Susanna Egan, *Mirror Talk: Genres of Crisis in Contemporary Autobiography* (Chapel Hill: Univ. of North Carolina Press, 1999).

11. Ibid., 4. See Anthony Paul Kerby, *Narrative and the Self* (Bloomington: Indiana Univ. Press, 1991); and Jean Starobinski, "The Style of Autobiography," *Autobiography: Essays Theoretical and Critical*, ed. James Olney (Princeton: Princeton Univ. Press, 1980), 73–83.

12. Egan, *Mirror Talk*, 4–7.

13. Both Lyotard's and Langer's quotations can be found in Lawrence L. Langer, *Admitting the Holocaust: Collected Essays* (New York: Oxford Univ. Press, 1995), 15.

14. Barbara Harlow, *Resistance Literature* (New York: Methuen, 1987), 182.

15. Michael M. J. Fischer, "Autobiographical Voices (1, 2, 3) and Mosaic Memory: Experimental Sondages in the (Post)modern World," *Autobiography and Postmodernism*, ed. Kathleen Ashley, Leigh Gilmore, Gerald Peters (Amherst: Univ. of Massachusetts Press, 1994), 120.

16. An example of writing to record a life well lived is evidenced in Ben Franklin's assertion in his autobiography that his life was worthy enough to live over again in the same way he lived it. Given the impossibility of this, the next best thing was to write the story.

17. See, for example, Susan Stanford Friedman, "Women's Autobiographical Selves: Theory and Practice," *The Private Self: Theory and Practice of Women's Autobiographical Writings*, ed. Shari Benstock (Chapel Hill: Univ. of North Carolina Press, 1988), 34–62.

18. See H. Porter Abbott, "Autobiography, Autography, Fiction: Groundwork

for a Taxonomy of Textual Categories," *New Literary History* 19 (1988): 597–615, for an excellent discussion of the illusions of autobiographical referentiality being taken for signs of "authentic" identity. Paul John Eakin, in *Fictions in Autobiography: Studies in the Art of Self-Invention* (Princeton: Princeton Univ. Press, 1985) and *Touching the World: Reference in Autobiography* (Princeton: Princeton Univ. Press, 1992), argues eloquently various ways that "fictions of the self" are the truths of the self and thus referential. On the role of metaphor, he writes, "When it comes to the self, then, autobiography is doubly structured, doubly mediated, a textual metaphor for what is already a metaphor for the subjective reality of consciousness" (*Touching theWorld*, 102).

19. Julia Kristeva, "Freud and Love: Treatment and Its Discontents," *The Kristeva Reader*, ed. Toril Moi, trans. Léon S. Roudiez (New York: Columbia Univ. Press, 1986), 247.

20. When the "object" consists of another person's speech, Kristeva is explicit about the result: "In being able to receive the other's words, to assimilate, repeat and reproduce them, I become like him: One. A subject of enunciation. Through psychic osmosis/identification. Through love" (244).

21. Kristeva is actually exploring how children come to understand themselves as an "I" and establish discrete spaces of identification for themselves. She distinguishes between the Lacanian notion of desire in metonynmic displacement and love in metaphorical identification. I am using the terms in a more general context.

22. Lili'uokalani states in her autobiography that she composed hundreds of songs. George S. Kanahele in *Hawaiian Music and Musicians* (Honolulu: Univ. of Hawai'i Press, 1979) indicates that more than one hundred of them have survived. Whatever the exact number of songs, Lili'uokalani could sight read, play numerous instruments, had perfect pitch, and was "the most prolific Hawaiian composer of the century" (30).

23. For example, a statewide convention to debate and draft sovereignty models was held on July 31, 1999. According to an article in the *Honolulu Advertiser* announcing the convention, models for debate include restoring the monarchy, creating an independent Hawaiian nation, or creating a nation within a nation (Lum). For important discussions of the usage of "Native," see Haunani-Kay Trask, *From a Native Daughter: Colonialism and Sovereignty in Hawai'i* (Monroe, Maine: Common Courage, 1993), 70, and Lilikalā Kame'eleihiwa, *Native Land and Foreign Desires: Pehea Lā E Pono Ai?* (Honolulu: Bishop Museum Press, 1992), 342n. 7.

24. President Bill Clinton signed a landmark piece of legislation in November 1993. It was a formal apology to Native Hawaiians for the illegal overthrow of Hawai'i in 1893. On February 23, 2000, the U.S. Supreme Court struck down the Hawai'i constitutional provision that limits voting of trustees of the Office of Hawaiian Affairs (under auspices of the state) to residents with Hawaiian blood.

25. Noenoe Silva, working in the late 1990s at the National Archives in Washington, D.C., located an 1897 petition against annexation. It has more than 21,000 signatures, almost all of them Native Hawaiians. See "*Kanaka Maoli* Resistance to Annexation," *'Ōiwi: A Native Hawaiian Journal* 1 (Dec. 1998): 40–76. Her forthcoming book on Hawai'i is based on extensive work with Hawaiian language sources.

26. H.D., *Palimpsest* (Paris: Contact, 1926); *Hedylus* (Boston: Houghton Mifflin, 1928); *Nights* (Dijon: Darantière, 1934); *Paint It Today*, ed. Cassandra Laity (New York: New York Univ. Press, 1992); *Asphodel*, ed. Robert Spoo (Durham: Duke Univ. Press, 1992).

27. Grete Weil, *My Sister, My Antigone*, trans. Krishna Winston (New York: Avon/Bard, 1984); *Last Trolley from Beethovenstraat*, trans. John Barrett (Boston: Godine, 1997).

28. Elyse Crystall, Jill Kuhnheim, and Mary Layoun, "An Interview with Isabel Allende," *Contemporary Literature* 33 (1992): 588.

29. Caren Kaplan opens her essay "Resisting Autobiography: Out-Law Genres and Transnational Feminist Subjects" by saying that the "troubles" of autobiography "seem to define it" (115). I use the term differently, of course, to designate the elements of catastrophe, but the source for my word choice is Kaplan's essay in Sidonie Smith and Julia Watson, eds., *De/Colonizing the Subject: The Politics of Gender in Women's Autobiography* (Minneapolis: Univ. of Minnesota Press, 1992), 115–38.

30. Egan discusses life writing and tropes in her introduction.

31. Paul de Man, "Autobiography as De-facement," *MLN* 94 (1979): 921.

32. Sidonie Smith, *Subjectivity, Identity, and the Body: Women's Autobiographical Practices in the Twentieth Century* (Bloomington: Indiana Univ. Press, 1993), 21–22.

33. Leslie A. Adelson, *Making Bodies, Making History: Feminism and German Identity* (Lincoln: Univ. of Nebraska Press, 1993), 1.

34. Ibid., 34.

35. Ibid., 7.

36. Gerald Prince, *Dictionary of Narratology* (Lincoln: Univ. of Nebraska Press, 1987), 80. Prince's succinct explanation of "cultural code" derives from Barthes's *S/Z*.

37. Michal is one of the least studied women of the Old Testament. She appears a number of times in 1 and 2 Samuel and 1 Chronicles. She is given to David as his bride for his triumphing over Goliath.

38. The implicit aligning of David's mass killings to create a Jewish nation and Hitler's policies during World War II is quite provocative and reflects Weil's personal ambivalence regarding her Christian/German identification and the treatment she received from the Nazis in the late 1930s that caused her and her husband to flee Germany.

39. Couser, in *Recovering Bodies: Illness, Disability, and Life Writing* (Madison: Univ. of Wisconsin Press, 1997), cites troping as part of the experience of illness. "Reductive synecdoche," for example, refers to the patient by singling out the malfunctioning body part (26). He looks at metaphors of illness, particularly war metaphors, in numerous books, including Paul Monette's *Borrowed Time: An AIDS Memoir* (1988) and Emmanuel Dreuilhe's *Mortal Embrace* (1988). Susan Sontag's *Illness as Metaphor* (New York: Farrar, 1978) is an important earlier study of how we identify disease through figurative modes of thought and language.

40. Sarah Cornell, "Hélène Cixous' *Le Livre de Promethea*," *Writing Differences: Readings from the Seminar of Hélène Cixous*, ed. Susan Sellers (New York: St. Martin's, 1988), 127–40.

41. Ibid., 134.

42. Stressing in this context the body's corporeal grounding, I am also thinking of Elizabeth Grosz's analyses of the body in *Space, Time, and Perversion: Essays
on the Politics of Bodies* (New York: Routledge, 1995) as "a concrete, material ani-
mate organization of flesh, organs, nerves, and skeletal structure, which are given
a unity, cohesiveness, and form through the psychical and social inscription of the
body's surface" (104). Grosz sees the biological body as "amorphous, a series of
uncoordinated potentialities that require social triggering, ordering, and long-
term 'administration'" (104). The transpositioning of the body into text is, as
I see it, an ordering and form of social triggering. This applies not only to the
actual result but to the effort of transpositioning, which is a form of tropological
activity. See also Adelson, in *Making Bodies, Making History*, responding to Judith
Butler (15).

43. Certain kinds of conceptual and performative art could be considered
exceptions to this distinction between "art" and "life," but I am thinking of the
works of this study only.

44. De Man, "Autobiography as De-facement," 920.

45. Françoise Lionnet, *Autobiographical Voices: Race, Gender, Self-Portraiture*
(Ithaca: Cornell Univ. Press, 1989), xi.

46. Even Lili'uokalani, who ruled Hawai'i, did so because her older brother,
King Kalākaua, had died while overseas. From that point on she challenged her
largely Caucasian political adversaries who wanted annexation as soon as possible and who were unprepared for the force of her resistance. Allende's magical
realism, which works miracles in her fiction, can do little to keep her daughter
alive, while Weil loses her husband to the death camps. For H.D. and Banti, the
bombs and destruction around them shatter any sense of their city as a fortifica-
tion in which they find protection.

47. In addition to "Resisting Autobiography," see Kaplan and Inderpal Grewal,
eds., *Scattered Hegemonies: Postmodernity and Transnational Feminist Practices*
(Minneapolis: Univ. of Minnesota Press, 1994).

48. Lionnet, "Dissymmetry Embodied," *Borderwork: Feminist Engagements
with Comparative Literature*, ed. Margaret R. Higonnet (Ithaca: Cornell Univ.
Press, 1994), 41; and see also "The Politics and Aesthetics of *Métissage*," *Autobiographical Voices*, 1–29.

49. Harlow, *Resistance Literature*, 118–53.

50. Lejeune, "The Autobiographical Pact," 131.

51. H.D., "Writing on the Wall," *Tribute to Freud* (New York: New Directions,
1984), 21.

1. AUTOBIOGRAPHY AS POLITICAL DISCOURSE

1. *Hawaii's Story by Hawaii's Queen* (Boston: Lee and Shepard, 1898; Honolulu:
Mutual, 1990). Passages quoted from the 1990 edition will be cited with page numbers in parentheses in the text. Although I refer to this paperback edition
throughout my discussion, this chapter is based on two original typescripts,
"Hawaii's Story" and "Variegated Leaves," housed at the Hawai'i State Archives,

'Iolani Palace Grounds, Honolulu. These typescripts total approximately six hundred pages and exhibit many editorial changes. Lili'uokalani's private and professional correspondence with her editors, also in the collection, reveals the rapid completion of her book while shedding light on pertinent issues and decisions regarding editorial and legal decisions, the appendixes, genealogies, use of other documents, and publication.

2. "Among the Books: *Hawaii's Story by Her ex-Queen,*" *The Watchman*, Feb. 10, 1898, 14.

3. Susanna Egan, *Mirror Talk: Genres of Crisis in Contemporary Autobiography* (Chapel Hill: Univ. of North Carolina Press, 1999), 4–5.

4. By 1897 the oligarchy controlling Hawai'i's legislature had actually declared the country a "Republic." Haunani-Kay Trask writes in *From a Native Daughter: Colonialism and Sovereignty in Hawai'i* (Monroe, Maine: Common Courage Press, 1993) that when President Cleveland did not move forward on annexation, "the all-white provisional government became the all-white oligarchy renamed, euphemistically, the Republic of Hawai'i. Of course, the alleged 'republic' was actually an oligarchy, with a franchise limited by property and language requirements and a loyalty oath that effectively excluded most Natives" (20).

5. M. M. Bakhtin, *The Dialogic Imagination,* ed. Michael Holquist, trans. Caryl Emerson and Michael Holquist (Austin: Univ. of Texas Press, 1981). See in particular the chapter "Discourse and the Novel."

6. My approach to this text is, for the most part, reader oriented, working from the assumption that since Lili'uokalani wrote for a Caucasian (*haole*) American audience, the strategies I identify in this chapter are highly relevant. Additional readings will emerge as the book receives the attention it deserves from life writing critics. Native Hawaiian scholars will be the most important readers in the examination of subversive strategies grounded in indigenous traditions. For example, in an unpublished essay written at the University of Hawai'i, Nohealani Kawahakui examines how the book uses the Hawaiian *mo'olelo* form of narrating history.

7. Estelle C. Jelinek's *Women's Autobiography: Essays in Criticism* (Bloomington: Indiana Univ. Press, 1980) proceeds from the assumption that there is a canon of women's life writing and that gender accounts for distinct differences between the writings of men and women. Like many American feminists in the 1970s, Jelinek focuses on gender with little attention to social class, race, religion, or ethnicity. Among the earliest studies that take up positionality and factors other than gender are Sidonie Smith, *A Poetics of Women's Autobiography: Marginality and the Fictions of Self-Representation* (Bloomington: Indiana Univ. Press, 1987); Françoise Lionnet, *Autobiographical Voices: Race, Gender, Self-Portraiture* (Ithaca: Cornell Univ. Press, 1989); Sidonie Smith and Julia Watson, eds., *De/Colonizing the Subject: Politics of Gender in Women's Autobiography* (Minneapolis: Univ. of Minnesota Press, 1992); and Bella Brodzki and Celeste Schenck, eds., *Life/Lines: Theorizing Women's Autobiography* (Minneapolis: Univ. of Minnesota Press, 1988). Domna C. Stanton's edited collection, *The Female Autograph* (New York: New York Literary Forum, 1984), was especially useful in the early stages of my own design of *The Text Is Myself* for its breadth of geographical and generic coverage.

8. Caren Kaplan, "Resisting Autobiography: Out-Law Genres and Transnational Feminist Subjects," in *De/Colonizing the Subject: Politics of Gender in Women's Autobiography*, ed. Smith and Watson, 119.

9. Robin L. Bott's essay "'I know what is due to me': Self-fashioning and Legitimization in Queen Liliuokalani's *Hawaii's Story by Hawaii's Queen*," *Remaking Queen Victoria*, ed. Margaret Homans and Adrienne Munich (Cambridge: Cambridge Univ. Press, 1997), argues that Lili'uokalani constructs herself, with poor judgment, after the most famous monarch of her time, Queen Victoria. Bott attributes this to a desire for the deference and "homage of the American people" (140) and discusses the strategies in the book as ultimately alienating the American public. Bott presents the book as part history but predominantly as indulgent self-characterization. Though she and I may occasionally agree on certain details of the narrative, Bott's conclusions are contrary to mine. She believes the book is "not so much a political or historical tract as it is a memoir and swan song of a deposed queen" and that Lili'uokalani "may have enjoyed, remembered, and possibly preferred the celebrity of being a queen over the political responsibility of governing a nation" (154).

10. Helena G. Allen, *The Betrayal of Liliuokalani: Last Queen of Hawaii, 1838–1917* (Honolulu: Mutual, 1982), 266 (emphasis added).

11. Lucien Young, *The Real Hawaii: Its History and Present Condition* (New York: Doubleday, 1899), 64. Young's first sentence that the 1893 revolution overthrew a "semi-barbaric monarchy" sets the tone for the rest of the book.

12. Allen indicates that Lili'uokalani was "without doubt" the best educated woman in the Hawaiian islands. In addition to Hawaiian and English, she was "familiar with French and German, and had some knowledge of Greek and Latin" (241–42).

13. Allen describes how she was accused of sorcery, along with "planning a political assassination, adultery, promiscuity, savagery, dealing in the occult, treason, and misprision" (242).

14. Lili'uokalani, ed., trans., and intro., *The Kumulipo: An Hawaiian Creation Myth* (Boston: Lee and Shepard, 1898; Kentfield, Calif.: Pueo Press, 1978). Another translation is Martha Warren Beckwith (Chicago: Univ. of Chicago Press, 1951; Honolulu: Univ. of Hawai'i Press, 1972). In the chapter entitled "My Literary Occupation" in *Hawaii's Story*, the narrator describes the book as one of the three literary projects she has been working on while living in exile (350).

15. The oldest school on the island of O'ahu, originally called the Chiefs' Children's School, it was founded in 1839 during the reign of King Kamehameha III to give the future leaders of Hawai'i a Western style of education. In 1850 it moved from its location near 'Iolani Palace and began accepting children who were not royal descendents. Today it is the Royal Elementary School and part of the state school system.

16. Elsewhere in the autobiography the same point is repeated with a larger cast of former missionaries and similar sarcasm toward their hypocrisy: "Dr. G. P. Judd, Mr. W. Richards, and Mr. R. Armstrong, men who originally came to Hawaii with no other avowed object than that of teaching the religion of Jesus Christ; but they soon resigned their meagre salaries from the American Board of

Commissioners for Foreign Missions, and found positions in the councils or cabinets of the Kamehamehas more lucrative and presumably more satisfactory to them" (232).

17. A century and a half later Castle and Cooke, Inc. and its subsequent mutations continue to play a role in the economy of Hawai'i. The island of Lana'i is owned by one of these companies. The irony is that the accumulated wealth was built on food production and distribution (sugar and pineapple), precisely the activity that Lili'uokalani criticizes her missionary teachers for neglecting. Land development has also been a central activity of the commercial descendents of her missionary teachers.

18. George S. Kanahele, ed., *Hawaiian Music and Musicians: An Illustrated History* (Honolulu: Univ. of Hawai'i Press, 1979), 229–30.

19. Kaplan, "Resisting Autobiography," 130.

20. They accompanied Queen Kapi'olani, the wife of Lili'uokalani's brother Kalākaua, who reigned from 1874 to 1891. The sequence is long but extremely useful. Correspondence pertaining to the editorial work done on Lili'uokalani's typescript shows an editor's or reader's critical response to the length and detailing of the trip. Despite this, few cuts were made and the sequence remained fairly intact.

21. Queen Victoria had previously corresponded with Queen Emma, wife of King Alexander Liholiho (Kamehameha IV), who ruled from 1855 until he died in 1863. Victoria was godmother to Emma and Alexander Liholiho's only son, Albert, who died at the age of four in 1862. The correspondence between the two queens, with some gaps, lasted approximately twenty years. See Rhoda E. A. Hackler, "'My Dear Friend': Letters of Queen Victoria and Queen Emma," *The Hawaiian Journal of History* 22 (1988): 101–30.

22. Egan, *Mirror Talk*, 226–27.

23. The editorial is dated September 5, 1887, and contains the following statements: "The government of the Sandwich Islands appears to have passed from the hands of the king into the hands of a military oligarchy that is more domineering than Kalakaua ever was. Before the recent revolt of the Europeans in Honolulu the press of the city was very plain spoken. It printed unadorned truths about the king, and the latter made no effort to suppress such unpleasant utterances. . . . It seems incredible, but it is an actual fact, that not one of the Honolulu journals dared to reprint the comments of the American press on the so-called revolution, although such comment would have been very interesting reading to all Hawaiians. . . . In a word, the freedom of the press of Honolulu is a myth under the reform party, and the man who looks for the facts in the Honolulu journals will not find them" (375).

24. The important exceptions to this are cited, foremost among them Grover Cleveland, who wanted Lili'uokalani restored to the throne.

25. Curtis Pi'ehu Iaukea and Lorna Kahilipuaokalani Iaukea Watson, *By Royal Command: The Official Life and Personal Reminiscences of Colonel Curtis Pi'ehu Iaukea at the Court of Hawai'i's Rulers*, ed. Niklaus R. Schweizer (Honolulu: Hui Hanai, Queen Lili'uokalani Children's Center, 1988). Iaukea says that Dominis was a tempering force on his wife and that "his influence might have changed the history of Hawai'i and preserved the Monarchy" (143).

26. In a diary entry of March 19, 1885, for example, she writes: "Glad to get him to sleep at last instead of being bored to death by his silly maudlin stories. What a life to bear still I am happy to think that I should have so much forbearance and patience. Patience always has its reward" (MS MC Lili'uokalani Diaries, Bishop Museum Archives, Honolulu). Aldyth Morris, in her play Lili'uokalani (Honolulu: Univ. of Hawai'i Press, 1993), dramatizes the discrepancy between the private and public nature of the marriage. She has Lili'uokalani reflect on her mother-in-law's refusal to attend the wedding and her request that Lili'uokalani establish a household separate from Washington Place (where mother, son, and wife lived together for a time): "I am not completely banished. That would be a scandal. I have my room here—but when I am with John, I feel I am a visitor. When he comes to see me, he is my visitor. Sometimes, we sit together in his carriage for half an hour or so. Then he goes his way, and I go mine. As I told him once, I have a husband, but no one to wake up to" (12–13).

27. Carolyn G. Heilbrun makes this point, drawing from Jill Conway's "Convention versus Self-Revelation: Five Types of Autobiography by Women of the Progressive Era" (1983), Writing a Woman's Life (New York: Ballantine, 1988), 24–25.

28. Paul de Man, "Autobiography as De-facement," MLN 94 (1979): 923.

29. In The Real Hawaii: Its History and Present Condition, Lucien Young, a U.S. Marine lieutenant, describes her as a "baleful, degrading influence, exalting immorality, drunkenness, heathenism, and race hatred" (64).

30. Lili'uokalani realized the role of race in American history and was concerned over the status of Hawaiians if the two countries were joined. In "A Change of Scene to Forget Sorrow" she alludes to the legacy of slavery, asking why the United States would "extinguish the nationality of my poor people, many of whom have now not a foot of land which can be called their own. And for what? In order that another race-problem shall be injected into the social and political perplexities with which the United States in the great experiment of popular government is already struggling? In order that a novel and inconsistent foreign and colonial policy shall be grafted upon its hitherto impregnable diplomacy? or in order that a friendly and generous, yet proud-spirited and sensitive race... shall be crushed under the weight of a social order and prejudice with which even another century of preparation would hardly fit it to cope?" (310). In "Hawaiian Autonomy" she refers to the Native American population, expressing her fear that Hawaiians would be "relegated to the condition of the aborigines of the American continent" (369). Trask points out that when the Crown Prince Liholiho had traveled with his brother Prince Lot by train through the United States, he was ejected "because of his skin color." "Keenly aware of American racism because of haole [foreigner, Caucasian] treatment of American Indians and of enslaved African peoples on the Continent, Hawaiians understood they would be classified with other 'colored races'" (From a Native Daughter, 11–12).

31. Sidonie Smith, Subjectivity, Identity, and the Body: Women's Autobiographical Practices in the Twentieth Century (Bloomington: Indiana Univ. Press, 1993), 143.

32. The subsequent chapter again introduces personal narrative concerning her prison life. It begins by informing readers that the charge of treason was reduced

to misprision of treason (having knowledge of conspiracy). She received a fine of five thousand dollars and a sentence of five years' imprisonment at hard labor. Lili'uokalani comments that these sentences were not carried out but served instead "to terrorize the native people and to humiliate me" (289). The prosecution's goal, to persuade her to renounce her claim to the throne, succeeded. By abdicating, she secured leniency for others who were involved in the revolt. Approximately 180 people were prosecuted and convicted, some sentenced up to thirty-five years (*Trial of a Queen: 1895 Military Tribunal* [Honolulu: Judiciary History Center, Hawai'i State Judiciary, and the Friends of the Judiciary History Center, 1995]).

33. Craig Howes studies ways in which ideological accounts of the overthrow appear even in children's books. See "The Emperor's New Clothes: A Short History of History in American Children's Books About Hawaii," in *Literature and Hawaii's Children: Imagination—A Bridge to Magic Realms in the Humanities*, ed. Cristina Bacchilega and Steven Curry (Honolulu: Literature and Hawaii's Children, 1988), 118–26. He finds that the "white-collar revolution that overthrew the Hawaiian monarchy" is repeatedly justified. For more comprehensive information on children's literature representing Hawai'i shortly after annexation, see Craig Howes, "Hawaii through Western Eyes: Orientalism and Historical Fiction for Children," *The Lion and the Unicorn: A Critical Journal of Children's Literature* 11 (1987): 68–87.

34. Tom Coffman, in *Nation Within: The Story of America's Annexation of the Nation of Hawai'i* (Kāne'ohe, Hawai'i: Epicenter, 1998) says that the Blount Report was forgotten by historians until the late 1970s, and since then it has been widely studied (142–43). Lili'uokalani's references to it were also forgotten. Her second appendix contains extracts from the statement she sent to Blount and that he relied on when writing his own crucial report. Even more ironic, given the neglect of the Blount report, which favored the Native position and criticized the missionary party, is the narrator's explicit reference to it. In the chapter "Hawaiians Plead for a New Constitution" she speaks of Blount's visit to the island and informs readers, "All the evidence can be reviewed by any person who may wish to do so, and a judgment formed of the men who caused this revolution, as it has been bound in volumes, and can be seen at the Library of Congress in the Capitol at Washington" (236).

35. The court, a military commission composed of seven men, is called "a kangaroo court" in *Trial of a Queen: 1895 Military Tribunal.* The section by Jon M. Van Dyke and Paula Henderson entitled "The Trial of Lili'uokalani, February 1895" explains that "it is improper to try civilians in military courts under martial law unless ongoing fighting is occurring." It adds that the scheduling of the trial did not leave adequate time for the queen's lawyer to prepare her defense and that the men who judged the queen were "clearly disposed to find Lili'uokalani guilty" (7).

36. Allen quotes from an unidentified source that Lili'uokalani was so skillful that the cross-examination of her was "resultless." The queen, according to Allen, gave her testimony in Hawaiian, presumably in defiance of the Caucasian men who were trying her (334). Albertine Loomis writes in *For Whom Are the Stars?*:

Revolution and Counterrevolution in Hawai'i, 1893–95 (Honolulu: Univ. of Hawai'i Press and Friends of the Library of Hawai'i, 1976) that she delivered "all her testimony" in Hawaiian on the third day of her trial and it was the court interpreter who issued a translation. The court adjourned to study the text and the next morning demanded that certain paragraphs be deleted. On the blatant censorship of historical records, Loomis concludes: "Never again would the government consent to receive, as it had on January 17, 1893, a document embodying this version of the overthrow." The queen's lawyer objected to the deletion of any section but was overruled, "and the expurgated statement went into the court records." Anticipating that this would happen, he had already sent the full and complete version out of Hawai'i by steamer (209).

37. Native Hawaiian groups quickly organized mass meetings and petition drives throughout the islands. The petitions were presumed lost until Noenoe K. Silva located them in the files of the Senate Committee on Foreign Affairs in 1997. The 38,000 signatures represent nearly all of the Native population. See Noenoe K. Silva, "Kanaka Maoli Resistance to Annexation," *'Ōiwi: A Native Hawaiian Journal* 1 (1998): 40–71.

38. Lilikalā Kame'eleihiwa, *Native Land and Foreign Desires: Pehea Lā E Pono Ai?* (Honolulu: Bishop Museum Press, 1992), presents an indispensable and comprehensive history of how land in Hawai'i was transformed from traditional, communal use to that of private ownership.

39. Identified as W. O. Kinney, he was the judge advocate in her trial and in early 1897 was part of the commission sent from Hawai'i to lobby the new U.S. president for an annexation treaty.

40. Iaukea recalls in *By Royal Command* his own reaction to the queen's having to sign the abdication document with the name Dominis as "shock," because it was "indefinsible [*sic*] treatment of the Queen" (208).

41. Smith, *Subjectivity, Identity, and the Body,* 50.

42. W. A. Russ, Jr. records this episode more fully in *The Hawaiian Republic (1894–98) and Its Struggle to Win Annexation* (1961; reprint, Selinsgrove, Pa.: Susquehanna Univ. Press, 1992). Lili'uokalani tried to see President McKinley in July 1897, just a few weeks after he sent the treaty to Congress. She quotes from her subsequent letter to him, dated July 24, 1897: "It would have been a pleasure to me to have met you in person, and it was expected on the part of the Hawaiian nation that I would have had the opportunity to tell you of their great trust in the United States government, their love of their independence, and their hopes that although they are without official representatives in Washington, you would be pleased willingly to listen to their prayers" (194). The visit she describes occurred after her initial unsuccessful attempt to see him.

43. Allen reports that the queen was eventually allowed to buy back certain pieces of jewelry. She also reports that the building, Washington Place, was "so violently assaulted" that the foundation had to be repaired at a later date. Even the queen's songs were taken on the pretext they might have hidden messages to her people in them. Also see Loomis, *For Whom Are the Stars?* 182–84.

44. Items belonging to the queen and other royalty are slowly being returned to 'Iolani Palace, and one day more of the queen's documents may surface. In the

mid-1990s the quilt that Lili'uokalani worked on during her imprisonment was returned anonymously and is now on continuous exhibit in 'Iolani Palace. As both a material and textual life document, the quilt bears witness to Lili'uokalani's sentence and survival. It bears the embroidered testimony "Imprisoned at Iolani Palace. We began this quilt there" along with important dates in the queen's life and names of her supporters and the women who helped in making the quilt. The quilt is briefly described in Robert Shaw's *Hawaiian Quilt Masterpieces* (Westport, Conn.: Hugh Lauter Levin, 1996).

45. Lorrin A. Thurston, *Memoirs of the Hawaiian Revolution*, ed. Andrew Farrell (Honolulu: Advertiser, 1936).

46. Palmer visited Hawai'i as a "special correspondent." He wrote *Memories of Hawaii and Hawaiian Correspondence* (Boston: Lee and Shepard), 1894; *Again in Hawaii* (Boston: Lee and Shepard, 1895); and *Hawaii: The Story of a National Wrong* (Boston: Nathan Sawyer, 1896).

47. Allen believes that "differences in culture were deleted" (358), and this is borne out by the ways in which the autobiographical character is presented to readers for at least part of the book.

48. Felicity A. Nussbaum, "Toward Conceptualizing Diary," *Studies in Autobiography*, ed. James Olney (New York: Oxford Univ. Press, 1988), 137.

49. For details of the importance of using primary materials when studying older documents, see Miriam Fuchs, "The Diaries of Queen Lili'uokalani," *Profession 95* (1995): 38–40.

50. The correspondence indicates that the outside reader judged the narrative on the royal trip to England to attend Queen Victoria's Jubilee to be too long, but neither he nor Lee made substantial cuts.

51. One of the two typescripts of the autobiography is a continuous manuscript with no sections. The second typescript shows the addition of chapter titles, and Sara Lee's letters refer to the work involved in doing this.

52. Letter from Lili'uokalani, Nov. 11, 1897, to William Lee, MS MC Lili'uokalani Files, Hawai'i State Archives, Honolulu.

53. The actual title of Appendix B is "Extracts from Statement Made by the Queen to Minister Blount."

54. Owana Ka'ohelelani, "The Hawaiian Mind: Insights," *Honolulu Advertiser*, April 29, 1994, A18.

55. Judith Binney, "Maori Oral Narratives, Pakeha Written Texts: Two Forms of Telling History," *New Zealand Journal of History* 20 (1987): 19.

56. Kame'eleihiwa, *Native Land and Foreign Desires*, 2–3, 19–20.

57. Ibid., 22.

58. In her diary entry of February 27, 1898, she expresses herself in a similar way. With the Hawaiian resistance leaders leaving Washington, she writes, "Faces turned toward the homeland, the things done by them in Washington against Annexation and for the welfare of the people are made known" (translated from Hawaiian by Jason Achiu; MS MC Lili'uokalani Diaries 1898, Bishop Museum Archives).

59. H. Porter Abbott, "Autobiography, Autography, Fiction: Groundwork for a Taxonomy of Textual Categories," *New Literary History* 19 (1988): 597–615.

60. Thomas J. Osborne, *Annexation Hawaii: Fighting American Imperialism* (Waimānalo, Hawai'i: Island Style, 1998), attributes the lack of information on the Senate session in early 1898 to the fact that nine weeks of discussion were held in a closed executive session, and no transcript of the speeches was made (103).

61. Other factors included Japan's opposition to annexation, for the Japanese population outnumbered the American population by twelve to one; in overall terms, the Americans were outnumbered "roughly fifty to one" although their influence was "omnipresent" (Coffman, *Nation Within*, 259–60). Coffman emphasizes Theodore Roosevelt's aggressive stance toward annexation. In addition, the treaty said that further immigration from China would be stopped, meaning that the Chinese Exclusion Act of 1882, which was operating in the United States, would thenceforth apply to Hawai'i (253). Race, as well as commercial and military interests, played a role in all sorts of ways. Coffman quotes Roosevelt saying, as months of indecision ensued in Congress, "If America missed this opportunity . . . it will show that we either have lost, or else wholly lack, the masterful instinct which alone can make a race great" (261). When the USS *Maine* was blown up in February 1898 in Cuba, national attention turned to the Spanish-American War and fighting in the Philippines in April 1898.

62. Though historical accounts tend to say that Richard Pettigrew, a Democrat from South Dakota, brought the petitions to the Senate, Silva did not find them in the National Archives or the Pettigrew Museum in South Dakota (Silva, "Kanaka Maoli Resistance to Annexation," 71).

63. There was more support for the resolution in the House of Representatives, where the vote on June 15, 1898, was 209 in favor and 91 against. See Coffman, *Nation Within*, 311. Osborne makes the point that the decision on Hawai'i opened the way for immediate and aggressive U.S. imperialism. Within seven months the United States had acquired Guam, the Philippines, Puerto Rico, and Wake Island (136).

64. Her unofficial lobbying and giving of receptions continued. Diary entries for early 1898 refer intermittently to the congressional debates. On January 10, for example, two representatives of the Hawaiian resistance groups were in the Senate only a few minutes before the Senate went into closed session. Lili'uokalani loaned or gave her autobiography to various people, and by mid-March she records hearing that the annexation bill will be tabled and brought back as a joint resolution.

2. AUTOBIOGRAPHICAL FICTION AS TESTIMONY

1. Caroline Zilboorg's *Richard Aldington and H.D.: The Early Years in Letters* (Bloomington: Indiana Univ. Press, 1992) traces the literary collaboration of Aldington and H.D., including their editorship of *The Egoist*, throughout the First World War. As Zilboorg makes clear, Aldington blamed Britain's politics for the emotional, creative, and physical damage to his generation of men, though he himself missed the worst of the fighting. The Battle of the Somme began while he was in basic training in England and ended just before he was sent abroad. During the Battle of Flanders he returned to England for officers' training, and

during the Third Battle of Ypres he was in London or on leave (108–9). His letters describe the nightmare of living in the trenches, and Aldington suffered shell shock or post-traumatic stress disorder and physical ailments from exposure to mustard gas. His feelings underlie the novels he wrote over the next twenty years, such as *Death of a Hero* (1929), *The Colonel's Daughter* (1931), *All Men Are Enemies* (1933), *Women Must Work* (1934), and *Rejected Guest* (1939). Aldington explained that he chose to live primarily in America and France because of his "wartime anger and blame" (172).

2. *Tribute to Freud* (New York: New Directions, 1984), 40.

3. One of these manuscripts, *Asphodel*, was edited by Robert Spoo and posthumously published in 1992 (Durham: Duke Univ. Press, 1992). A discussion of the ethics of publishing and critiquing a work that H.D. did not want published took place on the Hilda Doolittle Society Discussion List (HDSOC-L) in early Fall 2001. Susan Stanford Friedman, *Psyche Reborn: The Emergence of H.D.* (Bloomington: Indiana Univ. Press, 1981), 7.

4. Friedman, *Penelope's Web: Gender, Modernity, H.D.'s Fiction* (New York: Cambridge Univ. Press, 1990), 217. Friedman calls the publication history of H.D.'s prose volumes a "story of partial revelation, endless deferral, fragmentation, destruction, and suppression" (23). She also believes that we are unlikely ever to know how many prose manuscripts H.D. destroyed in the 1920s and 1930s (22).

5. Bryher, in *The Days of Mars: A Memoir, 1940–1946* (New York: Harcourt, 1972), calls the war years that she and H.D. were living together "the days of Mars." "Now for the 'days of Mars,' we were together 'inside the citadel' as many people called London, near the park guns and, though we did not know it then, an unexploded bomb .... She could have left us easily, but she stayed" (116). Bryher (1894–1983) adopted and helped raise H.D.'s daughter. Although they generally lived apart after the war years, they remained extremely close until H.D. died in 1961.

6. Her first book, *Sea Garden*, a collection of Imagist poems, was published in London by Constable in 1916. Donna Krolik Hollenberg attributes H.D.'s decision to stay in London during the war to these same reasons but also points out that in 1913, when H.D. married Aldington, she became a British subject. See *Between History and Poetry: The Letters of H.D. and Norman Holmes Pearson* (Iowa City: Univ. of Iowa Press, 1997), 13n. 27.

7. H.D., "Spring 1941," *Within the Walls* (Iowa City: Windhover, 1993), 44.

8. In one part of *Within the Walls*, dated January 1941, H.D. contemplates why she fails to take steps to ensure the safety of her manuscripts. On the one hand she is concerned over their possible loss, but, on the other hand, she is dissatisfied with them and denigrates their importance. She calls her previous writing "dead wood," which she feels she cannot even "decently bury" ("Dream of a Book" 6).

9. Bryher, *The Days of Mars*, 8.

10. H.D. composed some of her finest poetry after she started *The Gift*, and she published her verse successively as *The Walls Do Not Fall* (London: Oxford Univ. Press, 1944); *Tribute to the Angels* (London: Oxford Univ. Press, 1945); and *The Flowering of the Rod* (London: Oxford Univ. Press, 1946).

11. *The Gift by H.D.: The Complete Text*, ed. and annotated by Jane Augustine

(Gainesville: Univ. Press of Florida, 1998). Unless noted otherwise, all references will be to this edition and will be cited with page numbers in parentheses in the text.

12. See this chapter, 214nn. 3, 4 for Friedman's books. See also Rachel Blau DuPlessis, *H.D.: The Career of That Struggle* (Bloomington: Indiana Univ. Press, 1986), and Susan Stanford Friedman and Rachel Blau DuPlessis, *Signets: Reading H.D.* (Madison: Univ. of Wisconsin Press, 1990).

13. Suzette A. Henke, *Shattered Subjects: Trauma and Testimony in Women's Life-Writing* (New York: St. Martin's, 1998), 25.

14. Jean Gallagher, *The World Wars Through the Female Gaze* (Carbondale: Southern Illinois Univ. Press, 1998), 97–115.

15. Henry Pelling, *Britain and the Second World War* (London: Collins, 1970), 97.

16. Angus Calder, *The People's War: Britain 1939–1945* (New York: Pantheon, 1969), 210–14. The May 10, 1941, attack damaged buildings such as Westminster Abbey, the Law Courts, the War Office, the Mint, and the Tower of London. Calder estimates that a quarter of a million books of the British Museum were burned; one-third of Greater London's streets became impassable; 155,000 citizens were without gas, water, or electricity. "Not for eleven days were the last pumps withdrawn from the fires, while exhausted civil defenders and a badly shaken population waited for the blow which must surely finish off the capital; the blow which never came" (214).

17. My own essays on this text assume the importance of the air war over London, but they do not distinguish between crisis and catastrophe. See "H.D.'s *The Gift*: 'Hide-and-Seek' with the 'Skeletal Hand of Death,'" *Redefining Autobiography in Twentieth-Century Fiction by Women,* ed. Colette T. Hall and Janice Morgan (New York: Garland, 1991), 85–102, and "H.D.'s Self-Inscription: Between Time and 'Out-of-Time' in *The Gift," Southern Review* 26 (July 1990): 542–54.

18. The resistant and resolute nature of the British under wartime pressure has become legendary. Throughout *Battle of Britain* (London: Rainbird, 1980), Len Deighton characterizes the period of regular bombing in the spring and summer 1940 as something to which the British became conditioned. Most citizens remained in their own homes during the attacks, with just 4 percent using the Tube shelters (202).

19. See Calder, *The People's War,* 169, 174. In an August 9, 1943, letter to Norman Holmes Pearson, H.D. explains that even though she worked on and off at this manuscript for twenty years, it began to take shape only when she discarded all the early work and began again during what she calls the "bad raids" (Hollenberg 26). This indicates that she started to write the extant version of *The Gift* during the Battle of Britain in the fall of 1940 but did not make enough progress to include 1940 on the final page of the seven chapters that constitute the autobiographical fiction and precede the "Notes" section.

20. The last page of the seven chapters of autobiographical fiction specifically confines the time of the writing to 1941 and 1943; conspicuously omitted are 1940 and 1942. While the last page of the "Notes" (coming after the seven chapters) dates the whole manuscript "London—1940–44," presumably this is a more general way to indicate the longer duration for which the manuscript remained unfinished.

21. H.D. was writing the poems collected in *The Walls Do Not Fall,* the first volume of *Trilogy.* In 1942 the drama was taking place on the Russian front in the battle for Stalingrad. Calder describes occasional minor raids after the main Blitz, with bombers flying in low and touching over different parts of the country (286–87). According to Pelling, "the war was being fought in distant theatres of the world which people could not visualize, instead of taking place in the skies above their homes. Air attack on Britain in 1942 was on a very much diminished scale, being merely tip-and-run raids and a few deliberate reprisals on non-industrial targets such as Canterbury, Bath, and Exeter" (158–59). Called the "Baedeker raids," these strikes were ordered by Hitler in retaliation for Britain's attack on the historic Baltic port of Lubeck. See Sarah H. S. Graham, "'We have a secret. We are alive': H.D.'s Trilogy as a Response to War," *Texas Studies in Literature and Language* 44 (2002): 161–210, for a recent study linking the resurgence of H.D.'s poetic energies to the war. The most important dates for writing *Trilogy,* however, are 1942 and 1944, which partially overlap with only the "Notes" section of *The Gift.*

22. Deighton argues that Germany's erratic bombing worked to the advantage of Britain. In fact, he goes so far as to call the bombing of London and of cities such as Coventry and Plymouth as "an erratic pattern that defied logic" (203).

23. Much critical work on *The Gift* uses psychobiographical and psychoanalytical approaches, studying the actions of the autobiographical protagonist, Hilda, as well as the voice of the adult narrator relative to both Hilda and H.D., as author. Other important approaches stress the prophetic and spiritual purposes of the book. Augustine's characterization, in her introduction to *The Gift by H.D.: The Complete Text,* sums up much of what we know concerning H.D.'s motivations: "To change the course of history, to expunge suffering and pain from a world radically divided between good and evil, as in Gnostic thought—these are H.D.'s motives for writing *The Gift.* She wrote in order to rebuild the world of her childhood, guaranteed by the piety and high purpose of eighteenth-century Moravianism. The values of the Moravian Church define the good that she summons up against the evil of World War II" (4).

24. My interpretation, using the restored sections, stresses one aspect of the book, which is in line with the thesis of my larger study. Richly allusive, *The Gift* will continue to stimulate a wide range of critical responses. Critics even differ on the book's generic classification. H.D., in "H.D. by Delia Alton," published in *Iowa Review* 16 (Fall 1986), calls it an autobiographical fantasy (189). DuPlessis, in "A Note on the State of H.D.'s The Gift," *Sulfur* 9 (1984): 178–82, calls it an autobiographical meditation (178), while Barbara Guest describes it in *Herself Defined: The Poet H.D. and Her World* (Garden City: Doubleday, 1984) as "the reconstruction of her childhood" (266). Diana Collecott, reviewing its spiritual, memoirist, and sexual dimensions, finally settles on calling it "wholly original" (x) in her introduction to the British edition of *The Gift,* abr. ed. (London: Virago, 1984). Although Henke in *Shattered Subjects* says it is an "autobiographical testimony" (26), she nevertheless emphasizes its fictional dimensions and psychoanalytic resonances: "At every stage, Hilda acknowledges the fantasmatic nature of her imaginary projections. Freud, after all, continually assured her [H.D.] that fact and fantasy bear equal weight in the world of the unconscious" (39). Henke also works

to interpret the more obscure memories within the book, paying attention to the Freudian symbols.

25. Jean Gallagher's chapter on *The Gift* in *The World Wars Through the Female Gaze* examines how the context of the Blitz led H.D. to discover different forms of visuality. Gallagher then links the narrator's views of wartime violence with those of the patriarchal family of her childhood, while positing gendered vision (female) against gendered violence (male). Some of the narrator's memories, like the one of the girl in a burning crinoline, work as parables of female disempowerment (97–115).

26. H.D. comments further on the relationship between the lulls between bomb attacks and her "psychic wonderings and probing and exacerbated nerves" in a July 26, 1941, letter to May Sarton. Quoted in Sarton's "Letters from H.D.," *H.D.: Woman and Poet*, ed. Michael King (Orono, Maine: National Poetry Foundation, 1986), 53.

27. Indeed, what is arguably the central incident that she recalls, her grandmother transmitting to her the message of the "gift," may or may not have actually taken place. In *Majic Ring*, as H.D. describes a spiritual or "supernormal" experience in Greece, she explains that she worked her psychic experience into "reconstructed memories that I made my grandmother tell me, as if in reverie or half-dream or even trance." Despite the embellishments, "the story held, it rang true" (Augustine 27n. 34).

28. H.D. did some preliminary writing prior to this time frame, and because she did not publish the manuscript in her lifetime, she was also able to return to it in the years following the war. The most substantial work was, however, already accomplished. See this chapter, 215n. 19, for her references to this in a letter to Pearson.

29. To keep track of the progression and structure of *The Gift*, I sometimes refer to the chapters by number rather than title. It should be noted that H.D. did just the opposite, entitling the seven chapters on her typescript but not numbering them. For many useful details on existing typescripts, readers should consult Augustine's excellent and comprehensive introduction in *The Gift by H.D.: The Complete Text* (1–28).

30. Adalaide Morris's work on *The Gift* emphasizes its purpose as prophecy. In "A Relay of Power and of Peace: H.D. and the Spirit of the Gift," *Contemporary Literature* 27 (Winter 1986): 493–524 and "Autobiography and Prophecy," *H.D.: Woman and Poet*, 227–36) she discusses the commingling of myth, history, and autobiography as a way to "offer society a vision capable of addressing and resolving crisis" (235). The first essay was reprinted in Friedman and DuPlessis, eds., *Signets: Reading H.D.*, 52–82.

31. Shoshana Felman and Dori Laub, *Testimony: Crises of Witnessing in Literature, Psychoanalysis, and History* (New York: Routledge, 1992), xiv–xv. Felman's discussion of novels by Dostoevsky and Camus, poetry by Mallarmé, and Freud's *Interpretation of Dreams* illustrates ways that different genres may all perform as historical and autobiographical testimony.

32. Ibid., xv.

33. "H.D. by Delia Alton," 192.

34. Friedman's chapter in *Penelope's Web* on *The Gift* emphasizes H.D.'s psychoanalytic approach and modes of self-analysis.

35. "H.D. by Delia Alton," 192.

36. The historical notes to "Dark Room" explain that the Moravian school where her grandfather was the principal and which was founded in the mid–eighteenth century, was known as The Seminary. He was vice principal for five years and principal for twenty years "in the period that preceded, included and followed the Civil War" (228).

37. Gallagher, concentrating on the book's visual imagery, stresses the fact that the other female students witness the girl's terrible death and that the witnessing activity, as well as the tragedy, motivates H.D. to open her book with this incident (103). It should be noted that H.D. did not observe this incident herself. It took place a few years before her birth and was therefore relayed to her as story.

38. DuPlessis, in *H.D.: The Career of That Struggle*, describes burning as the most powerful image of *The Gift* (77).

39. The exception to this easing of the air war was the Baedeker series of raids in the spring of 1942; see this chapter, 216n. 21. Barbara Guest notes that during the erratic bombing of 1941, the city of Plymouth was among the sites badly hit. Frances Gregg and her mother were killed by exploding bombs. H.D. had come to Europe with Mrs. Gregg and Frances, who was one of her earliest female lovers (*Herself Defined: The Poet H.D. and Her World*, 230). Frances Gregg was portrayed as Fayne Rabb in H.D.'s *HERmione*, written in the late 1920s and posthumously published by New Directions in 1981.

40. Augustine, *The Gift by H.D.: The Complete Text*, 1.

41. H.D., *The Gift*, abr. ed., intro. by Perdita Schaffner (New York: New Directions, 1982), xiv.

42. The exception to this is Friedman and DuPlessis's publication of the original version of chapter 1 ("Dark Room") with the relevant entries from "Notes" in *Montemora* 8 (1981): 57–76. However, these entries necessarily follow the individually published chapter, and this gives the impression that the historical notes come at the end of each chapter in the original typescript. This is not the case. Instead, they comprise, all together, the final section of *The Gift*.

43. In the late 1980s an editor at New Directions talked briefly about the changes to the manuscript and indicated to me that a scholarly edition would be a welcome addition to the existing trade edition.

44. For details on the excisions, readers should consult Rachel Blau DuPlessis, "A Note on the State of H.D.'s *The Gift*." DuPlessis writes: "the publication of the New Directions *Gift*, given the level and pertinacity of the cuts sustained, does substantially alter our picture of this important, finished autobiographical meditation. These cuts are further complicated by being veiled: no explanatory note by the editor is set forth, no in-text indications are offered; no principle of exclusion or excision is developed. Yet the work we read is rather less than H.D. wrote" (178).

45. Henke, for instance, sees the playing out of male mastery and sexual dominance and female subservience (33). Dianne Chisholm, in *H.D.'s Freudian Poetics:*

Psychoanalysis in Translation (Ithaca: Cornell Univ. Press. 1992), analyzes the monster imagery throughout the chapter most particularly as an allegory of primal, sexual fantasy (135–47).

46. H.D. does, however, hold Germany responsible for mass persecution in the sketch entitled "Escape" and dated January 1941 in *Within the Walls:* "The average English person is amazed and surprised by stories of the concentration camps. The newspapers only now begin to hint of the depth of depravity. I quote from *I Accuse.* 'The enormity and ferocity of these tortures are almost beyond belief'" (8–9).

47. In the "Notes" to chapter 6 ("What It Was"), H.D. calls the details of her grandmother's testimony "reconstructed memory or re-invoked fantasy" (271).

48. The "Notes" explains the geography of the site in the mid-eighteenth century as follows: "This island was in the Monocacy Creek, at the foot of the present grounds in the rear of the Young Ladies' Seminary. It is marked on the oldest map of the locality, and a depression in the grounds reveals where the inside channel of the stream then was. A rustic footbridge was constructed across it to the island, and there many interesting social meetings, official conferences and important interviews with Indians took place. Its name, 'the Island of the Wounds,' meant that it was dedicated to the remembrance of the wounds of Jesus, as then dwelt upon in certain special liturgies and hymns" (262).

49. Leslie A. Adelson, *Making Bodies, Making History* (Lincoln: Univ. of Nebraska Press, 1993), 1.

50. Felman, *Testimony,* 5.

51. Agnes Heller, *A Theory of History* (London: Routledge, 1982), 44.

52. Felman and Laub, *Testimony,* 57.

53. See, for example, Friedman, *Penelope's Web,* 340–44, and Chisholm, 127–29.

54. *The Times,* Jan. 18, 1943, 4.

55. With H.D. writing the preceding chapters predominantly in 1941 and "Morning Star" in and after January 1943, the gap between some of the material could be longer than two years.

56. The passage reads as follows: "No, I was unprotected. I had no steel-helmet and I had no mother-of-pearl shell around me. I was broken open, the mollusc or oyster or clam that was my perceptive abstract self or soul, had neither the super-human reasoning nor the human habitation; I was not clothed in the spiritual armour of light, nor was I clothed in intellectual armour of abstraction" (215).

57. In "Blue Lights," a January 1941 sketch in *Within the Walls,* H.D. repeatedly links the fear of random death to her wartime creativity. She describes a flame in her skull, which ignites a mnemonic process: "People [who] write from America ... will not understand that this is burning, that this is a flame in a skull, and that this flame must meet another flame" (14–15).

58. Mieke Bal, "Memories in the Museum: Preposterous Histories for Today," *Acts of Memory: Cultural Recall in the Present,* ed. Mieke Bal, Jonathan Crewe, and Leo Spitzer (Hanover: Univ. Press of New England, 1999), 173.

59. DuPlessis, *H.D.: The Career of That Struggle,* 77.

60. H.D., in "H.D. by Delia Alton," refers to *The Gift* as an unpublished

manuscript. "This book was written in London, during the days of the bombard-
ment. It is autobiographical, 'almost.' The author has the privilege of trimming or
paring, of concentrating or expanding, where it will best suit his purpose or where
his purpose will suit him—*suit* perhaps, in the old Victorian *Sartor Resartus* manner" (188).

61. Winston Churchill's term for the V-1 was "robot bomber," but the conno-
tations were so ominous that the word was rarely used. See Peter G. Cooksley,
Flying Bomb: The Story of Hitler's V-Weapons in World War II (New York: Scribners,
1979), 69.

62. October 5, 1943, letter to Norman Holmes Pearson, Hollenberg, *Between
History and Poetry*, 29.

63. In "The New Air Weapon: First Official Detail," *The Times*, June 20, 1944,
the writer quotes a description of the flying bomb from the Air Ministry, which also
criticizes the weapon as "unmilitary" because of its dependence on chance (4).

64. Evelyn Waugh, from *Unconditional Surrender*, in Calder, *The People's War*,
560.

65. Bryher remarks that calling the bombs "doodlebugs" did not lessen her
apprehension at all. She quotes from one of her own letters to a friend: "One is
peacefully typing or eating one's supper, or even sitting of a late afternoon in the
park watching old dames exercising their Pekes, there is a noise like an express train
and then the earth heaves up and you don't know where you are. Most people say
that there is a red light and as it gets over your head, the red light goes out, the
tail wags and then you are blown to high heaven but the authorities say no, we
exaggerate. Anyhow there are fierce fights between people who would rather have
the Blitz and people who would rather face the bugs. I think the bugs are worse
myself but it is a moot point. We are pretty evenly divided and as with a real bug,
or cockroach, you can't get away from them anywhere" (*Days of Mars* 133).

66. In the restored edition, twenty-seven pages of "Notes" precede the reference
to flying bombs, which is dated June 29, 1944. Twenty-four pages come afterward.

67. The "Notes" ends with a citation of the writing site and time, "London—
1940–44."

68. Silvia Dobson's "'Shock Knit Within Terror': Living Through World War
II," *Iowa Review* 16 (Fall 1986): 232–45, traces personal correspondence with H.D.
in this period. Dobson quotes from a letter H.D. wrote soon after D-Day in which
she refers to the new stage of the war: "The LIBERATION means so much to me
and to Br—though to me especially, as it was to France I first went from USA
before I saw England. Here, they are excited because it means victory and the war
ending soon (D.V. [*Deo Volente*]) but to me it is something special and regener-
ating" (238).

69. Friedman's "Dating H.D.'s Writing" gives a comprehensive and detailed
timeline of H.D.'s works, categorized by dates of composition as well as publication dates, which are often far apart (in *Signets*, ed. Friedman and DuPlessis,
46–51).

70. Elie Wiesel, "The Holocaust as a Literary Inspiration," *Dimensions of the
Holocaust* (Evanston: Northwestern Univ. Press, 1977), 9.

71. Felman and Laub, *Testimony*, 7.

3. BIOGRAPHICAL FICTION AS AUTOBIOGRAPHICAL PALIMPSEST

1. Anna Banti was the pseudonym of Lucia Longhi Lopresti, who lived from 1895–1985. She was a prolific and varied writer, publishing her first novel, *Itinerario di Paolina*, in 1937. After attending the University of Rome, she married the prominent art historian, Roberto Longhi, whose 1916 article on the Gentileschis is still used by scholars. Longhi also founded the influential journal, *Paragone*, which Banti coedited and took over after his death. According to JoAnn Cannon (See n. 18), Banti's treatment of Artemisia implicitly refutes Longhi's conclusion that Artemisia's talents and intellect were inferior to her father's. Banti's date of death is usually shown as 1985 even though the dust jacket for the Univ. of Nebraska's *Artemisia* indicates 1978. For brief biographical summaries, in addition to Caracciolo's Afterword to *Artemisia* (215–19), see Daria Valentini's Introduction to Banti's *A Piercing Cry: Translation of Un Grido Lacerante*, trans. Daria Valentini and S. Mark Lewis (New York: Peter Lang, 1996), v-xv, and Beverly Ballaro, "Anna Banti," in *Italian Women Writers: A Bio-Bibliographical Sourcebook*, ed. Rinaldina Russell (Westport, Conn.: Greenwood, 1997), 35–43.

2. Her 1940 short story volume, *Il coraggio delle donne*, was followed by *Sette lune* in 1941 and *Le monache cantano* in 1942.

3. Anna Banti, *Artemisia*, trans. Shirley D'Ardia Caracciolo (Lincoln: Univ. of Nebraska Press, 1988). References will be cited with page numbers in parentheses in the text. The book was originally published in Florence in 1947 by Sansoni.

4. Increased interest in Artemisia is evidenced by the recent exhibit on Artemisia and Orazio Gentileschi, which began in Rome in Fall 2001, traveled to the New York Metropolitan Museum of Art in Spring 2002, and to the St. Louis Art Museum in Summer. The byproduct of the exhibit was *Orazio and Artemisia Gentileschi*, ed. Keith Christiansen (New Haven: Yale Univ. Press, 2001).

5. Alexandra Lapierre's research notes to *Artemisia: A Novel*, trans. Liz Heron (New York: Grove, 2000) describe new documents pertaining to a second phase of the rape trial (386–95). According to Lapierre, Tassi was in and out of prison many times, including a charge of incest brought by his own sister (380). Other fictional treatments centering on Artemisia include Susan Vreeland's *The Passion of Artemisia* (New York: Viking, 2002); Marine Bramley's *Artemisia, or the Passion of Painting*, trans. C. Dickson (New York: Welcome Rain, 2000); and Sally Clark's *Life without Instruction: A Play* (Vancouver: Talon, 1994).

6. Recent documentary evidence suggests that Artemisia probably gave birth to four children, two of whom died and two daughters whom she raised (Lapierre, 399).

7. Mary D. Garrard, "Artemisia Gentileschi: The Artist's Autograph in Letters and Paintings," *The Female Autograph*, ed. Domna C. Stanton (New York: New York Literary Forum, 1984), 91. The major studies of Artemisia Gentileschi are Mary D. Garrard, *Artemisia Gentileschi: The Image of the Female Hero in Italian Baroque Art* (Princeton: Princeton Univ. Press, 1989) and R. Ward Bissell, *Artemisia Gentileschi and the Authority of Art: Critical Reading and Catalogue Raisonné* (University Park: Pennsylvania State Univ. Press, 1999). Bissell also published *Orazio Gentileschi and the Poetic Tradition in Caravaggesque Painting* (University Park: Pennsylvania State Univ. Press, 1981). Garrard's *Artemisia Gentileschi*

Around 1622: The Shaping and Reshaping of an Artistic Identity (Berkeley: Univ. of California Press, 2001) focuses on attribution problems of the Seville Mary Magdalene and the Burghley House Susanna and the Elders. Although the book centers on a period later in Artemisia's career than the 1630 self-portrait, it is a fascinating study of issues concerning female identity construction and female creativity. Earlier publications by Garrard include "Artemisia Gentileschi's 'Self-Portrait as the Allegory of Painting,'" *Art Bulletin* 62 (1980): 97–112 and, coedited with Norma Broude, *Feminism and Art History* (New York: Harper, 1982). Garrard wrote the Introduction to *Artemisia Gentileschi* (New York: Rizzoli, 1993). Other useful studies are Alfred Moir, *The Italian Followers of Caravaggio*, 2 vols. (Cambridge: Harvard Univ. Press, 1967); Richard E. Spear, *Caravaggio and His Followers* (Cleveland: Cleveland Museum of Art, 1971); Germaine Greer, *The Obstacle Race: The Fortunes of Women Painters and Their Work* (New York: Farrar, 1979); Ann Sutherland Harris and Linda Nochlin, *Women Artists, 1550–1950* (New York: Knopf, 1981); and Frances Borzello, *Seeing Ourselves: Women's Self-Portraits* (New York: Abrams, 1998), 53–56.

8. This chapter discusses the Allied Campaign in Italy solely as it pertains to Banti's references to it. For more extensive treatment, consult Bruce E. Egger and Lee Macmillan Otts, *G. Company's War: Two Personal Accounts of the Campaigns in Europe, 1944–1945*, ed. Paul Roley (Tuscaloosa: Univ. of Alabama Press, 1992); G. A. Shepperd, *The Italian Campaign 1943–45: A Political and Military Re-assessment* (New York: Praeger, 1968); and Eric Linklater, *The Campaign In Italy* (London: Unwin, 1977). In July 1943, Allied forces landed in Sicily, and after thirty-eight days of fighting began the advance in Southern Italy. Linklater traces the slow progress during the summer of 1944 toward Florence. By August 3, 1944, the South African Divisions (as Banti also describes them) had penetrated the southern edge of Florence and reached the river bank. "All the bridges had been ruthlessly destroyed except the Ponte Vecchio, the approaches to which on either side had been blocked by the demolition of many old and gracious houses. German snipers and machine-gunners opened fire from the northern part of the city as the South African Division closed on the river" (337).

9. The literary critic, R. W. B. Lewis, who was a liaison officer with a British intelligence unit in Italy during the Allied advance, gives an account that matches Banti's. In *The City of Florence* (New York: Holt, 1995), he recounts driving a jeep just after the fighting across one of the few bridges left standing, to find Florence "ferociously shattered by German dynamite" (5). He starts with July 29, when the German command ordered over a hundred thousand people living along the Arno River to evacuate, and, as Banti also recalls, many of them refugees occupying the Palazzo Pitti. On August 3 a state of emergency was declared, with German paratroopers firing on civilians. According to Lewis, "Altogether, the Germans destroyed five bridges, 267 shops, 71 workshops, 123 houses containing four hundred living quarters, about a dozen medieval towers, and some twenty old palazzi. Among the human casualties were a number killed by land mines left in the ruins" (51). Lewis continues, uncannily echoing Banti: "The Florentines were exhausted, stunned by the violence done to the bridges and their surroundings, and desperate for water. I watched them, women mostly, queuing up on Lungarno for water

supplied by American pumps; their heads drooped, they seemed unable to raise their eyes from the ground" (55).

10. Because my approach stresses ways that the life writing component of this work incorporates all of its other constitutive elements, I have not designated each time Banti departs from the historical record. In any case, Banti informs readers that her own emotions and life have become part of the text, and thus trying to separate the threads would be counterproductive. Thanks to scholarly research in the past twenty years, we know much more about Artemisia's life than Banti knew at mid-century.

11. Thomas Peterson refers to Banti's use of internal dialogue in her late auto-biographical *Un grido lacerante* (*A Piercing Scream*) in "*The 'Feminine' Writing of Anna Banti: Un Grido Lacerante.*" *NEMLA Italian Studies* 11–12 (1987–88): 87–96.

12. The appendices in Garrard's *Artemisia Gentileschi* (1989) provide English translations of the following archival material: twenty-eight letters by the artist written from 1620 to 1651, personal correspondence with patrons, and the testimony of the 1612 rape trial (translated by Efrem G. Calingaert). The latter includes court transcripts of Artemisia's testimony, witnesses' accounts for and against the defendant, the midwives' report of the physical examination of Artemisia, and evidence that Artemisia was "tested" for truthfulness by a sibille, which is a thumbscrew device. Tassi, the defendant, was not given any such test (404–5).

13. Throughout this chapter I refer to Artemisia Gentileschi as Artemisia in line with Garrard's commentary in *Artemisia Gentileschi* (1989) on the practice of naming, "not in the spirit of the deplorable literary habit of calling women artists by their first names (and men by their last), but partly to distinguish Artemisia from her father Orazio" and "because art historians commonly use Italian Renaissance artists' first names, as in Piero (della Francesca) or Michelangelo (Buonarroti)" (489n. 1).

14. Garrard (1989) devotes a chapter to the work, discussing it as a combination of self-portraiture and allegorical representation. Artemisia portrays her own likeness while also giving herself attributes of "pittura," the female personification of the art of painting, in such details as the chain and pendent she wears and her unruly hair. "Pittura, or the allegorical representation of the art of painting as a female figure, made her appearance in Italian art in the first half of the sixteenth century, along with the equally new female personifications of sculpture and architecture" (340).

15. For a recent collection of essays on cultural memory, especially in regard to trauma, war, and political narratives, see Mieke Bal, Jonathan Crewe, and Leo Spitzer, eds. *Acts of Memory: Cultural Recall in the Present* (Hanover: Univ. Press of New England, 1999). Van Alphen's "Symptoms of Discursivity: Experience, Memory, and Trauma" (24–38) stresses ways in which experience and discourse are inseparable. "Discourse has a fundamental role in the process that allows experiences to come about and in shaping their form and content" (25), and reveals memory as "not something we have, but something we produce *as individuals sharing a culture*" (37, italics in original). This applies to *Artemisia*, for the "thing" being remembered no longer has any "real" existence and comes to life entirely through discourse shared by numerous speakers.

16. Garrard in *Artemisia Gentileschi* (1989) simply notes Banti's book as a fictional romance (519n. 243).

17. Valeria Finucci, "'Portrait of the Artist as a Female Painter': The Kunstler-roman Tradition in A. Banti's *Artemisia*," *Quaderni d'italianistica* 8 (1987): 167–93. In another study, "From Mother to Daughter: The Emergence of a Female Geneal-ogy in Anna Banti's *Artemisia* and Alba de Céspedes's *Dalla parte di lei*," Anna Marie Torriglia discusses the book as a novel (*Italica* 73 [1996]: 369–87).

18. JoAnn Cannon, "*Artemisia* and the Life Story of the Exceptional Woman," *Forum Italicum* 28 (1994): 322–41.

19. The quotation (46) is from Heller's "History, Art, and Fiction in Anna Banti's *Artemisia*," *Contemporary Women Writers in Italy: A Modern Renaissance*, ed. Santo L. Aricò (Amherst: Univ. of Massachusetts Press, 1990): 45–60. A varia-tion of this essay, "Remembering Artemisia: Anna Banti and Artemisia Gen-tileschi," appears in *Donna: Women in Italian Culture*, ed. Ada Testaferri (Toronto: Dovehouse, 1989), 99–108. Claire Marrone's essay "Women Writing Auto/biogra-phy: Anna Banti's *Artemisia* and Eunice Lipton's *Alias Olympia*," in *Life Writing/ Writing Lives*, ed. Bette H. Kirschstein (Malabar, FL: Krieger, 2001), examines the book as a hybrid work of "creative" biographical and autobiographical writing. In contrast to my own view that emphasizes history, especially current catastrophe and devastation, Marrone believes *Artemisia* subordinates historical particulars and specific sites, commenting: "Because of the two temporal moments at play— the Second World War and Renaissance Italy—the dominant themes of the text are ahistorical" (116).

20. Sidonie Smith, *Subjectivity, Identity, and the Body: Women's Autobiographi-cal Practices in the Twentieth Century* (Bloomington: Indiana Univ. Press, 1993), 3.

21. Lewis refers also to the heat and dry conditions. He recalls Allied troops able to cross the river bed into the city because the river was nearly dry. After August 4, 1944, there was ready access into the city, but Allied forces delayed enter-ing because they had lost a quarter of their forces (51).

22. Lewis presents the scene of the same day with some additional details: "At 10:30 P.M., the Florentines, shut up in their homes, heard tremendous rumblings from the vicinity of the river. Half an hour later there was a colossal explosion, and this was followed by periodic earthshocks until 5 A.M." (50).

23. Shoshana Felman and Dori Laub, *Testimony: Crises of Witnessing in Litera-ture, Psychoanalysis, and History* (New York: Routledge, 1992), 69.

24. When Artemisia settled in Naples it was the second largest city in Europe and a thriving art center. She received many commissions from aristocratic and royal patrons including Charles I of England and Don Antonio Ruffo of Sicily, to whom some of her extant letters are addressed (Garrard, *Artemisia Gentileschi* [1989], 88–110, 390–401).

25. Michael M. J. Fischer, "Autobiographical Voices (1, 2, 3) and Mosaic Mem-ory: Experimental Sondages in the (Post)modern World," in *Autobiography and Postmodernism*, ed. Kathleen Ashley, Leigh Gilmore, and Gerald Peters (Amherst: Univ. of Massachusetts Press, 1994), 79.

26. Barbara Kosta, *Recasting Autobiography: Women's Counterfictions in Con-temporary German Literature and Film* (Ithaca: Cornell Univ. Press, 1994), 10.

27. An October 24, 1637, letter asks for news of her husband in Rome, whether he is alive or dead (Garrard, *Artemisia Gentileschi* [1989], 387–88)

28. Rita Felski, *Beyond Feminist Aesthetics: Feminist Literature and Social Change* (Cambridge: Harvard Univ. Press, 1989), 151.

29. Charles I was an art collector and patron, with strong ties to Italy, a liking for Italian Renaissance art, and a habit of inviting Italian artists to work in his court. Garrard (*Artemesia Gentileschi*, 1989) hypothesizes that the primary reason for Artemisia's time in England (1638 to ca. 1641) was to help her father, then in his midseventies, decorate the ceiling of the Queen's House in Greenwich. Orazio had been in England since 1626. The plan called for nine canvases across a forty-foot-square ceiling. Garrard points out that previous scholarship attributes only two or three of the figures to Artemisia and that official accounts list the commission as only Orazio's. Garrard believes Artemisia's contributions are more than what have been officially credited to her (112–21). Inventories after Charles I was executed show that the king owned numerous paintings by Artemisia, among them: a *Susanna and the Elders*, a *Tarquin and Lucretia*, a *Self-Portrait*, a *Pintura*, a *Saint Laying his Hand on Fruit*, and a *Bathsheba Bathing with Other Naked Figures*. Most of these were sold by midcentury. The painting still in the Royal Collection today is the famous *Self-Portrait* (111–12, 514nn. 190–93).

30. Carol Hanbery MacKay, "Biography as Reflected Autobiography: The Self-Creation of Anne Thackeray Ritchie," *Revealing Lives: Autobiography, Biography, and Gender,* ed. Susan Groag Bell and Marilyn Yalom (Albany: SUNY Press, 1990), 65–79, qtd. 66, 79.

31. According to Bissell and Garrard, Artemisia probably executed the self-portrait in the early 1630s. Lapierre conjectures that Artemisia brought the painting with her to London. It appears in the inventories of the royal collections after her time there, but not before (420).

32. Annella de Rosa was a Neopolitan painter. According to Richard Burt, documents do not support the "legend" that her husband, Agostino Beltrano, killed her, in "After Love Lives," accessed Nov. 24, 2000, www.unix.oit.umass.edu/~engl891/afterlovelivesnotes.htm.

33. Although Artemisia is distressed at being rejected and suffers, Banti emphasizes that she is not yet ready to embrace female sisterhood. She is hurt, for "after all her pride, whom has she had to lean on, confide in, subjugate? Men, worthless men.... Her thoughts wander as she drifts off to sleep" (107–8).

34. Carol Lazzaro-Weis, "Stranger Than Life? Autobiography and Historical Fiction," *Gendering Italian Fiction: Feminist Revisions of Italian History,* ed. Maria Ornella Marotti and Gabriella Brooke (Madison, N.J.: Fairleigh Dickinson Univ. Press, 1999), 31–48 (quote on p. 42). Lazzaro-Weis briefly refers to Artemisia in *From Margins to Mainstream: Feminism and Fictional Modes in Italian Women's Writings, 1968–1990* (Philadelphia: Univ. of Pennsylvania Press, 1993), 130–31.

35. Bissell reviews in *Artemisia and the Authority of Art* both sides of the debate (272–75) while offering his own argument, contrary to Garrard's, against the self-portrait actually depicting Artemisia. He dates the canvas 1638–39, which means that Artemisia would have executed it while in London and would have been considerably older than the woman shown.

36. Along these thematic lines, Banti's story "The Courage of Women" is included in *New Italian Women: A Collection of Short Fiction,* ed. Martha King (New York: Italica, 1989), 1–22. See also *"The Signorina" and Other Stories,* ed. Carol Lazzaro-Weis (New York: Modern Language Association, 2001).

37. Heller and Finucci hardly mention the conclusion. D'Ardia Caracciolo justifies its vagueness on the basis that no biographical documentation exists on Artemisia's life after her time in England.

38. Cannon, "*Artemisia* and the Life Story of the Exceptional Woman," 337.

39. Sharon O'Brien, *Willa Cather: The Emerging Voice* (Cambridge: Harvard Univ. Press, 1997), xviii. This biography was initially published in 1987, but O'Brien's preface to the later edition offers valuable insights into feminist biography and the relation of the biographer to her subject. Banti, of course, wrote biographical fiction, but many of O'Brien's points apply to this mode as well. See also O'Brien's essay (123–33) in *Contesting the Subject: Essays in the Postmodern Theory and Practice of Biography and Biographical Criticism,* William H. Epstein, ed. (West LaFayette, Ind.: Purdue Univ. Press, 1991).

40. Bissell notes that despite the paucity of documentary materials on Artemisia's last decade of life, there are thirteen letters from 1649 to 1651. Eight canvases are cited in these letters, but only two canvases have been identified (90). Bissell assumes that Artemisia returned to Italy in 1640 or thereabouts and lived in Naples until her death, which cannot be documented precisely. Garrard (1989) indicates that Artemisia's departure for England occurred after November 1637. Orazio had been there since 1626 (513–14n. 185).

4. BIBLICAL RENARRATIZATION AS AUTOBIOGRAPHICAL INTERTEXT

1. To compile this biographical summary, I have relied on the following sources: biographical information from the publisher, David R. Godine, Inc.; correspondence with John Barrett, English translator of two of Weil's books; various German-language reference works; Leslie A. Adelson's pages on Weil in *Yale Companion to Jewish Writing and Thought in German Culture, 1096–1996,* ed. Sander L. Gilman and Jack Zipes (New Haven: Yale Univ. Press, 1997): 749–55; and Dagmar C. G. Lorenz, *Keepers of the Motherland: German Texts by Jewish Women Writers* (Lincoln: Univ. of Nebraska Press, 1997), 278–85.

2. For a discussion of the changing status, constituencies, and role of the Jewish population in postwar Germany, see Sander L. Gilman, *Jews in Today's German Culture* (Bloomington: Indiana Univ. Press, 1995); and Sander L. Gilman and Karen Remmler, eds., *Reemerging Jewish Culture in Germany: Life and Literature Since 1989* (New York: New York Univ. Press, 1994).

3. Grete Weil, *Der Brautpreis: Roman* (Zurich: Nagel and Kimche, 1988); *The Bride Price: A Novel,* trans. John Barrett (Boston: Godine, 1991). The author was awarded the Geschwister Scholl Prize for this volume. References to this volume will be cited with page numbers in parentheses in the text.

4. Edith Milton, "Cutting Giants Down to Size," *The Women's Review of Books* 9 (July 1992): 37. Milton also refers to the problematic reception of Weil's books, which I discuss later in the chapter. According to Milton, the author is better

known in the United States for having returned to Germany after the war than for her writings. Jewish literary circles in America have criticized Weil for her decision and "cannot sympathize with Weil's profound but paradoxical evaluation of her own Judaism and see her German citizenship as treachery."

5. Feminist critics Alicia Suskin Ostriker, Mieke Bal, and others have rehabilitated women's stories from the Old Testament. They have, however, largely focused on figures such as Esther, Ruth, and Judith, who play more prominent roles than Michal does and are, in some ways, less problematic. See Bal, *Anti-Covenant: Counter-Reading Women's Lives in the Hebrew Bible* (Sheffield, U.K.: Almond-Sheffield, 1981) and *Lethal Love: Feminist Literary Readings of Biblical Love Stories* (Bloomington: Indiana Univ. Press, 1987); Ostriker, *The Nakedness of the Fathers: Biblical Visions and Revisions* (New Brunswick: Rutgers Univ. Press, 1994) and *Feminist Revision and the Bible* (Cambridge: Blackwell, 1993); and Alice Bach, ed., *The Pleasure of Her Text: Feminist Readings of Biblical and Historical Texts* (Philadelphia: Trinity Press, 1990). J. Cheryl Exum has researched extensively the story of Michal, with her chapter in *Fragmented Women: Feminist (Sub)Versions of Biblical Narratives* (Valley Forge, Pa.: Trinity, 1993) covering the basic issues and questions.

6. David J. A. Clines summarizes in "Michal Observed: An Introduction to Reading Her Story," in *Telling Queen Michal's Story: An Experiment in Comparative Interpretation*, ed. David J. A. Clines and Tamara C. Eskenazi (Sheffield, U.K.: JSOT Press, 1991), Michal's appearances in the pertinent sections, which are confined to four episodes and three "notations" in 1 and 2 Samuel with an additional reference in 1 Chronicles (26).

7. There have been numerous literary treatments of the Michal-David story, most recently *Queenmaker,* by India Edghill (Talitho, 1999; New York: St. Martin's, 2002), a historical fiction that similarly presents David through the eyes of Michal. Treatments in Hebrew literature include Y. L. Gordon's nineteenth-century epic poem, translated as "The Love of David and Michal"; A. Ashman's three-act drama, *Michal, the Daughter of Saul* (1940); and the historical novels *A King's Heart* (1977) by I. A. Malkiely and *King David* (1984) by Yakob Goren. Eskenazi summarizes these texts in "Michal in Hebrew Sources," *Telling Queen Michal's Story,* ed. Clines and Eskenazi, 157–74.

8. Elke Liebs points out in "Grete Weil: A Jewish Antigone," in *Facing Fascism and Confronting the Past: German Women Writers from Weimar to the Present,* ed. Elke P. Frederiksen and Martha Kaarsberg Wallach (Albany: SUNY Press, 2000), that the question was particularly aggravated because Weil did not aggressively try to get the Nazis to free her husband or seek retribution after his death at Mauthausen (238).

9. Lawrence L. Langer, *Holocaust Testimonies: The Ruins of Memory* (New Haven: Yale Univ. Press, 1991), xv.

10. Michael M. J. Fischer, "Autobiographical Voices (1, 2, 3) and Mosaic Memory: Experimental Sondages in the (Post)modern World," *Autobiography and Postmodernism,* ed. Kathleen Ashley, Leigh Gilmore, Gerald Peters (Amherst: Univ. of Massachusetts Press, 1994), 79–129.

11. Fischer, "Autobiographical Voices," 92.

12. Adele Berlin, in "Characterization in Biblical Narrative: David's Wives" (Clines and Eskenazi, eds., *Telling Queen Michal's Story*), notes the importance of Michal regardless of the brevity of her appearances. Her love for David, which she makes known twice in 1 Samuel, presents the only time in the Bible that a woman actually makes her own choice of a marriage partner. Berlin also points out that there is little evidence anywhere in the Bible that David responds in kind to Michal's emotion; he seems more interested in being a son-in-law to King Saul and thus motivated by practical considerations (91–93).

13. One of the ironies of Michal's obscurity is that despite the ambiguities and brevity of her appearances in the Old Testament, Michal exhibits remarkable traits. Clines says that Michal was the first woman in ancient Israel to be both a king's daughter and a king's wife, giving her an enormous patriarchal burden (8). Consequently, her rebellion against her father, King Saul, and her plan to get her husband safely into exile become all the more extraordinary accomplishments. In direct contrast to Clines's insistence that Michal has virtually no story, just fragmented references, Exum uses a feminist analysis in "Murder They Wrote: Ideology and the Manipulation of Female Presence in Biblical Narrative" (Clines and Eskenazi, eds., *Telling Queen Michal's Story*, 176–98) to explore Old Testament gender ideology and to reconstruct a story with enormous historical symbolism pertinent to Israel. Exum focuses on the scene in 2 Samuel, where Michal speaks scathingly to David during the celebration bringing the ark to Jerusalem and where the narration provides readers with access to her thoughts. The New Oxford English Bible presents the episode as follows: "As the ark of the Lord came into the city of David, Michal daughter of Saul looked out of the window, and saw King David leaping and dancing before the Lord; and she despised him in her heart" (2 Samuel 6.16), and then "David went to bless his household. But Michal the daughter of Saul came out to meet David, and said, 'How the king of Israel honored himself today, uncovering himself today before the eyes of his servants' maids, as any vulgar fellow might shamelessly uncover himself!' David said to Michal, 'It was before the Lord, who chose me in place of your father and all his household, to appoint me as prince over Israel, the people of the Lord, that I have danced before the Lord. I will make myself yet more contemptible than this, and I will be abased in my own eyes; but by the maid of whom you have spoken, by them I shall be held in honor.' And Michal the daughter of Saul had no child to the day of her death" (2 Samuel 6.20–23). Critics have debated this heated exchange, but Exum stresses that the moment marks the end of any balance between Saulide and Davidic values, for Michal, who once symbolized compromise, is given no further role in the Old Testament.

14. Dagmar C. G. Lorenz quotes from a 1989 interview, following the German publication of *The Bride Price*, in which Weil confirms what her text explores, the difficulties of being both German and Jewish: "I have not been raised in the Jewish tradition. My parents always believed in the German-Jewish symbiosis, as did most everybody at that time. And I always identified with German culture—with Goethe and Schiller" (*Keepers of the Motherland*, 278–79).

15. Robert Alter discusses in "Characterization and the Art of Reticence" (Clines and Eskenazi, eds., *Telling Michal's Story*) the unique status of the biblical

Michal due to her being the "only instance in all biblical narrative in which we are explicitly told that a woman loves a man" (68). Alter, though, also points to the opaque nature of the relationship between her and David, for the Bible gives no specific reasons why she starts to love him; Weil makes effective use of this absence by portraying her own version of Michal as vacillating between love and hate for her husband over the years.

16. Zafrira Ben-Barak investigates the historical and legal background of Michal's second marriage and her subsequent return to David in "The Legal Background to the Restoration of Michal to David," in Clines and Eskenazi, eds., *Telling Queen Michal's Story* (74–90).

17. *My Sister, My Antigone,* trans. Krishna Winston (New York: Avon/Bard, 1984); *Last Trolley from Beethovenstraat,* trans. John Barrett (Boston: Godine, 1997).

18. John Barrett, letter to the author, June 23, 1999.

19. Lorenz, *Keepers of the Motherland,* 284.

20. The question of Michal's second marriage to Paltiel, a man of no status or wealth, and her reunion with David after many years is much discussed by critics as to its legal, moral, and social implications.

21. Elaine Scarry, *The Body in Pain: The Making and Unmaking of the World* (New York: Oxford Univ. Press, 1985), 38–42.

22. Lawrence L. Langer, *Admitting the Holocaust: Collected Essays* (New York: Oxford Univ. Press, 1995), 9.

23. The autobiographical narrator recalls her prewar belief that she would be immune from persecution because of her strong nationalism and weak religious faith: "Strange: even during the persecution I did not have the feeling they could mean me. Each time I left the house I had to make it clear to myself again: I look Jewish, my (forged) identification card is not good enough so that they'll accept it. If I go out into the street, they'll stop me and send me to the east. (The east, our word in those days for Auschwitz and other camps which, with few exceptions, we did not know by name)" (143).

24. Langer alludes to the converging of David and Hitler in his review "A Stranger in Her Own Land" (*Book World,* April 26, 1992), though less forcefully than Lorenz does in her study. He comments suggestively that the biographical portrait is one sided, slanted very heavily to expose David as a "primitive and warlike leader," with "little of the heroic in David's achievement, and less to admire in the Jahwe he worships" (5). Langer refers to certain "facts" that are obscured by the fictional dimensions of the book, but he is not more explicit concerning the nature of those facts or the specific way that the storytelling has, presumably, altered them.

25. Lorenz, *Keepers of the Motherland,* 283.

26. Ibid., 284.

27. For references to David's wives and children, see 1 Chronicles 2.3. Weil's renarratization focuses on four of his wives: Michal, Abigail, Maacha, and Bathsheba.

28. Elke Liebs, in "Grete Weil: A Jewish Antigone," points to a similar dichotomy in Weil's *My Sister, My Antigone,* and finds Weil's contradictory attitude toward wartime victimization—and her own experiences—very disturbing. The

author "exposes the sentimentality of the victims, and the absurdity of (Jewish) survivors' syndrome, from which she herself suffers so much" (236). This section of *The Bride Price* exhibits a similar contradiction, acknowledging and denying a bond with other Jewish women who survived the Nazi genocide.

29. Lorenz, *Keepers of the Motherland*, 285. For an excellent summary of the Historians' Debate, see Dominick LaCapra, "The Historians' Debate (*Historikerstreit*)," Gilman and Zipes, eds., *Yale Companion*, 812–19.

5. AUTOBIOGRAPHICAL DISCOURSE AS BIOGRAPHICAL TRIBUTE

1. Allende describes in *Paula* as well as in numerous interviews the circumstances that led her to write her first novel. During an interview later printed in *Conversations with Isabel Allende*, ed. John Rodden (Austin: Univ. of Texas Press, 1999), she said that on January 8, 1981, she received the phone call that her grandfather was dying: "And I decided to write a letter about all the things he told us when we were young. I was working two shifts, twelve hours per day, and I wrote at night. I had five hundred pages by the end of the year. And it was *The House of the Spirits*" ("After Paula," 412).

2. *The House of the Spirits*, trans. Magda Bogin (New York: Knopf, 1985); *La casa de los espiritus* (Barcelona: Plaza y Janés, 1982). *Of Love and Shadows*, trans. Margaret Sayers Peden (New York: Knopf, 1987); *De amor y de sombra* (Barcelona: Plaza y Janés, 1984). *Eva Luna*, trans. Margaret Sayers Peden (New York: Knopf, 1988); *Eva Luna* (Barcelona: Plaza y Janés, 1987). *The Stories of Eva Luna*, trans. Margaret Sayers Peden (New York: Atheneum, 1991); *Cuentos de Eva Luna* (Buenos Aires: Editorial Sudamericana and Barcelona: Plaza y Janés, 1989); *The Infinite Plan*, trans. Margaret Sayers Peden (New York: HarperCollins, 1993); *El plan infinito* (Buenos Aires: Editorial Sudamericana and Barcelona: Plaza y Janés, 1991).

3. Elyse Crystall, Jill Kuhnheim, and Mary Layoun, "An Interview with Isabel Allende," *Contemporary Literature* 33 (Winter 1992): 585–600.

4. Ibid., 586–87.

5. Allende recalls that her family became aware of porphyria in the early 1980s after a niece was diagnosed with it in North America. Allende's first husband, son, and daughter all tested positive (280). Most people who know about the disease, which derives from an enzyme disorder, associate it with the British royal family, including George III and George IV.

6. *Paula*, trans. Margaret Sayers Peden (New York: HarperCollins, 1995); *Paula* (Buenos Aires: Editorial Sudamericana, 1994). Citations from the English-language translation will be placed in parentheses in the text. In an interview before the U.S. edition of *Paula* came out, Allende explained that she did not begin writing with the goal of publication. In the book, and in this 1994 interview with Rosa Pinol, she credits her literary agent with the idea to write as an "escape valve" during the first few months of Paula's illness ("A Mother's Letter of Loss," *Conversations*, ed. Rodden, 400). It should be added that Allende has explained *My Invented Country: A Nostalgic Journey through Chile* as a response to the catastrophic destruction of the World Trade Center. In this book's introduction she notes the coincidence of the tragedy of September 11, 2001, to September 11,

1973, the date of the military coup in Chile. Both were life-changing events for Allende.

7. Geoffrey Dean, *The Porphyrias: A Story of Inheritance and Environment* (Philadelphia: Lippincott, 1971). Dean stresses that patients who carry the gene should do everything possible to avoid the onset of an acute attack. "Once an acute attack has commenced, the patient's life is in great danger and a very high level of medical and nursing care will be required" (133–34). After initial difficulty in speaking, the patient will experience respiratory paralysis and need a tracheotomy and respirator.

8. Allende describes the writing time in more detail in her interview with John Rodden, entitled "The Writer as Exile, and Her Search for Home" (*Conversations*, 427–38). The manuscript went through two drafts, but there was "very little editing" after she wrote out the first draft: "With nonfiction, everything is just given to you" (435). In her interview with Virginia Invernizzi ("I Remember Emotions, I Remember Moments," 438–61) in the same volume, Allende again describes writing the first part of the book at the hospital in Madrid and the rest of it in her home in California. This information confirms the dates that she provides in *Paula* relative to her writing times and locations.

9. The genre category for *Paula* warrants discussion since the text relies on different modes. Rodden indicates that in Germany and the Netherlands, for example, the book was published as a work of fiction (*Conversations*, 3).

10. See G. Thomas Couser, *Recovering Bodies: Illness, Disability, and Life Writing* (Madison: Univ. of Wisconsin Press, 1997), 5. He uses the term "autopathography" in "Autopathography: Women, Illness, Lifewriting" (65) in his guest-edited *Illness, Disability, and Lifewriting: a/b Autobiography Studies* 6 (1991), which leads logically to the complementary term "biopathography."

11. Paul John Eakin, *How Our Lives Become Stories* (Ithaca: Cornell Univ. Press, 1999), 160.

12. Doris Grumbach, "Farewell My Daughter," *Los Angeles Times Book Review*, Apr. 30, 1995, 3.

13. Suzanne Ruta, "The Long Goodbye," *New York Times Book Review*, May 21, 1995, 11.

14. The essays in Shari Benstock's collection, *The Private Self: Theory and Practice of Women's Autobiographical Writings* (Chapel Hill: Univ. of North Carolina Press, 1988), map out important foundational work in women's autobiographical studies. Susan Stanford Friedman, in "Women's Autobiographical Selves: Theory and Practice," examines how individualistic identity paradigms fail to take into account the psychological and social development of women and minorities (34–62). For a more recent discussion of relationality and a response to Friedman, see Eakin's second chapter, "Relational Selves, Relational Lives: Autobiography and the Myth of Autonomy," in *How Our Lives Become Stories*.

15. Matthew Norman's review of the documentary on BBC 1, directed by Mischa Scorer, exemplifies this point of view. In "Missing Paula, Missing the Point," Norman criticizes the documentary for failing to "paint a vibrant picture" of Paula, who seems "little more than the peg" on which Allende's own history rests (*Evening Standard*, Sept. 19, 1995, 45).

16. Linda Wagner-Martin, *Telling Women's Lives: The New Biography* (New Brunswick: Rutgers Univ. Press, 1994).

17. Diane Wood Middlebrook, "Telling Secrets," *The Seductions of Biography*, ed. Mary Rhiel and David Suchoff (New York: Routledge, 1996), 123–29. See also Middlebrook's essay "Postmodernism and the Biographer," *Revealing Lives: Autobiography, Biography, and Gender*, ed. Susan Groag Bell and Marilyn Yalom, eds.,(Albany: SUNY Press, 1990), 155–65.

18. Phyllis Rose, "Confessions of a Burned-Out Biographer," *The Seductions of Biography*, ed. Rhiel and Suchoff, 136.

19. Middlebrook, "Telling Secrets," 129.

20. Crystall et al., "An Interview," 591. Allende repeats this point in her interview with Invernizzi in *Conversations with Isabel Allende.*

21. Elaine Scarry, *The Body in Pain: The Making and Unmaking of the World* (New York: Oxford Univ. Press, 1985).

22. Ibid., 4–5.

23. Gérard Genette, *Narrative Discourse: An Essay in Method*, trans. Jane E. Lewin (Ithaca: Cornell Univ. Press, 1980), 219.

24. L. L. Langness and Gelya Frank, *Lives: An Anthropological Approach to Biography* (Novato, Calif.: Chandler and Sharp, 1981), 96.

25. Janet Malcolm, *The Silent Woman: Sylvia Plath and Ted Hughes* (New York: Knopf, 1994), 8–9. The full statement applies to biographies of persons who, in contrast to Paula, are already deceased: "Biography is the medium through which the remaining secrets of the famous dead are taken from them and dumped out in full view of the world. The biographer at work, indeed, is like the professional burglar, breaking into a house, rifling through certain drawers that he has good reason to think contain the jewelry and money, and triumphantly bearing his loot away. The voyeurism and busybodyism that impel writers and readers of biography alike are obscured by an apparatus of scholarship designed to give the enterprise an appearance of blanklike blandness and solidity." Rose's term, "psychic exploitation," comes from "Confessions of a Burned-Out Biographer," 136.

26. Ruta, "The Long Goodbye," 11.

27. Wilson Snipes, "The Biographer as a Center of Reference," *Biography: An Interdisciplinary Quarterly* 5.3 (Summer 1982): 217.

28. Genette, *Narrative Discourse*, 216–19.

29. Eakin, *How Our Lives*, 85.

30. "I Remember Emotions, I Remember Moments," in *Conversations*, ed. Rodden, 444–45.

31. Gusdorf's 1956 essay is translated and reprinted as "Conditions and Limits of Autobiography," in *Autobiography: Essays Theoretical and Critical*, ed. James Olney (Princeton: Princeton Univ. Press, 1980), 24–48. See also Georg Misch, *History of Autobiography*, trans. E. W. Dickes (1907; rpt. London: Routledge and Kegan Paul, 1950).

32. Philippe Lejeune, *On Autobiography*, ed. Paul John Eakin, trans. Katherine Leary (Minneapolis: Univ. of Minnesota Press, 1989), 4.

33. Despite the fact that the Allende family always called Salvador Allende "uncle," he and Isabel Allende were actually second cousins. Her father, who abandoned

the family when she was a child, and Salvador Allende were first cousins. Salvador Allende was also her godfather (*Conversations*, ed. Rodden, 29n. 15).

34. Ruta, "The Long Goodbye," 11.

35. Georges Gusdorf, "Conditions and Limits of Autobiography," in *Autobiography*, ed. Olney, 30.

36. Allende is unconcerned with issues of accuracy or exaggeration. "You, Paula, have given me this silence in which to examine my path through the world, to return to the true and the fantastic pasts, to recover memories others have forgotten, to remember what never happened and what still may happen" (162).

37. Oliver Sacks, *The Man Who Mistook His Wife for a Hat and Other Clinical Tales* (London: Picador, 1986), 105–6, 4.

38. Genette, *Narrative Discourse*, 217–18.

39. Allende began *The House of the Spirits* on January 8, 1981: "I also began my second novel on an eighth of January, and since have not dared change that auspicious date, partly out of superstition, but also for reasons of discipline" (9).

40. Scarry, *The Body in Pain*, 13.

41. Susanna Egan, *Mirror Talk: Genres of Crisis in Contemporary Autobiographies* (Chapel Hill: Univ. of North Carolina Press, 1999), 25.

42. Ibid., 227.

43. Suzette A. Henke, in *Shattered Subjects: Trauma and Testimony in Women's Life-Writing* (New York: St. Martin's Press, 1998), for instance, studies how repressed traumas manifest themselves in feminist life narratives that reconstruct the subject (xiii, 144).

44. Egan, *Mirror Talk*, 198.

45. Lejeune, *On Autobiography*, 5.

46. Arthur W. Frank, *The Wounded Storyteller: Body, Illness, and Ethics* (Chicago: Univ. of Chicago Press, 1995), 115.

47. Scarry, *The Body in Pain*, 307.

48. Brian McHale, *Postmodernist Fiction* (London: Routledge, 1987), 135.

49. Julia Kristeva, "Freud and Love: Treatment and Its Discontents," *The Kristeva Reader*, ed. Toril Moi (New York: Columbia Univ. Press, 1986), 244.

50. In the book, the date of Paula's death is cited as December 6. A number of other sources, including Allende herself in interviews, give December 8 as the date (Rodden, *Conversations*, 410, 416, 427). Rodden confirms the date as December 8 in his chapter "The Chilean Scheherazade," *Performing the Literary Interview: How Writers Craft their Public Selves* (Lincoln: Univ. of Nebraska Press, 2001), 206.

51. George C. Rosenwald and Richard L. Ochberg, eds., *Storied Lives: The Cultural Politics of Self-Understanding* (New Haven: Yale Univ. Press, 1992), 8, 286.

52. Rodden quotes Allende as she explains in an interview that she composed the notes for *Paula* as a private activity. "I was not thinking of publishing ... my only goal was to survive; that is the only time that I have written something without thinking of a reader" (*Conversations*, 17).

Works Cited

Abbott, H. Porter. "Autobiography, Autography, Fiction: Groundwork for a Taxonomy of Textual Categories." *New Literary History* 19 (1988): 597–615.

Adelson, Leslie A. *Making Bodies, Making History: Feminism and German Identity.* Lincoln: Univ. of Nebraska Press, 1993.

———. "1971 *Ein Sommer in der Woche der Itke K.* by American-born author Jeannette Lander is published." Gilman and Zipes 750–55.

Allen, Helena G. *The Betrayal of Liliuokalani: Last Queen of Hawaii 1838–1917.* Honolulu: Mutual, 1982.

Allende, Isabel. "After Paula." Interview with John Rodden. Rodden, *Conversations* 409–20.

———. *Eva Luna.* Trans. Margaret Sayers Peden. New York: Knopf, 1988; *Eva Luna.* Barcelona: Plaza y Janés, 1987.

———. *The House of the Spirits.* Trans. Magda Bogin. New York: Knopf, 1985; *La casa de los espiritus.* Barcelona: Plaza y Janés, 1982.

———. "I Remember Emotions, I Remember Moments." Interview with Virginia Invernizzi. Rodden, *Conversations* 438–61.

———. *The Infinite Plan.* Trans. Margaret Sayers Peden. New York: HarperCollins, 1993; *El plan infinito.* Barcelona: Plaza y Janés, 1991.

———. *Of Love and Shadows.* Trans. Margaret Sayers Peden. New York: Knopf, 1987; *De amor y de sombra.* Barcelona: Plaza y Janés, 1984.

———. "A Mother's Letter of Loss." Interview with Rosa Piñol. Rodden, *Conversations* 399–401.

———. *My Invented Country: A Nostalgic Journey through Chile.* Trans. Margaret Sayers Peden. New York: HarperCollins, 2003; *Mi País Inventado: Un Paseo Nostalgico por Chile.* Barcelona: Areté, 2003.

———. *Paula.* Trans. Margaret Sayers Peden. New York: HarperCollins, 1995. *Paula.* Buenos Aires: Editorial Sudamericana, 1995.

———. *The Stories of Eva Luna.* Trans. Margaret Sayers Peden. New York: Atheneum, 1991; *Cuentos de Eva Luna.* Barcelona: Plaza y Janés, 1989.

———. "The Writer as Exile, and Her Search for Home." Interview with John Rodden. Rodden, *Conversations* 427–38.

Alter, Robert. "Characterization and the Art of Reticence." Clines and Eskenazi 64–73. Rpt. from *The Art of Biblical Narrative*. London: George Allen, 1981. 114–25.

"Among the Books: *Hawaii's Story by Her ex-Queen*." *The Watchman*, Feb. 10, 1898, 14.

Aricò, Santo L., ed. *Contemporary Women Writers in Italy: A Modern Renaissance*. Amherst: Univ. of Massachusetts Press, 1990.

Ashley, Kathleen, Leigh Gilmore, and Gerald Peters, eds. *Autobiography and Postmodernism*. Amherst: Univ. of Massachusetts Press, 1994.

Augustine, Jane, ed. *The Gift by H.D.: The Complete Text*. Gainesville: Univ. Press of Florida, 1998.

Bach, Alice, ed. *The Pleasure of Her Text: Feminist Readings of Biblical and Historical Texts*. Philadelphia: Trinity Press, 1990.

Bakhtin, M. M. *The Dialogic Imagination*. Ed. Michael Holquist. Trans. Caryl Emerson and Michael Holquist. Austin: Univ. of Texas Press, 1981.

Bal, Mieke, ed. *Anti-Covenant: Counter-Reading Women's Lives in the Hebrew Bible*. Sheffield, U.K.: Almond-Sheffield, 1981.

———. *Lethal Love: Feminist Literary Readings of Biblical Love Stories*. Bloomington: Indiana Univ. Press, 1987.

———. "Memories in the Museum: Preposterous Histories for Today." Bal, Crewe, and Spitzer 171–90.

Bal, Mieke, Jonathan Crewe, and Leo Spitzer, eds. *Acts of Memory: Cultural Recall in the Present*. Hanover: Univ. Press of New England, 1999.

Banti, Anna. *Artemisia*. Florence: Sansoni, 1947. Trans. Shirley D'Ardia Caracciolo. Lincoln: Univ. of Nebraska Press, 1988.

———. "The Courage of Women." Martha King 1–22.

John Barrett. Letter to Miriam Fuchs. June 23, 1999.

Beckwith, Martha Warren, ed. *The Kumulipo: A Hawaiian Creation Chant*. Chicago: Univ. of Chicago Press, 1951; Honolulu: Univ. of Hawai'i Press, 1972.

Bell, Susan Groag, and Marilyn Yalom, eds. *Revealing Lives: Autobiography, Biography, and Gender*. Albany: SUNY Press, 1990.

Bellaro, Beverly. "Anna Banti (Lucia Lopresti Longhi) (1895–1985)." *The Feminist Encyclopedia of Italian Literature*. Ed. Rinaldina Russell. Westport, Conn.: Greenwood, 1997. 26–27.

———. "Anna Banti." *Italian Women Writers: A Bio-Bibliographical Sourcebook*. Ed. Rinaldina Russell. Westport, Conn.: Greenwood, 1994. 35–43.

Ben-Barak, Zafrira. "The Legal Background to the Restoration of Michal to David." Clines and Eskenazi 74–90. Rpt. from *Studies in the Historical Books*. Ed. J. A. Emerton. Leiden, The Netherlands: Brill, 1979. 15–29.

Benstock, Shari, ed. *The Private Self: Theory and Practice of Women's Autobiographical Writings*. Chapel Hill: Univ. of North Carolina Press, 1988.

Berlin, Adele. "Characterization in Biblical Narrative: David's Wives." Clines and Eskenazi 91–93. Excerpted from *Journal for the Study of the Old Testament* 23 (1982): 69–85.

Beverley, John. "The Margin at the Center: On *Testimonio*." Smith and Watson, *De/Colonizing the Subject* 91–114.

Binney, Judith. "Maori Oral Narratives, Pakeha Written Texts: Two Forms of Telling History." *New Zealand Journal of History* 20 (1987): 16–20.

Bissell, R. Ward. *Artemisia Gentileschi and the Authority of Art: Critical Reading and Catalogue Raisonné*. University Park: Pennsylvania State Univ. Press, 1999.

———. *Orazio Gentileschi and the Poetic Tradition in Caravaggesque Painting*. University Park: Pennsylvania State Univ. Press, 1981.

Borzello, Frances. *Seeing Ourselves: Women's Self Portraits*. New York: Abrams, 1998.

Bott, Robin L. "'I know what is due to me': Self-Fashioning and Legitimization in Queen Lili'uokalani's *Hawaii's Story by Hawaii's Queen*." Homans and Munich 140–56.

Bramley, Marine. *Artemisia, or the Passion of Painting*. Trans. C. Dickson. New York: Welcome Rain, 2000.

Brodzki, Bella, and Celeste Schenck, eds. *Life/Lines: Theorizing Women's Autobiography*. Ithaca: Cornell Univ. Press, 1988.

Bryher. *The Days of Mars: A Memoir, 1940–1946*. New York: Harcourt, 1972.

Burt, Richard. "After Love Lives." www.unix.oit.umass.edu/~engl891/afterlove livesnotes.htm. Accessed Nov. 24, 2000.

Calder, Angus. *The People's War: Britain 1939–1945*. New York: Pantheon, 1969.

Cannon, JoAnn. "*Artemisia* and the Life Story of the Exceptional Woman." *Forum Italicum* 28 (1994): 322–41.

Caracciolo, Shirley D'Ardia. Afterword. *Artemisia*. Lincoln: Univ. of Nebraska Press, 1988. 215–19.

Caruth, Cathy, ed. *Trauma: Explorations in Memory*. Baltimore: Johns Hopkins Univ. Press, 1995.

———. *Unclaimed Experience: Trauma, Narrative, and History*. Baltimore: Johns Hopkins Univ. Press, 1996.

Chisholm, Dianne. *H.D.'s Freudian Poetics: Psychoanalysis in Translation*. Ithaca: Cornell Univ. Press, 1992.

Christiansen, Keith. *Orazio and Artemisia Gentileschi*. New Haven: Yale Univ. Press, 2001.

Clark, Sally. *Life Without Instruction: A Play*. Vancouver: Talon, 1994.

Clines, David J. A., and Tamara C. Eskenazi, eds. *Telling Queen Michal's Story: An Experiment in Comparative Interpretation*. Sheffield, U.K.: JSOT Press, 1991.

Coffman, Tom. *Nation Within: The Story of America's Annexation of the Nation of Hawai'i*. Kāne'ohe, Hawai'i: Epicenter, 1998.

Collecott, Diana. Introduction. *The Gift* [abridged]. London: Virago, 1984. vii–xix.

Cooksley, Peter G. *Flying Bomb: The Story of Hitler's V-weapons in World War II*. New York: Scribners, 1979.

Cornell, Sarah. "Hélène Cixous' *Le Livre de Promethea*." Sellers 127–40.

Couser, G. Thomas. *Recovering Bodies: Illness, Disability, and Life Writing*. Madison: Univ. of Wisconsin Press, 1997.

Crystall, Elyse, Jill Kuhnheim, and Mary Layoun. "An Interview with Isabel Allende." *Contemporary Literature* 33 (Winter 1992): 585–600.

Culbertson, Roberta. "Embodied Memory, Transcendence, and Telling: Recounting Trauma, Re-establishing the Self." *New Literary History* 26 (1995): 169–95.

Dean, Geoffrey. *The Porphyrias: A Story of Inheritance and Environment.* Philadelphia: Lippincott, 1971.

de Man, Paul. "Autobiography as De-facement." *MLN* 94 (1979): 919–30.

Deighton, Len. *Battle of Britain.* London: Rainbird, 1980.

Dobson, Silvia. "'Shock Knit Within Terror': Living Through World War II." *Iowa Review* 16 (Fall 1986): 232–45.

DuPlessis, Rachel Blau. *H.D.: The Career of That Struggle.* Bloomington: Indiana Univ. Press, 1986.

———. "A Note on the State of H.D.'s *The Gift.*" *Sulfur* 9 (1984): 178–82.

Eakin, Paul John. *Fictions in Autobiography: Studies in the Art of Self-Invention.* Princeton: Princeton Univ. Press, 1985.

———. *How Our Lives Become Stories.* Ithaca: Cornell Univ. Press, 1999.

———. *Touching the World: Reference in Autobiography.* Princeton: Princeton Univ. Press, 1992.

Edghill, India. *Queenmaker.* 1999. New York: St. Martin's, 2002.

Egan, Susanna. *Mirror Talk: Genres of Crisis in Contemporary Autobiography.* Chapel Hill: Univ. of North Carolina Press, 1999.

Egan, Susanna, and Gabriele Helms, eds. Special Issue on "Autobiography and Changing Identities." *Biography: An Interdisciplinary Quarterly* 24.1 (Winter 2001).

Egger, Bruce E., and Lee MacMillan Otts. *G. Company's War: Two Personal Accounts of the Campaigns in Europe, 1944–1945.* Ed. Paul Roley. Tuscaloosa: Univ. of Alabama Press, 1992.

Engel, Susan. *Context Is Everything: The Nature of Memory.* New York: Freeman, 1999.

Epstein, William H., ed. *Contesting the Subject: Essays in the Postmodern Theory and Practice of Biography and Biographical Criticism.* West LaFayette: Purdue Univ. Press, 1991.

Exum, J. Cheryl. *Fragmented Women: Feminist (Sub)Versions of Biblical Narratives.* Valley Forge: Trinity, 1993.

———. "Murder They Wrote: Ideology and the Manipulation of Female Presence in Biblical Narrative." Clines and Eskenazi 176–98. Rpt. from Bach 55–68.

Felman, Shoshana, and Dori Laub. *Testimony: Crises of Witnessing in Literature, Psychoanalysis, and History.* New York: Routledge, 1992.

Felski, Rita. *Beyond Feminist Aesthetics: Feminist Literature and Social Change.* Cambridge: Harvard Univ. Press, 1989.

Finucci, Valeria. "'A Portrait of the Artist as a Female Painter': The Kunstlerroman Tradition in A. Banti's *Artemisia.*" *Quaderni d'italianistica* 8 (1987): 167–93.

Fischer, Michael M. J. "Autobiographical Voices (1, 2, 3) and Mosaic Memory: Experimental Sondages in the (Post)modern World." Ashley, Gilmore, and Peters 79–129.

Frank, Arthur W. *The Wounded Storyteller: Body, Illness, and Ethics.* Chicago: Univ. of Chicago Press, 1995.

Frederiksen, Elke P., and Martha Kaarsberg Wallach, eds. *Facing Fascism and*

Confronting the Past: German Women Writers from Weimar to the Present. Albany: SUNY Press, 2000.

Friedman, Ellen G., and Miriam Fuchs, eds. *Breaking the Sequence: Women's Experimental Fiction.* Princeton: Princeton Univ. Press, 1989.

Friedman, Susan Stanford. *Penelope's Web: Gender, Modernity, H.D.'s Fiction.* New York: Cambridge Univ. Press, 1990.

———. *Psyche Reborn: The Emergence of H.D.* Bloomington: Indiana Univ. Press, 1981.

———. "Women's Autobiographical Selves: Theory and Practice." Benstock 4–62.

Friedman, Susan Stanford, and Rachel Blau DuPlessis, eds. *Signets: Reading H.D.* Madison: Univ. of Wisconsin Press, 1990.

Fuchs, Miriam. "The Diaries of Queen Lili'uokalani." *Profession 95* (1995) 38–40.

———. "H.D.'s *The Gift*: 'Hide-and-Seek' with the 'Skeletal Hand of Death.'" Hall and Morgan 85–102.

———. "H.D.'s Self-Inscription: Between Time and 'Out-of-Time' in *The Gift*." *Southern Review* 26 (July 1990): 542–54.

———. "Recalling the Past and Rescuing the Self: Autobiographical Slippage in Grete Weil's *The Bride Price: A Novel*." *Shofar: Journal of the Western Jewish Studies Association* 17 (Winter 1999): 73–83.

Gallagher, Jean. *The World Wars Through the Female Gaze.* Carbondale: Southern Illinois Univ. Press, 1998.

Garrard, Mary D. "Artemisia Gentileschi: The Artist's Autograph in Letters and Paintings." Stanton 81–95.

———. *Artemisia Gentileschi: The Image of the Female Hero in Italian Baroque Art.* Princeton: Princeton Univ. Press, 1989.

———. *Artemisia Gentileschi around 1622: The Shaping and Reshaping of an Artistic Identity.* Berkeley: Univ. of California Press, 2001.

———. "Artemisia Gentileschi's 'Self-Portrait as the Allegory of Painting.'" *Art Bulletin* 62 (1980): 97–112.

———. Introduction. *Artemisia Gentileschi.* New York: Rizzoli, 1993.

Garrard, Mary D., and Norma Broude, eds. *Feminism and Art History.* New York: Harper, 1982.

Genette, Gérard. *Narrative Discourse: An Essay in Method.* Trans. Jane E. Lewin. Ithaca: Cornell Univ. Press, 1980.

Gilman, Sander L. *Jews in Today's German Culture.* Bloomington: Indiana Univ. Press, 1995.

Gilman, Sander L., and Steven T. Katz. *Anti-Semitism in Times of Crisis.* New York: New York Univ. Press, 1991.

Gilman, Sander L., and Karen Remmler, eds. *Reemerging Jewish Culture in Germany: Life and Literature Since 1989.* New York: New York Univ. Press, 1994.

Gilman, Sander L., and Jack Zipes, eds. *Yale Companion to Jewish Writing and Thought in German Culture, 1096–1996.* New Haven: Yale Univ. Press, 1997.

Gilmore, Leigh. "Limit-Cases: Trauma, Self-Representation, and the Jurisdictions of Identity." Egan and Helms, 128–39.

———. *The Limits of Autobiography: Trauma and Testimony.* Ithaca: Cornell Univ. Press, 2001.

Greer, Germaine. *The Obstacle Race: The Fortunes of Women Painters and Their Work*. New York: Farrar, 1979.

Grosz, Elizabeth A. *Space, Time, and Perversion: Essays On the Politics of Bodies*. New York: Routledge, 1995.

Grumbach, Doris. "Farewell My Daughter." *Los Angeles Times Book Review*, Apr. 30, 1995, 3.

Guest, Barbara. *Herself Defined: The Poet H.D. and Her World*. Garden City: Doubleday, 1984.

Gusdorf, Georges. "Conditions and Limits of Autobiography." Trans. James Olney. Olney, *Autobiography* 28–48.

Hackler, Rhoda A. E. "'My Dear Friend': Letters of Queen Victoria and Queen Emma." *The Hawaiian Journal of History* 22 (1988): 101–30.

Hall, Colette T., and Janice Morgan, eds. *Redefining Autobiography in Twentieth-Century Fiction by Women*. New York: Garland, 1991.

Harlow, Barbara. *Resistance Literature*. New York: Methuen, 1987.

Harris, Ann Sutherland, and Linda Nochlin. *Women Artists: 1550–1950*. L.A. County Museum of Art. New York: Knopf, 1976.

Haskel, Francis. "Artemisia's Revenge?" *New York Review of Books*, July 20, 1989, 36–38.

Hawkins, Anne Hunsaker. *Reconstructing Illness: Studies in Pathography*. West Lafayette, Ind.: Purdue Univ. Press, 1993.

H.D. (Hilda Doolittle). *Asphodel*. Ed. and introd. Robert Spoo. Durham: Duke Univ. Press, 1992.

———. *The Flowering of the Rod*. London: Oxford, 1946.

———. *The Gift* [abridged]. Intro. Perdita Schaffner. New York: New Directions, 1982.

———. "H.D. by Delia Alton." *Iowa Review* 16 (Fall 1986): 174–221.

———. *Hedylus*. Boston: Houghton Mifflin, 1928.

———. *Helen in Egypt*. New York: Grove, 1961.

———. *Hermetic Definition*. New York: New Directions, 1972.

———. *HERmione*. New York: New Directions, 1981.

———. *Nights*. Dijon: Darantière, 1934.

———. *Paint It Today*. Ed. Cassandra Laity. New York: New York Univ. Press, 1992.

———. *Palimpsest*. Paris: Contact, 1926.

———. *Sea Garden*. London: Constable, 1916.

———. *Tribute to Freud*. 1956. New York: New Directions, 1984.

———. *Tribute to the Angels*. London: Oxford Univ. Press, 1945.

———. *Trilogy* (*The Walls Do Not Fall*; *Tribute to the Angels*; *The Flowering of the Rod*). New York: New Directions, 1973.

———. *The Walls Do Not Fall*. London: Oxford Univ. Press, 1944.

———. *Within the Walls*. Iowa City: Windhover, 1993.

Heilbrun, Carolyn G. *Writing a Woman's Life*. New York: Ballantine, 1988.

Heller, Agnes. *A Theory of History*. London: Routledge, 1982.

Heller, Deborah. "History, Art, and Fiction in Anna Banti's *Artemisia*." Aricò 45–60.

———. "Remembering *Artemisia*: Anna Banti and Artemisia Gentileschi." Testaferri 99–108.

Henke, Suzette A. *Shattered Subjects: Trauma and Testimony in Women's Life-Writing.* New York: St. Martin's, 1998.

Herman, Judith Lewis. *Trauma and Recovery.* New York: Basic, 1992.

Higonnet, Margaret R., ed. *Borderwork: Feminist Engagements with Comparative Literature.* Ithaca: Cornell Univ. Press, 1994.

Hollenberg, Donna Krolik. *Between History and Poetry: The Letters of H.D. and Norman Holmes Pearson.* Iowa City: Univ. of Iowa Press, 1997.

Homans, Margaret, and Adrienne Munich, eds. *Remaking Queen Victoria.* Cambridge: Cambridge Univ. Press, 1997.

Howes, Craig. "The Emperor's New Clothes: A Short History in American Children's Books about Hawaii." *Literature and Hawaii's Children: Imagination—A Bridge to Magic Realms in the Humanities.* Ed. Cristina Bacchilega and Steven Curry. Honolulu: 1988, 118–26.

———. "Hawaii Through Western Eyes: Orientalism and Historical Fiction for Children." *The Lion and the Unicorn: A Critical Journal of Children's Literature* 11 (1987): 68–87.

Iaukea, Curtis Pi'ehu, and Lorna Kahilipuaokalani Iaukea Watson. *By Royal Command: The Official Life and Personal Reminiscences of Colonel Curtis Pi'ehu Iaukea at the Court of Hawaii's Rulers.* Ed. Niklaus R. Schweizer. Honolulu: Hui Hanai, Queen Lili'uokalani Children's Center, 1988.

Jelinek, Estelle, C., ed. *Women's Autobiography: Essays in Criticism.* Bloomington: Indiana Univ. Press, 1980.

Jolly, Margaretta, ed. *The Encyclopedia of Life Writing.* London: Fitzroy Dearborn, 2001.

Kame'eleihiwa, Lilikalā. *Native Land and Foreign Desires: Pehea Lā E Pono Ai?* Honolulu: Bishop Museum Press, 1992.

Kanahele, George S., ed. *Hawaiian Music and Musicians: An Illustrated History.* Honolulu: Univ. of Hawai'i Press, 1979.

Ka'ohelelani, Owana. "The Hawaiian Mind: Insights." *Honolulu Advertiser,* Apr., 1994, A18.

Kaplan, Caren. "Resisting Autobiography: Out-Law Genres and Transnational Feminist Subjects." Smith and Watson, *De/Colonizing the Subject* 115–38.

Kaplan, Caren, and Inderpal Grewal, eds. *Scattered Hegemonies: Postmodernity and Transnational Feminist Practices.* Minneapolis: Univ. of Minnesota Press, 1994.

Kawahakui, Nohealani. Unpublished essay. Dept. of English, University of Hawai'i. 1997.

Kerby, Anthony Paul. *Narrative and the Self.* Bloomington: Indiana Univ. Press, 1991.

King, Martha, ed. *New Italian Women: A Collection of Short Fiction.* New York: Italica, 1989.

King, Michael, ed. *H. D.: Woman and Poet.* Orono, Maine: National Poetry Foundation, 1986.

Kirschstein, Bette H., ed. *Life Writing/Writing Lives.* Malabar, Fla.: Krieger, 2001.

Kosta, Barbara. *Recasting Autobiography: Women's Counterfictions in Contemporary German Literature and Film.* Ithaca: Cornell Univ. Press, 1994.

Kristeva, Julia. "Freud and Love: Treatment and Its Discontents." Trans. Léon S. Roudiez. Moi 238–71.

Kualapai, Lydia K. *Cast in Print: The Nineteenth-Century Hawaiian Imaginary.* Diss. Univ. of Nebraska, 2001. Ann Arbor: UMI. 3034383 (2002).

LaCapra, Dominick. "The Historians' Debate (*Historikerstreit*)." Gilman and Zipes 812–19.

Langer, Lawrence L. *Admitting the Holocaust: Collected Essays.* New York: Oxford Univ. Press, 1995.

———. *Holocaust Testimonies: The Ruins of Memory.* New Haven: Yale Univ. Press, 1991.

———. "A Stranger in Her Own Land." *Book World*, Apr. 26, 1992, 5.

Langness, L. L., and Gelya Frank. *Lives: An Anthropological Approach to Biography.* Novato, Calif.: Chandler and Sharp, 1981.

Lapierre, Alexandra. *Artemisia: A Novel.* Trans. Liz Heron. New York: Grove, 2000.

Lazzaro-Weis, Carol. *From Margins to Mainstream: Feminism and Fictional Modes in Italian Women's Writings, 1968–1990.* Philadelphia: Univ. of Pennsylvania Press, 1993.

———. "Stranger Than Life? Autobiography and Historical Fiction." Marotti and Brooke 31–48.

Lejeune, Philippe. *On Autobiography.* Ed. and intro. Paul John Eakin. Trans. Katherine Leary. Minneapolis: Univ. of Minnesota Press, 1989.

———. "The Autobiographical Pact (*bis*)." 1981. Lejeune 119–37.

Lewis, R. W. B. *The City of Florence: Historical Vistas and Personal Sightings.* New York: Holt, 1995.

Liebs, Elke. "Grete Weil: A Jewish Antigone." Frederiksen and Wallach 235–43.

Lili'uokalani. Diaries. Bernice Pauahi Bishop Museum. Honolulu, Hawai'i; Hamilton Library (translated photocopies). University of Hawai'i, Honolulu, Hawai'i. Other materials in Hawai'i State Archives, MS MC Lili'uokalani Files. 'Iolani Palace Grounds, Honolulu.

———. "Hawaii's Story." Typescript. Hawai'i State Archives. Honolulu, Hawai'i.

———. *Hawaii's Story by Hawaii's Queen.* Boston: Lee and Shepard, 1898; Honolulu: Mutual, 1990.

———, ed. *The Kumulipo: An Hawaiian Creation Myth.* Trans. and introd. Lili'uokalani. Boston: Lee and Shepard, 1898; Kentfield, Calif.: Pueo, 1978.

———. November 11, 1897, letter to William Lee. Hawai'i State Archives. 'Iolani Palace Grounds, Honolulu.

———. "Variegated Leaves, from the Diary of Liliuokalani of Hawaii." Typescript. Hawai'i State Archives. 'Iolani Palace Grounds, Honolulu.

Linklater, Eric. *The Campaign In Italy.* London: Unwin, 1977.

Lionnet, Françoise. *Autobiographical Voices: Race, Gender, Self-Portraiture.* Ithaca: Cornell Univ. Press, 1989.

———. "Dissymmetry Embodied." Higonnet 19–41.

Loomis, Albertine. *For Whom Are the Stars?: Revolution and Counterrevolution in Hawaii, 1893–1895.* Honolulu: Univ. of Hawai'i Press and Friends of the Library of Hawai'i, 1976.

Lorenz, Dagmar C. G. *Keepers of the Motherland: German Texts by Jewish Women Writers.* Lincoln: Univ. of Nebraska Press, 1997.

Lum, Curtis. "Sovereignty Event Schedule July 31." *Honolulu Advertiser*, June 15, 1999, B1, B4.

MacKay, Carol Hanbery. "Biography as Reflected Autobiography: The Self-Creation of Anne Thackeray Ritchie." Groag and Yalom 65–79.

Malcolm, Janet. *The Silent Woman: Sylvia Plath and Ted Hughes.* New York: Knopf, 1994.

Marotti, Maria Ornella, and Gabriella Brooke, eds. *Gendering Italian Fiction: Feminist Revisions of Italian History.* Madison, N.J.: Fairleigh Dickinson Univ. Press, 1999.

Marrone, Claire. "Women Writing Auto/biography: Anna Banti's *Artemisia* and Eunice Lipton's *Alias Olympia.*" Kirschstein 115–30.

McHale, Brian. *Postmodernist Fiction.* London: Routledge, 1987.

Middlebrook, Diane Wood. "Postmodernism and the Biographer." Bell and Yalom 155–65.

————. "Telling Secrets." *The Seductions of Biography.* Rhiel and Suchoff 123–29.

Milton, Edith. "Cutting Giants Down to Size." *Women's Review of Books* 9 (1992): 37.

Misch, Georg. 1907. *History of Autobiography.* London: Routledge, 1950.

Moi, Toril, ed. *The Kristeva Reader.* Trans. Léon S. Roudiez. New York: Columbia Univ. Press, 1986.

Moir, Alfred. *The Italian Followers of Caravaggio.* 2 vols. Cambridge: Harvard Univ. Press, 1967.

Morris, Adalaide. "Autobiography and Prophecy." Michael King 227–36.

————. "A Relay of Power and of Peace: H.D. and the Spirit of the Gift." *Contemporary Literature* 27 (Winter 1986): 493–524.

Morris, Aldyth. *Liliʻuokalani.* Honolulu: Univ. of Hawaiʻi Press, 1993.

"The New Air Weapon: First Official Detail." *The Times,* June 20, 1944, 4.

Norman, Matthew. "Missing Paula, Missing the Point." *Evening Standard,* Sept. 19, 1995, 45.

Nussbaum, Felicity A. "Toward Conceptualizing Diary." Olney, *Studies in Autobiography* 128–40.

O'Brien, Sharon. "Feminist Theory and Literary Biography." Epstein 123–33.

————. *Willa Cather: The Emerging Voice.* 1987. Cambridge: Harvard Univ. Press, 1997.

Olney, James, ed. *Autobiography: Essays Theoretical and Critical.* Princeton: Princeton Univ. Press, 1980.

————, ed. *Studies in Autobiography.* New York: Oxford Univ. Press, 1988.

Osborne, Thomas J. *Annexation Hawaii: Fighting American Imperialism.* 1981. Waimānalo, Hawaiʻi: Island Style, 1998.

Ostriker, Alicia Suskin. *Feminist Revision and the Bible.* Cambridge: Blackwell, 1993.

————. *The Nakedness of the Fathers: Biblical Visions and Revisions.* New Brunswick: Rutgers Univ. Press, 1994.

Palmer, Julius A., Jr. *Again in Hawaii.* Boston: Lee and Shepard, 1895.

————. *Hawaii: The Story of a National Wrong.* Boston: Nathan Sawyer, 1896.

————. *Memories of Hawaii and Hawaiian Correspondence.* Boston: Lee and Shepard, 1894.

Pelling, Henry. *Britain and the Second World War.* London: Collins, 1970.

Peterson, Thomas. "The 'Feminine' Writing of Anna Banti: *Un Grido Lacerante.*" *NEMLA Italian Studies* 11–12 (1987–88): 87–96.

Prince, Gerald. *A Dictionary of Narratology.* Lincoln: Univ. of Nebraska Press, 1987.

Rhiel, Mary, and David Suchoff, eds. *The Seductions of Biography.* New York: Routledge, 1996.

Rodden, John, ed. *Conversations with Isabel Allende.* Trans. Virginia Invernizzi. Austin: Univ. of Texas Press, 1999.

————. "The Chilean Scheherazade: Isabel Allende." *Performing the Literary Interview* 203–26.

————. *Performing the Literary Interview: How Writers Craft their Public Selves.* Lincoln: Univ. of Nebraska Press, 2001.

Rose, Phyllis. "Confessions of a Burned-Out Biographer." Rhiel and Suchoff 131–36.

Rosenwald, George C., and Richard L. Ochberg, eds. *Storied Lives: The Cultural Politics of Self-Understanding.* New Haven: Yale Univ. Press, 1992.

Russ, W. A., Jr. *The Hawaiian Republic (1894–98) and Its Struggle to Win Annexation.* 1961. Reprint, Selinsgrove, Pa.: Susquehanna Univ. Press, 1992.

Russell, Rinaldina, ed. *The Feminist Encyclopedia of Italian Literature.* Westport, Conn.: Greenwood, 1997.

————, ed. *Italian Women Writers: A Bio-Bibliographical Sourcebook.* Westport, Conn.: Greenwood, 1994.

Ruta, Suzanne. "The Long Goodbye." *New York Times Book Review,* May 21, 1995, 11.

Sacks, Oliver. *The Man Who Mistook His Wife for a Hat and Other Clinical Tales.* London: Picador, 1986.

Sarton, May. "Letters from H.D." Michael King 49–57.

Sayre, Robert F. "Autobiography and America." Olney, *Autobiography* 146–68.

Scarry, Elaine. *The Body in Pain: The Making and Unmaking of the World.* New York: Oxford Univ. Press, 1985.

Sellers, Susan S., ed. *Writing Differences: Readings from the Seminar of Hélène Cixous.* New York: St. Martin's, 1988.

Shaw, Robert. *Hawaiian Quilt Masterpieces.* Westport, Conn.: Hugh Lauter Levin, 1996.

Shepperd, G. A. *The Italian Campaign 1943–45: A Political and Military Reassessment.* New York: Praeger, 1968.

Silva, Noenoe K. "*Kanaka Maoli* Resistance to Annexation." *'Ōiwi: A Native Hawaiian Journal* 1 (1998): 40–71.

Smith, Sidonie. *Moving Lives: Twentieth-Century Women's Travel Writing.* Minneapolis: Univ. of Minnesota Press, 2001.

————. *A Poetics of Women's Autobiography: Marginality and the Fictions of Self-Representation.* Bloomington: Indiana Univ. Press, 1987.

————. *Subjectivity, Identity, and the Body: Women's Autobiographical Practices in the Twentieth Century.* Bloomington: Indiana Univ. Press, 1993.

Smith, Sidonie, and Julia Watson, eds. *De/Colonizing the Subject: The Politics of Gender in Women's Autobiography.* Minneapolis: Univ. of Minnesota Press, 1992.
———. *Getting a Life: Everyday Uses of Autobiography.* Minneapolis: Univ. of Minnesota Press, 1996.
———. *Interfaces: Women, Autobiography, Images, Performance.* Ann Arbor: Univ. of Michigan Press, 2002.
———. *Reading Autobiography: A Guide for Interpreting Life Narratives.* Minneapolis: Univ. of Minnesota Press, 2001.
———. *Women, Autobiography, Theory: A Reader.* Madison: Univ. of Wisconsin Press, 1998.
Snipes, Wilson. "The Biographer as a Center of Reference." *Biography: An Interdisciplinary Quarterly* 5.3 (Summer 1982): 215–25.
Sontag, Susan. *Illness as Metaphor.* New York: Farrar, 1978.
Spear, Richard E. *Caravaggio and His Followers.* Cleveland: Cleveland Museum of Art, 1971.
Stanton, Domna C., ed. *The Female Autograph: Theory and Practice of Autobiography from the Tenth to the Twentieth Century.* Chicago: Univ. of Chicago Press, 1987; New York: New York Literary Forum, 1984.
Starobinski, Jean. 1971. "The Style of Autobiography." Olney, *Autobiography* 73–83.
The Times. Jan. 18, 1943, 4.
Testaferri, Ada, ed. *Donna: Women in Italian Culture.* Toronto: Dovehouse, 1989.
Thurston, Lorrin A. *Memoirs of the Hawaiian Revolution.* Ed. Andrew Farrell. Honolulu: Advertiser, 1936.
Torriglia, Anna Maria. "From Mother to Daughter: The Emergence of a Female Genealogy in Anna Banti's *Artemisia* and Alba de Céspedes's *Della parte di lei.*" *Italica* 73 (1996): 369–87.
Trask, Haunani-Kay. *From a Native Daughter: Colonialism and Sovereignty in Hawai'i.* Monroe, Maine: Common Courage, 1993.
Trial of a Queen: 1895 Military Tribunal. Honolulu: Judiciary History Center, Hawai'i State Judiciary, and Friends of the Judiciary History Center, 1995.
Van Alphen, Ernst. "Symptoms of Discursivity: Experience, Memory, and Trauma." Bal, Crewe, and Spitzer 24–38.
Van der Kolk, Bessell, Alexander C. McFarlane, and Lars Weisaeth, eds. *Traumatic Stress: The Effects of Overwhelming Experience on Mind, Body, and Society.* New York: Guilford, 1996.
Van Dyke, Jon M., and Paula Henderson. "The Trial of Lili'uokalani, February 1895." *Trial of a Queen* 1–8.
Valentini, Daria, and S. Mark Lewis. Introduction. *A Piercing Cry: Translation of Un Grido Lacerante.* By Anna Banti. New York: Peter Lang, 1996. v–xv.
Vreeland, Susan. *The Passion of Artemisia.* New York: Viking, 2002.
Wagner-Martin, Linda. *Telling Women's Lives: The New Biography.* New Brunswick: Rutgers Univ. Press, 1994.
Weil, Grete. *The Bride Price: A Novel.* Trans. John Barrett. Boston: Godine, 1991; *Der Brautpreis: Roman.* Zurich: Nagel and Kimche, 1988.
———. *Last Trolley from Beethovenstraat.* Trans. John Barrett. Boston: Godine, 1997.

————. *My Sister, My Antigone.* Trans. Krishna Winston. New York: Avon/Bard, 1984.

Wiesel, Elie. "The Holocaust as a Literary Inspiration." *Dimensions of the Holocaust.* Evanston: Northwestern Univ. Press, 1977. 5–19.

Wood, Mary Elene. *The Writing on the Wall: Women's Autobiography and the Asylum.* Urbana: Univ. of Illinois Press, 1994.

Young, Lucien. *The Real Hawaii: Its History and Present Condition.* New York: Doubleday, 1899.

Zilboorg, Caroline. *Richard Aldington and H.D.: The Early Years in Letters.* Bloomington: Indiana Univ. Press, 1992.

Index

Abbott, H. Porter, 75
Adelson, Leslie A., 19, 25, 96
air attacks (London blitz): Baedeker
raids, 215n. 16; as catastrophe, 3,
80–81; as context of writing, 12,
14–15, 81–82, 94–95, 100–101, 103–4,
218n. 39, 219n. 57; irregularity of
attacks, 3, 89, 216nn. 21–22;
newspaper accounts of, 99–100,
104; pictured, 85, 86
Aldington, Richard (H.D.'s husband),
78, 213n. 1
Prince Alfred, Duke of Edinburgh,
38–39
Allen, Helena G., 64
Allende, Isabel: on autobiography, 178;
daughter's illness as catastrophe,
163; ethical dilemmas of biographical project, 164–65, 167, 170, 173, 176,
183, 189–90; pictured, 166; on process
of writing Paula, 231n. 8, 233n. 52;
self-imposed restrictions on writing,
22, 167; self-representation of,
182–83; spiritual beliefs of, 169;
writing career of, 17, 162, 230n. 1.
See also Paula (Allende)
Allende, Paula: as agent, 167, 191–93; as
audience for Paula, 17, 163, 170–73,
177, 180, 183, 186, 189; as author,
191–93; as collaborator, 184, 185;

191–93; death of, 195, 233n. 50; as
heroine of Paula, 177–78; as
inaccessible biographical subject,
169–70, 177; as persona rather than
person in Paula, 184; representations
of in Paula, 163, 171, 173–74, 176,
186–87, 189, 191–92
annexation of Hawai'i: Blount Report,
210n. 34; as catastrophe, 31, 54–55;
ceremony of, 29; as context of
Hawaii's Story by Hawaii's Queen,
14, 30, 31–32, 47, 54–56, 60–61, 75–76;
formal apology to Hawaiians, 203;
global sociopolitical context, 76; as
historical event, 29–31, 54, 75–77;
opposition to, 41, 203n. 25, 211n. 37,
213n. 62, 213nn. 61–62; petitions
against, 203n. 25, 211n. 37, 213n. 62;
treaty of annexation, proposed,
54–57, 75–76, 211n. 42
antagonists: adversaries as characters
in life writing, 53–54; audience as
antagonist, 53
Anti-Semitism in Times of Crisis
(Gilman and Katz), 6
appendixes in Hawaii's Story by
Hawaii's Queen, 45–47, 51, 54, 67–68
Artemisia (Banti): as ahistorical, 224n.
19; authorial control in, 120–21; as
autobiographical, 111, 115–16, 135–36,

Wisconsin Studies in Autobiography

William L. Andrews
General Editor

Robert F. Sayre
The Examined Self: Benjamin Franklin, Henry Adams, Henry James

Daniel B. Shea
Spiritual Autobiography in Early America

Lois Mark Stalvey
The Education of a WASP

Margaret Sams
Forbidden Family: A Wartime Memoir of the Philippines, 1941–1945
Edited, with an introduction, by Lynn Z. Bloom

Charlotte Perkins Gilman
The Living of Charlotte Perkins Gilman: An Autobiography
Introduction by Ann J. Lane

Mark Twain
Mark Twain's Own Autobiography: The Chapters from the North American Review
Edited, with an introduction, by Michael Kiskik

Journeys in New Worlds: Early American Women's Narratives
Edited by William L. Andrews

American Autobiography: Retrospect and Prospect
Edited by Paul John Eakin

Caroline Seabury
The Diary of Caroline Seabury, 1854–1863
Edited, with an introduction, by Suzanne L. Bunkers

Marian Anderson
My Lord, What a Morning
Introduction by Nellie Y. McKay

William Herrick
Jumping the Line: The Adventures and Misadventures of an American Radical

Women, Autobiography, Theory: A Reader
Edited by Sidonie Smith and Julia Watson

Carson McCullers
Illumination and Night Glare: The Unfinished Autobiography of Carson McCullers
Edited by Carlos L. Dews

Marie Hall Ets
Rosa: The Life of an Italian Immigrant

Yi-Fu Tuan
Who Am I?: An Autobiography of Emotion, Mind, and Spirit

Henry Bibb
The Life and Adventures of Henry Bibb: An American Slave
With a new introduction by Charles J. Heglar

Suzanne L. Bunkers
Diaries of Girls and Women: A Midwestern American Sampler

Jim Lane
The Autobiographical Documentary in America

Sandra Pouchet Paquet
Caribbean Autobiography: Cultural Identity and Self-Representation

Miriam Fuchs
The Text Is Myself: Women's Life Writing and Catastrophe